Apple Training Series

Mac OS X Server
Essentials Second Edition

Schoun Regan with David Pugh

Apple
Certified

Apple Training Series: Mac OS X Server Essentials, Second Edition
Schoun Regan with David Pugh
Copyright © 2008 by Apple Inc.

Published by Peachpit Press. For information on Peachpit Press books, contact:

Peachpit Press
1249 Eighth Street
Berkeley, CA 94710
510/524-2178
510/524-2221 (fax)

Find us on the Web at: www.peachpit.com.
To report errors, please send a note to errata@peachpit.com.
Peachpit Press is a division of Pearson Education.

Project Editor: Rebecca Freed
Production Editor: Laurie Stewart, Happenstance Type-O-Rama
Copyeditor: Patricia Pane
Tech Editor: Joel Rennich
Proofreader: Darren Meiss
Compositor: Craig Woods, Happenstance Type-O-Rama
Indexer: Beth Nauman-Montana
Cover design: Mimi Heft
Cover production: Happenstance Type-O-Rama

Notice of Rights

Notice of Liability

The information in this book is distributed on an "As Is" basis without warranty. While every precaution has been taken in the preparation of the book, neither the authors nor Peachpit shall have any liability to any person or entity with respect to any loss or damage caused or alleged to be caused directly or indirectly by the instructions contained in this book or by the computer software and hardware products described in it.

Trademarks

Many of the designations used by manufacturers and sellers to distinguish their products are claimed as trademarks. Where those designations appear in this book, and Peachpit was aware of a trademark claim, the designations appear as requested by the owner of the trademark. All other product names and services identified throughout this book are used in editorial fashion only and for the benefit of such companies with no intention of infringement of the trademark. No such use, or the use of any trade name, is intended to convey endorsement or other affiliation with this book.

ISBN 13: 978-0-321-49660-7
ISBN 10: 0-321-49660-4

9 8 7 6 5 4 3 2

Printed and bound in the United States of America

For Susan

Forever

—Schoun

To my lovely wife, Amanda.

—Dave

Acknowledgments

Schoun Regan Special thanks to Dave Pugh, LeRoy Dennison, Joel Rennich, Rebecca Freed, Robyn Thomas, and Hannah Onstad Latham.

Thanks to John Signa, Steve Brokaw, and Shane Ross for all their assistance.

I would also like to thank David Long, Simon Wheatley, André LaBranche, and Sohail Mamdani for all their tireless help.

Finally, a sincere and dear thank you to Juan Fernandez, Apple Enterprise System Engineer of the year for 2007. A well-deserved accolade. You earned it and I'm proud to call you my good friend.

Dave Pugh This book would not be possible without the continued support of everyone in the Mac community. Everyone plays their part in moving the OS forward by using it, improving it, creating products for it, and just plain standing behind it. I would especially like to salute those who actively promote the Mac platform: the publishers and their support staff, conference speakers, mailing list participants, and other authors, including those who are no longer with us. I would especially like to thank Schoun Regan for all of the opportunities he has given me. Without him, I wouldn't be where I am today, and would never be able to get to where I'll be tomorrow. Lastly, I can't give enough thanks to my wife, Amanda. She pushes me to be the best that I can be, and stands beside me through all of life's ups and downs. It is with her that I have shared the best experiences of my life—experiences that would not have happened without everything she has done for me.

Contents at a Glance

Table of Contents

Getting Started

Welcome to the official Mac OS X Server Essentials training course offered by Apple Computer. This book serves as a self-paced guide and is designed to help you build the basic skills you need to effectively administer Mac OS X Server. *Apple Training Series: Mac OS X Server Essentials* details the graphical tools that Apple provides to configure system services.

The primary goal of this book is to prepare technical coordinators and entry-level system administrators for the tasks demanded of them by Mac OS X Server. To become truly proficient, you need to learn the theory behind the tools you will use. For example, not only will you learn how to use Workgroup Manager—the tool for managing preferences for users, groups, and computer accounts and lists—but you will also learn about the ideas behind preference management, how to think about policies and control of resources, and how to set up preference and policy management to support your environment.

This book assumes that you have some knowledge of Mac OS X, because Mac OS X Server is built on top of Mac OS X. Therefore, basic navigation, troubleshooting of the system itself, and networking are all similar regardless of whether the system is Mac OS X or Mac OS X Server. The main differences you will encounter focus on the services provided with Mac OS X Server. For example, user creation is managed very differently in Mac OS X Server than in Mac OS X. While Windows file sharing and user management services are included in Mac OS X, Mac OS X Server adds a rich interface to configure and monitor these services; as such, this book will concentrate on the features that are unique to Mac OS X Server. When working through this book, a basic understanding and knowledge level of Mac OS X is preferred, including troubleshooting the operating system. Refer to *Apple Training Series: Mac OS X Support Essentials* from Peachpit Press if you need to develop a solid working knowledge of Mac OS X.

Finally, you will learn to develop processes to help you understand and work with the complexity of your system as it grows. Even a single Mac OS X Server computer can grow into a very complicated system, and creating documentation and charts can help you develop processes so that additions and modifications can integrate harmoniously with your existing system.

The Methodology

Apple Training Series books emphasize intense hands-on training. The exercises contained within this book are designed so that you can explore and learn the tools necessary to manage Mac OS X Server. They move along in a predictable fashion, starting with the installation and setup of Mac OS X Server and moving to more advanced topics such as multiprotocol file sharing, using access control lists, and permitting Mac OS X Server to be a centralized storage center for user information and authentication via LDAP and Password Server, and to become a Kerberos key distribution center. If you already have a Mac OS X Server set up, you can simply skip ahead to some of the later exercises in the book, provided you understand the change in IP addressing from our examples to your server and are not running your server as a production server.

Course Structure

This book serves as an introduction to Mac OS X Server and is not meant to be a definitive reference. Because Mac OS X and Mac OS X Server contain several open-source initiatives, it is impossible to include all the possibilities and permutations here. First-time users of Mac

OS X Server and users of other server operating systems who are migrating to Mac OS X Server have the most to gain from this book; still others who are upgrading from previous versions of Mac OS X Server will also find this book a valuable resource.

> **WARNING** ▸ The initial exercise in this book requires you to reformat a volume on which you will install Mac OS X Server. All data on this volume will be erased. Once past that point, the majority of the exercises in this book are designed to be nondestructive if followed correctly. However, some of the exercises are disruptive; for example, they may turn off or on certain network services suddenly. Other exercises, if performed incorrectly, could result in data loss or corruption to some basic services, possibly even erasing a disk or volume of a computer connected to the network on which Mac OS X Server resides. Thus, it is recommended that you run through the exercises on a Mac OS X Server that is not critical to your work or connected to a production network. This is also true of the Mac OS X computer you will use in these exercises. Please back up all your data if you choose to use a production machine for either the Mac OS X Server and/or the Mac OS X computers. Instructions are given for restoring your services to their preset state, but reasonable caution is recommended. Apple Computer and Peachpit Press are not responsible for any data loss or any damage to any equipment that occurs as a direct or indirect result of following the procedures described in this book.

Mac OS X Server is by no means difficult to set up and configure, but how you use Mac OS X Server should be planned out in advance. Accordingly, this book is divided into five sections:

▸ Lessons 1 and 2 cover installation, configuration, and setting up a basic domain name service (DNS) on your server, which in most circumstances is critical to the health and operation of Mac OS X Server.

▸ Lessons 3 and 4 define the differences between authentication and authorization, how to implement various types of access control, and Open Directory and the vast functionality it can provide.

▸ Lesson 5 covers the various file-sharing protocols—AFP, SMB, FTP, and NFS—and introduces the concept of sharing files and associating share points with users and groups.

▸ Lessons 6, 7, and 8 focus on setting up collaboration services such as mail, web, calendaring and chatting services, and a group Wiki.

▸ Lessons 9 and 10 teach you to manage user preferences, create a network startup disk, and deploy disk images.

Lesson Files

Lesson 3 makes use of a small text file; the file is available for download from http://www.peachpit.com/ats.leopardserver. You will have access to the file after registering for the site and registering this book. Place the file and its folder into your Users > Shared directory to use it in the Lesson 3 exercise.

System Requirements

This book assumes a basic level of familiarity with the Macintosh operating environment. All references to Mac OS X refer to Mac OS X v10.5, which is the primary operating system assumed throughout the book.

Here's what you will need to complete the lessons in this book:

▶   Two Macintosh computers, one with Mac OS X v10.5 installed and one on which to install Mac OS X v10.5 Server

▶   One USB or FireWire storage device for transferring files from one computer to the other

▶   An Ethernet switch to keep the two computers connected via a small private local network

▶   Two Ethernet network cables for connecting both computers to the switch

Certification

Apple Training Series: Mac OS X Server Essentials provides a thorough preparation for the Apple Mac OS X Server Essentials v10.5 certification exam, offered by Apple. Before you take the test, you should review the lessons and ideas in this book, and spend time setting up, configuring, and troubleshooting Mac OS X Server.

You should also download and review the Skills Assessment Guide, which lists the exam objectives, the score required to pass the exam, and how to register for it. To download the Skills Assessment Guide, visit http://train.apple.com/certification.

Earning Apple technical certification shows employers that you have achieved a high level of technical proficiency with Apple products. You'll also join a growing community of skilled professionals. In fact, Apple Mac OS X certification programs are among the fastest-growing certifications in the industry.

Passing any of the Mac OS X certification exams for OS X v10.3 or higher also qualifies you to join the new Mac OS X Certification Alliance, a free program that recognizes and supports the thousands of Mac OS X experts worldwide.

For more information, visit http://train.apple.com.

About the Apple Training Series

Apple Training Series: Mac OS X Server Essentials is part of the official training series for Apple products, which was developed by experts in the field and certified by Apple. The lessons are designed to let you learn at your own pace.

For those who prefer to learn in an instructor-led setting, Apple Authorized Training Centers, located around the globe, offer training courses. These courses, which typically use the Apple Training Series books as their curriculum, are taught by Apple-certified trainers, and balance concepts and lectures with excellent and intense hands-on labs and exercises. Apple Authorized Training Centers have been carefully selected and have met Apple's highest standards in all areas, including facilities, instructors, course delivery, and infrastructure. The goal of the program is to offer Apple customers, from beginners to the most seasoned professionals, the highest-quality training experience.

To find an Authorized Training Center near you, go to http://train.apple.com.

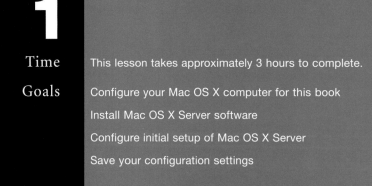

1

Time	This lesson takes approximately 3 hours to complete.
Goals	Configure your Mac OS X computer for this book
	Install Mac OS X Server software
	Configure initial setup of Mac OS X Server
	Save your configuration settings

Installing and Configuring Mac OS X Server

You can divide working with Mac OS X Server into three phases:

1. Planning and installation: Plan how the server will be set up, verify and configure the hardware, and install the server software.

2. Initial configuration: Use Server Assistant to perform the initial Mac OS X Server configuration. You can also use the Network preferences pane to update the interface configurations, including increasing performance by combining multiple Ethernet interfaces to act as one.

3. Maintenance: After the server is running, use utilities such as Server Admin and Workgroup Manager to perform ongoing server and account maintenance.

This lesson begins with the first two phases, the initial installation and configuration. Then it introduces the tools that you will use throughout the rest of this book to manage your server.

Preparing to Install Mac OS X Server

Installation of Mac OS X Server should be done in two steps:

1   Before you install the software, take the time to evaluate the server needs of your organization and the Mac OS X Server hardware requirements.

2   Then, use the Mac OS X Server Install DVD to install the operating system, server applications, and utilities.

We will not be covering the upgrade process in this book. Upgrading from an existing version of Mac OS X Server is an option available to administrators. It is always best practice to back up any existing setup prior to running the upgrade. Then you can restore should anything go wrong.

> **NOTE ▶** Updating the server software should be a planned event. Always run updates on a test system before rolling out into production. In some cases third-party solutions have not continued to operate smoothly with the new software. You should preflight the update in isolation first and roll out the update once you have tested your implementation.

Mac OS X Server can be installed using either of two methods: locally, while you are sitting at the server, or remotely, from another computer on the network (ideally, this will be a Mac OS X computer on your local network). Because both Mac OS X and Mac OS X Server—when booted from the install DVD—use Bonjour, Internet Protocol (IP) address differences are not a problem. Once the software is installed, configuration can take place. This can also be done either locally or remotely. Because a local installation and configuration does not force you to authenticate, you will be doing a remote installation in this lesson as if the server were in a server room or network closet down the hall from you, without a video card to rely on. You should already have a Mac OS X computer running Mac OS X v10.5 and have downloaded and installed the latest software updates. You will also want to install the Mac OS X Server Admin Tools. These tools, which can be either downloaded from the Apple Support webpage or obtained from the Mac OS X Server DVD, are what make the remote installation, configuration, and administration of Mac OS X Server possible. They require at least 179 megabytes (MB) of free disk space to be installed.

> **NOTE ▶** Mac OS X version 10.5 Server Administration software will not run on a computer running Mac OS X v10.4.

To install the Mac OS X Server Admin tools on Mac OS X:

1   Log in to your Mac OS X computer and insert the Mac OS X Server DVD or download the Server Admin Tools from Apple's website.

2   Open the DVD and install the package named ServerAdministrationSoftware.mpkg located inside the Other Installs folder, or install the package you downloaded from Apple's website. You do not need to restart.

3   Once the software is installed, you can locate the Server Admin Tools inside the /Applications/Server folder. The following tools are installed:

▶   Server Admin

▶   Server Assistant

▶   Server Monitor

▶   Server Preferences

▶   System Image Utility

▶   Workgroup Manager

▶   Xgrid Admin

Each of these tools, except Xgrid Admin, will be explained later in this lesson.

Configuring Mac OS X

After installing the Mac OS X Server Admin Tools, you'll want to set a network location for the lessons in this book so you can quickly refer back to them from any other network location. You will also be changing your computer name to make it easier to follow the examples in this book. Make sure your Mac OS X computer is up and running and plugged in to an

Ethernet switch. The computer that will be the Mac OS X server should also be plugged in to this switch.

1   If not already logged in, log in to your Mac OS X computer and open System Preferences.

2   Select the Sharing preferences pane and change the computer name to *XSE-CLIENT* (we are using XSE to stand for Mac OS X Server Essentials—the name of this book. You could name this location anything you like). You can always change it back anytime you want.

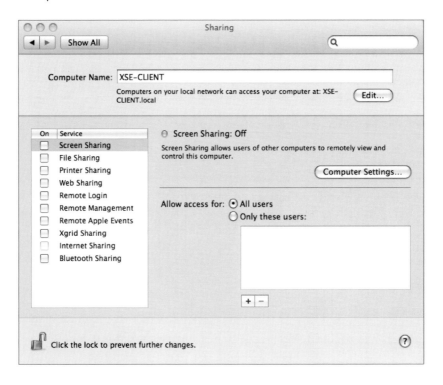

3   Click Show All and select the Network preferences pane.

4   Choose Edit Locations from the Locations pop-up menu, create a new location, and
name it *XSE Book*.

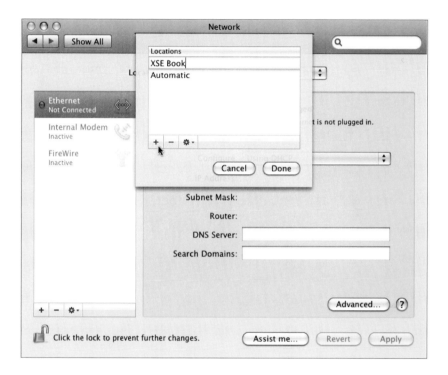

5   Use the Services action menu (the gear beneath the list of interfaces) to make all the
interfaces except Ethernet inactive.

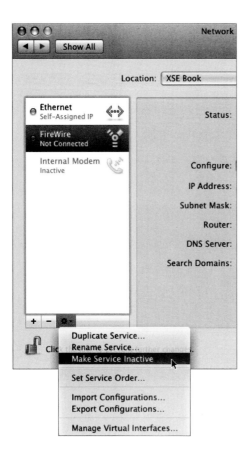

6   Select Ethernet from the list on the left. In the pane to the right, choose Using DHCP from the Configure pop-up menu if not already selected.

You should be getting a self-assigned address at this point in time, but since Mac OS X runs Bonjour, this will not currently be a problem.

7   Click Show All and select the Accounts preferences pane.

8   Select Login Options and choose Disabled from the "Automatic log in" pop-up menu, select Name and password from the "Display login window as," and enable fast user switching.

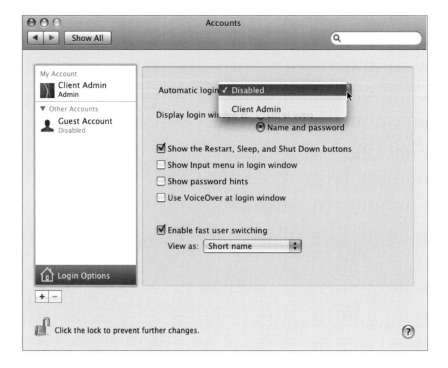

9   For these lessons, you may also want to change your Energy Saver preferences pane
settings to never have your Mac OS X computer go to sleep.

Evaluating Mac OS X Server Requirements

All desktop Macintosh computers are supported by Mac OS X Server v10.5, provided they
meet the requirements listed below. Although Mac OS X Server can be installed on a portable
Macintosh computer, Apple does not support or recommend this configuration.

Minimum Hardware Requirements

The basic installation requirements are as follows:

▶   PowerPC G4 (867 megahertz (MHz) or faster), G5, or Intel processor

▶   1 gigabyte (GB) of RAM; at least 1.5 GB of RAM for high-demand servers running
multiple services

▶   At least 20 GB of available disk space

You do not need a keyboard or display. As you will see later in this lesson, you can install Mac OS X Server using an administrator computer or another server.

Additional Hardware Considerations

Typical considerations when choosing server systems include network and system performance, disk space, and RAM.

Networking

Be sure to consider the speed of the network interface when making a server hardware decision. Many of Apple's products support Gigabit Ethernet. You can also "combine" two Ethernet interfaces to act as one, to double your aggregate network throughput for such services as Apple File Sharing.

Computer Speed

Although Mac OS X Server is supported on a wide variety of Macintosh computers, not all of them may be suitable for your needs. For a server that will only provide services for a few people, a Mac mini or older PowerMac G5 computer might meet your needs. For workgroups, you should use a Mac Pro. For demanding server environments, you might consider using the Xserve. Apple's Xserve is a 1U rackmount server that offers the ability to stack 42 Mac OS X Server systems in a typical server rack with dual Gigabit Ethernet interfaces, Lights-Out Management capabilities, and optional redundant power supplies.

> **NOTE ▶** Xserve, Power Mac G5, and any Macintosh Server G4 or Power Mac G4 released February 2000 or later include special hardware to detect an unexpected system shutdown and automatically restart the server machine. This feature works in conjunction with Mac OS X Server's ability to detect and restart after an error in server service.

Planning Your Mac OS X Server Deployment

A server administrator should follow certain steps when setting up Mac OS X Server. The first step is to review your organization's server needs. Will the server be used mainly for web services, QuickTime streaming, calendaring and Wiki services, file and print services, or something else? Will it be a dedicated server or will it have multiple uses?

When deciding how to use your Mac OS X Server, you might want to use the extensive planning document, which is located with the Mac OS X Server documentation included when you purchase Mac OS X Server.

NOTE ▶ Mac OS X Server v10.5 can be initially configured in three separate ways—Standard, Workgroup, or Advanced mode. Depending on the way you choose, the setup screens vary. Subsequently, not all the fields in Table 1.1 may have entries.

After reviewing the intended uses of the server, fill out a server worksheet detailing the following information in Table 1.1:

Table 1.1 Server worksheet

General information

Type of server setup (Standard, Workgroup, Advanced)

Server/Xserve hardware serial number

MAC address(es)

Mac OS X Server software serial number, Administration account information

Administrator long name

Administrator short name

Password

Network/Ethernet interface information

Whether TCP/IP will be active on various interfaces

IP address (for each interface to be used)

Subnet mask (for each interface to be used)

Router address (for each interface to be used)

DNS IP address (for each interface to be used)

DNS search domains (for each interface to be used)

Automatic or manual Ethernet connection speeds

IPv6 configuration

Table 1.1 **Server worksheet** (continued)

Lights-Out Management Interface (Xeon Xserves only)

IP address (for each channel to be used)

Subnet mask (for each channel to be used)

Router address (for each channel to be used)

Administrator name (for each channel to be used)

Password (for each channel to be used)

Naming information

Primary DNS name

Computer name

Bonjour (local) name (can be different than computer name)

Directory information—how this server uses or provides directory information (appears only in Advanced setup)

Standalone (local) only

Obtained from another server

Services to be started at startup (appears only in Standard and Workgroup setup)

Client computer backup server (appears only in Standard and Workgroup setup)

Table 1.1 **Server worksheet** (continued)

Authentication location (appears only in Workgroup setup)

Add user accounts (appears only in Standard and Workgroup setup)

After completing the server worksheet, you can proceed with the installation.

Installing Mac OS X Server

When booted from the Mac OS X Server v10.5 DVD, you have an array of utilities available to you when you click past the initial installation main language screen:

▶ Startup Disk

▶ Reset Password

▶ Firmware Password Utility

▶ Disk Utility

▶ Terminal

▶ System Profiler

▶ Network Utility

Verifying System Requirements

Before you can install Mac OS X Server, you should confirm the hardware requirements listed previously in this lesson. To do so, start up the Mac or Xserve from the Mac OS X Server DVD and choose System Profiler from the Utilities menu.

When the System Profiler application opens, you can check the CPU type and speed, amount of RAM, and locate the hardware serial number and Ethernet MAC address (which you should record for later use) from the Hardware Overview window.

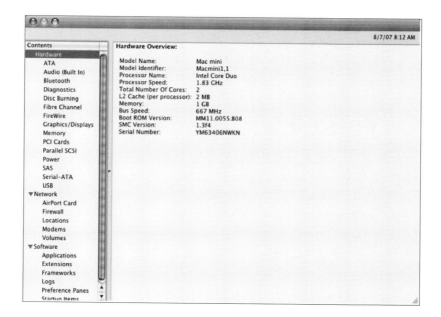

Then check available disk space from the ATA, SAS, or Serial-ATA contents list, depending on the type of hard drive(s) you have installed in your computer.

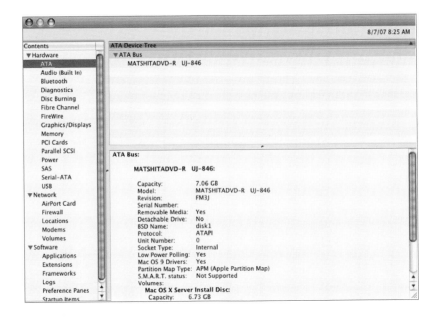

Formatting/Partitioning Drives

After you have confirmed your computer meets the hardware requirements, you can begin making decisions surrounding the devices and subsequent formatting of those devices prior to actually installing the software.

Like System Profiler, Disk Utility is also located under the Utilities menu when booted from the Mac OS X Server Install DVD. Using this utility, you can divide the hard disk into one or more partitions. Doing so allows you to first choose a partition scheme for your disk. Your choices are as follows:

▶ GUID Partition Table—used to start up Intel-based Macs

▶ Apple Partition Map—used to start up a PowerPC-based Mac

▶ Master Boot Record—used to start up DOS and Windows-based computers

Once you choose a partition scheme, you can divide your disk into as many as 16 logical drives, each with its own format. Subsequently, you are given the following format options for your partitions:

▶ Mac OS X Extended (Journaled)—This is the default option for Mac OS X and Mac OS X Server.

▶ Mac OS X Extended—This is the same as previous except there is no Journal written to the drive.

▶ Mac OS X Extended (Case-sensitive/Journaled)—Case-sensitive/ Journaled and Case-sensitive are used when you want your Mac OS X Server to be used primarily with other UNIX applications that require case sensitivity.

▶ Mac OS X Extended (Case-sensitive)—This is used when you want your Mac OS X Server to be used primarily with UNIX applications that require case sensitivity.

▶ MS-DOS file system (not bootable)

▶ Free (unformatted) Space (not bootable)

By using separate partitions, you can segregate your data from the operating system. Having the operating system on its own partition conserves space by keeping user accounts from filling up the startup partition. In case you need to perform a clean install of Mac OS X Server, you can erase the entire partition and install the operating system without touching the data on the other partitions. Having multiple partitions does not increase speed, but installing multiple drives may increase server performance. Simply select your hard disk, choose the number of partitions from the partition scheme menu, and choose the following for each partition:

▶ Name of partition—Using lowercase alphanumeric characters and removing spaces in volume names may help reduce troubleshooting of share points later down the road.

▶ Format of partition—See previous list for various acceptable Mac OS X Server partition formats.

▶ Size of partition—Again, Mac OS X Server requires at least 20 GB of space for installation.

Before you click the Apply button, remember, all previous data on the disk *may be erased*!

Installing the operating system on one drive and installing additional drives to store data can reduce connection times to the operating system and to data. If you add the second drive on a separate bus, the server can read and write to each of those buses independently.

Another installation option is to install on mirrored drives. Mirroring provides redundancy and increases uptime if one of the drives fails.

You begin the installation of Mac OS X Server v10.5 from a DVD, by starting up directly from the Mac OS X Server Install DVD. If you have purchased a new Xserve, the server software is already installed so you can proceed directly to the configuration. If you've already started up your server from the internal drive, insert the Mac OS X Server Install DVD and run the Install Mac OS X Server program. After you authenticate, the server reboots from the disc and proceeds with the installation process, starting with the selection of a language, and then prompting you for initial information. It then proceeds uninterrupted until it completes the installation.

RAID

Using a RAID (Redundant Array of Inexpensive [or Independent] Disks) configuration for your Mac OS X Server installation can help you avoid potential downtime and speed up throughput on your server, depending on how you configure the RAID.

This book does not go into detail on hardware RAID or using Apple's Xserve RAID hardware, but it is worth noting that software RAID can be used on certain hardware deployments that support more than one drive of the same size and bus type (SAS, or Serial Attached SCSI, and SATA, or Serial ATA drives) and permit RAIDs from FireWire devices.

Software RAID

If you have an Xserve, Mac Pro, or any other Apple computer with more than two drives of the same size and identical bus type, you can use Disk Utility to create a software RAID configuration. The choices you have are:

▶ Mirror, or RAID Level 1—where identical data is written to both drives. If one drive fails, the other contains the same data and therefore the operating system can still function.

▶ Stripe, or RAID Level 0—where data is written to both drives in a back-and-forth fashion, enabling the data to be written and retrieved faster than a single drive, such as when accessing large video files. However, if one drive fails, all data on both drives is lost.

▶ Concatenated Disk Set—where data is written to all drives in a 1,2,3-type fashion. When the first drive fills, the second drive is used, and so on. If one drive fails, data on that drive is lost.

Once you decide on the type of RAID array, you can choose a name for the logical volume and the format of that volume. Typically, only mirrored RAID setups are used for the boot volumes of servers.

Creating a Software RAID Mirrored Array

If you have a computer with more than one physical drive that meets the previously specified requirements, you can create a mirrored array.

1   Start up your computer with the Mac OS X Server v10.5 DVD and click the pointer to use the language you wish to see throughout the installation process.

2   Select Disk Utility from the Utilities menu and click any one of your disks on the left side of the window.

3   Click the RAID tab and drag in the volumes you want to use to create the RAID, choose a volume name and format type, and select Mirrored RAID Set as the RAID type.

4   Click the Create button and click past the window that informs you that you will lose all data on all drives associated with the array, and then view the completed RAID array.

5   You can then quit Disk Utility and proceed with your local installation.

Local Versus Remote Installation

You can choose to install Mac OS X Server either sitting locally in front of the computer on which you are installing the server software, or you can choose to install the software remotely. If you choose to install the software remotely, you must have network access to the computer.

Installing Locally

Local initial installation information that requires your input or response includes:

▶   Welcome/Read Me information

▶   License agreement

▶ Destination drive for server software

▶ Installation type—Easy Install or Customize

An Easy Install installs the following packages:

- Essential System Software

- Essential Server Software

- Server Administration Software

- Application Server Software

Easy Install also installs the following packages, but if you choose to customize the local installation, you will be able to disable them:

- X11—used to run Xwindows applications

- Language Translations—for French, German, and Japanese

- Printer Drivers—from various printer manufacturers

Installing Remotely

It is important to note that if you wish to install from any other computer, you will need both the hardware serial number (obtained earlier) and the Ethernet, or Media Access Control (MAC), address(es) of the computer that will host your server software. Repeat the method of launching System Profiler—similar to when you confirmed your hardware requirements—and click Network contents to obtain the Ethernet (MAC) address(es). Write the address on your Server Worksheet along with the hardware serial number and other pertinent information. You can also find this information on the label attached to the box of every Mac and Xserve sold.

When you install Mac OS X Server v10.5 on Apple's Xserve systems, there are additional items to consider. For example, Xserve is designed to be run "headless" (with no monitor) and with multiple Xserve systems installed on a server rack. Performing a local installation in this situation would require attaching a monitor and keyboard, so a more convenient method may be remote installation using Server Assistant.

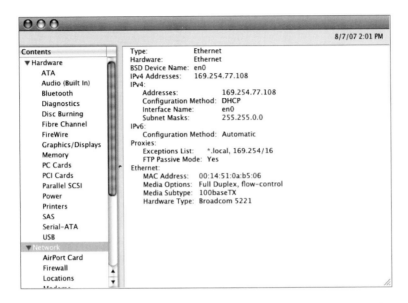

From any Mac OS X v10.5 computer with Server Admin Tools installed, you can use Server Assistant—located in the /Applications/Server folder inside the Applications folder—to install Mac OS X Server v10.5 on a remote computer that is started up from the Mac OS X Server Install DVD. Running a remote installation does not give you all the options that are available locally without additional software. For example, you can't run the Disk Utility application or customize the installation options such as removing extra print drivers.

NOTE ▶ You can use Apple Remote Desktop or third-party VNC software to connect to the computer started up from the Mac OS X Server DVD and take control of the keyboard and mouse, just as if you were sitting in front of the computer. This enables you to use the applications and tools under the Utilities menu. There is no user name for connecting to the computer, and the password is the first eight digits of the hardware serial number.

Server Assistant will search for and display all the computers on the local network that are started up from a Mac OS X Server Install DVD. You will now need to know the MAC address of your target computer to be able to choose it from the list of network computers if more than one computer is started up from a Mac OS X Server Install DVD. When Server Assistant contacts the target computer, you are asked for a password. The password is the first eight digits of the computer's hardware serial number, or 12345678 if you are installing onto an older machine that doesn't have a serial number or possibly onto a computer that has had its motherboard replaced.

Another option for remote installation is to use command-line tools such as the installer command from Terminal in Mac OS X. Alternatively, because Xserve is designed with a serial port, you can use command-line tools from an attached serial console, UNIX computer, or Windows computer.

> **NOTE** ▶ This book does not focus on command-line setup of Mac OS X Server v10.5.

Mac OS X Server v10.5 also includes the ability to have the Install DVD in the remote machine and not at the server. In this scenario, you do not need physical access to the server, nor is the server required to have an optical drive. You can, however, use other methods for remote installation. These include the following:

▶ Connect an external optical drive to the Xserve system via a FireWire or USB cable.

▶ Use an optical drive on a computer in Target Disk Mode connected to the Xserve system via a FireWire cable.

▶ Start the Xserve in Target Disk Mode and use another computer to install the server software on the Xserve system's mounted volume.

▶ Use another server with NetBoot services enabled to perform a network installation. As you will learn later, a server can be set up to install software onto other computers. This is extremely useful when you are setting up several servers—you can create one installation image and have it quickly replicated onto multiple computers.

Installer Issues

You can view the Installer log file during the installation process by selecting Installer Log from the Window menu. When you do so, a separate window appears at the bottom of the screen, allowing you to view three types of events within the log file:

▶ Show Errors Only

▶ Show Errors and Progress

▶ Show All Logs

You also have the option of saving the log file to a separate volume, such as an attached USB or FireWire device.

You should keep the installer log open on the computer on which Mac OS X Server is being installed to verify a successful install. Should the install fail for some reason, either select Show Errors Only from the menu on the left or select Show All Logs and use the Filter box to search for keywords, such as *fail*, *error*, *unable*, and *warning* that may indicate why the installation was not successful.

Installing Mac OS X Server Remotely

Remote management and installation is often a headache for system administrators. Mac OS X Server is designed to be easy to install and configure in remote installations or headless environments. You will use your computer running Mac OS X v10.5 to install Mac OS X Server on your server computer. You will want to have both your Mac OS X computer and your Mac OS X Server computer connected using Ethernet, not AirPort, to the same switch.

1   Write down the MAC address or addresses and hardware serial number (both can be found using System Profiler) of the computer on which Mac OS X Server is to be installed, or use the method discussed previously to obtain this information using the Install DVD.

2   Start up the target computer from the Mac OS X Server Install DVD by holding down the C key, just as you would to do a local install; do not touch the keyboard or mouse of the computer on which Mac OS X Server is to be installed. Everything else will be done remotely.

3   Launch Server Assistant (found in /Applications/Server) on your computer running Mac OS X v10.5.

Notice you did not have to worry about IP addresses. Bonjour takes care of that for you by automatically assigning 169.254.x.x addresses if an IP address is not already available from a Dynamic Host Configuration Protocol (DHCP) server.

4   Choose "Install Software on a remote server" if not already selected and click OK.

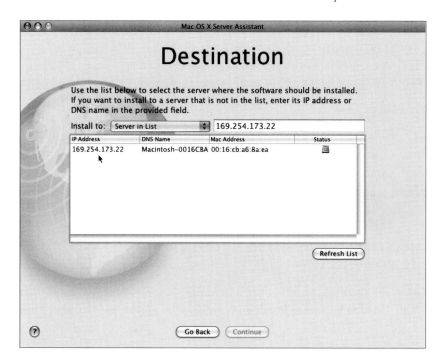

5   Select your intended server's computer from the Destination list and click Continue.
Enter the first eight digits of your server's hardware serial number in the field when
asked to authenticate (it is case sensitive).

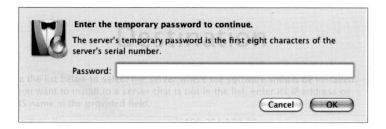

6   Choose the appropriate language for you.

7   Read the Important Information window.

8 Agree to the license agreement.

9 Select the disk or volume onto which Mac OS X Server will be installed. If you have another operating system on the disk or volume, you may be notified that the disk must be erased and you will be prompted to reformat the drive as Mac OS X Extended (Journaled). This is the option you selected when configuring your machine.

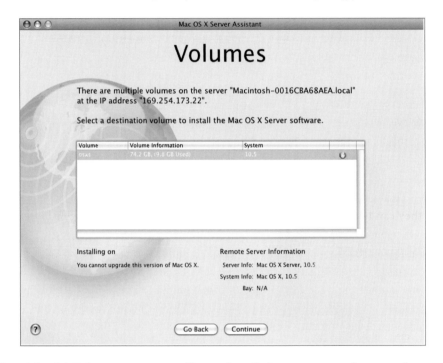

Your Mac OS X Server computer will now install the necessary software and automatically restart your server.

> **NOTE ▶** It is never a good idea to install Mac OS X Server without an active Ethernet connection.
>
> Also, be sure you install the Server Admin Tools on the machine that you will be using to configure the remote install. Do not merely copy the tools from another machine, because you won't necessarily get all the required files.

Initial Mac OS X Server Configuration

If you did a local installation, upon completion of the installation a Welcome screen appears prompting you to create a valid server configuration. In Mac OS X Server v10.5, initial configuration is completed using Server Assistant, which runs both as an installation assistant and, following a successful installation of Mac OS X Server, as a separate application used to install and configure remote computers. In each case, Server Assistant uses slightly different steps. It is Server Assistant that is used to configure the administrator account, computer names, network interfaces, and server configuration type. This makes the setup and configuration processes go quickly, provided you have already planned the configuration of your server.

Mac OS X Server v10.5 can be configured automatically using a configuration file generated by the Server Assistant application, which is available from the Server Admin Tools CD, or inside the /Applications/Server folder, which is on an existing Mac OS X Server v10.5 installation. The generated configuration file can be stored on another mounted volume, such as an iPod, USB or FireWire storage device, CD/DVD, or as a record in a directory service. The configuration files can be computer-specific, based on the MAC address, or they can be generic. If a configuration file is accessible to the newly installed server, Mac OS X Server will locate the file and automatically configure itself based on the settings in the configuration file. Later in this lesson you will save just such a server configuration file.

Choosing Setup Options

When using Server Assistant to set up a remote server, you are asked to select the destination computer and authenticate again using the first eight digits of the hardware serial number (or 12345678 if necessary for older computers). Local setup does not require these steps. At this point, both local and remote installations are similar, in that you now decide on how you wish your server to be configured initially. You have three options:

▶   Standard

▶   Workgroup

▶   Advanced

NOTE ▶ A fourth option appears if you're installing on a Mac with a Fibre Channel card installed. This allows the server to become a metadata controller for an Xsan. Xsan is not covered in this book.

Choosing one of these options will affect which windows appear later in the setup process.

The Standard configuration is useful for a novice Mac OS X Server administrator, initially supporting minimal services and requiring little background on how Mac OS X Server functions. This configuration uses the Server Preferences application to manage services and add local users and groups and is intended to be the only server, such as in a small business.

In general, the Workgroup configuration is useful when setting up a Mac OS X Server as a file, web, and calendaring server, and possibly relying on another server for user accounts and authorization. This configuration uses the Server Preferences application to manage services and add local users and groups and is intended for environments where the server supports a group or department that is part of a larger organization.

The Advanced configuration does not automatically configure any of the services for you. Instead, it allows separate configuration of each service and requires a deeper understanding of what Mac OS X Server can offer you. This configuration uses the Server Admin and Workgroup Manager tools to administer the server. You cannot use the Server Preferences tool for this configuration.

Table 1.2 shows which windows are available during each configuration.

Table 1.2 Mac OS X setup windows per configuration

Screen	Standard configuration	Workgroup configuration	Advanced configuration
Welcome	√	√	√
Destination (remote install only)	√	√	√
Server configuration	√	√	√
Language (remote install only)	√	√	√

Table 1.2 Mac OS X setup windows per configuration (continued)

Screen	Standard configuration	Workgroup configuration	Advanced configuration
Keyboard	√	√	√
Serial Number	√	√	√
Registration information	√	√	√
Additional requested information	√	√	√
Administrator Account	√	√	√
Network Address information	√	√	√
TCP/IP information per MAC address	√	√	√
Network Names	√	√	√
Time Zone	√	√	√
Date & Time	√	√	√
Server Backup	√	√	
Initial Mail Service	√		
VPN Remote Access	√		
Select Services to enable		√	
Directory Usage			√
Client Computer Backup	√	√	
Users and Authentication		√	
Add User Accounts	√	√	
Add New User Accounts	√	√	
Confirm Settings			√

We will now take a brief look at the Server Assistant setup windows, which are the more important ones.

Serial Number

The process to enter the serial number locally and remotely vary slightly. When using Server Assistant remotely, you can enter the serial number and associated names once, and then drag the small box in the lower-right corner of the screen to your desktop. Doing so creates a small text file that can be used to drag into this same screen on another server.

> **NOTE** ▶ You can also create this text file by hand. Its usefulness comes in when you must reinstall Mac OS X Server v10.5 and you cannot locate your original paperwork with the serial number.

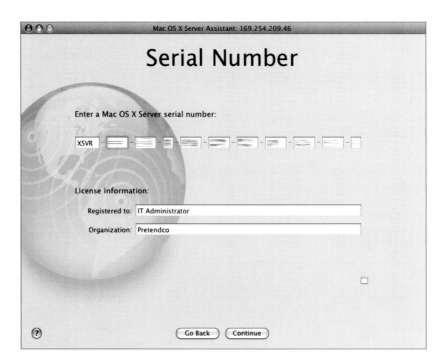

Services Questionnaire Screen

After the Serial Number screen and a registration screen appear, you are presented with a screen titled "A Few More Questions," which asks how the server will be used, what type of clients the server will support, and what services the server will host.

Mac OS X Server provides a wide range of services. These services can be launched at startup time to make sure they are available without administrator intervention. However, if you do not need a service, leave it off to reduce overhead and increase security.

With an initial installation, it is best not to enable any services during the installation process. Some services require proper supporting services, such as Domain Name Service (DNS) or DHCP, to be running and configured correctly. It is likely that none of the services will be configured exactly to your liking just by turning them on. It is best practice to always configure and thoroughly test your services before enabling them to start automatically.

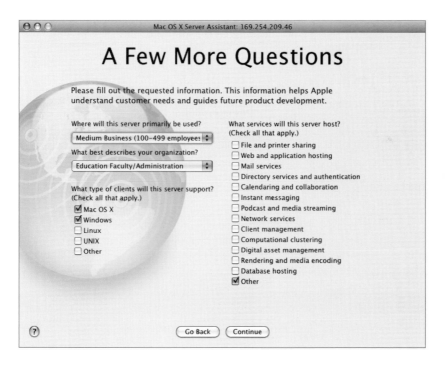

Table 1.3 shows what services are automatically enabled based on the type of server configuration you choose earlier:

Table 1.3 Default-enabled services per configuration

Screen	Standard configuration	Workgroup configuration	Advanced configuration
File and printer sharing	√	√	
Web and application hosting	√	√	
Mail services	√	√	
Directory services and authentication	√	√	
Calendaring and collaboration	√		
Instant messaging	√		
Podcast and media streaming			
Network services			
Client management			
Computational clustering			
Digital asset management			
Rendering and media encoding			
Database hosting			
Other			

Administrator Account

After the registration information and questionnaire windows, you are asked to enter initial account information. The first account that is created on Mac OS X Server v10.5 is a

local administrator account. However, the System Administrator account (root) is acti-
vated as well.

The password for System Administrator (root) is the same as the password for this initial
local administrator account, but they are not synchronized. If either the administrator or the
System Administrator's (root's) password is changed, the change does not affect the other
account's password.

Having the System Administrator (root) account active when Mac OS X Server is set up
has certain security implications. First, anyone who knows the initial local administrator
password can potentially log in as root and have unrestricted access to all contents of all
mounted volumes on that computer. Therefore, it is advisable that the root password be
changed after Mac OS X Server has been set up successfully. This can be done using the
Directory Utility located inside the Utilities folder.

NOTE ▶ The Edit Picture option appears only in the Standard and Workgroup
configurations.

Network Addressing

After setting the initial administrator account, you are prompted to choose whether your server will keep its current network configuration (set to DHCP by default), or to allow you to manually set up each interface. If a DHCP server is not present on your network, a self-allocated Bonjour address starting with 169.254.x.x will appear.

It is highly recommended that you choose a manual address for your servers, because dynamic addressing will reduce the number of services you can offer, and most services require a statically assigned address.

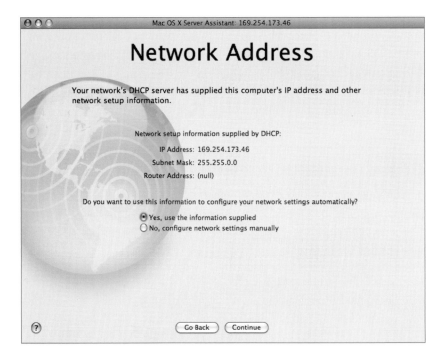

Network Interfaces

The next step in configuration of your server is the network setup.

Apple servers can use multiple interfaces for network access. Examples include computers with AirPort cards installed, Xserve systems with dual Gigabit Ethernet, and Mac OS X Server computers with 4-interface Ethernet cards.

The Server Assistant displays any interfaces it finds so the administrator can select whether TCP/IP should be enabled for each interface. You are prompted for detailed configuration information for each selected interface on subsequent windows.

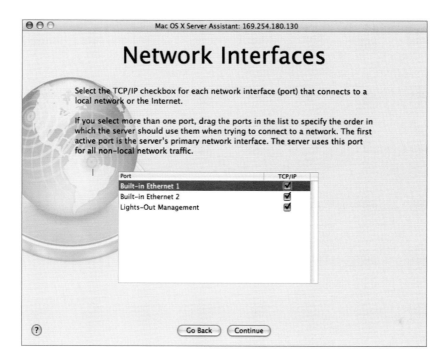

TCP/IP Connection

The screen shot below demonstrates how each Ethernet interface is displayed for configuration in the Server Assistant. Each interface has its own IP settings—for hosting different server services or dividing the amount of traffic supported over any one interface, including the ability to disable IPv6 and set your Ethernet interface to match the speed of your switch, should the need arise. You can also manually configure multiple interfaces or reconfigure network information later using the Network pane of System Preferences.

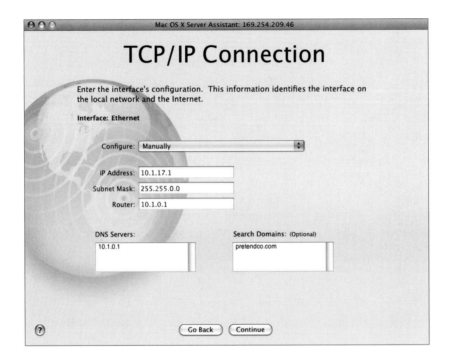

NOTE ▶ In the Network pane of System Preferences, you can also create multiple settings for a single interface. (To do so, you select the interface, and then click the Duplicate button.) This option is useful for assigning multiple IP addresses to the same Ethernet interface. One use of this is to host multiple websites, with unique IP addresses and unique webpages, from a single server with only one Ethernet interface. This configuration may require modifying DNS entries.

Lights-Out Management

On Intel Xserves, you also have the ability to connect to your server and manage rudimentary tasks via the Ethernet interfaces. What Apple calls Lights-Out Management (LOM), you are required to give this configuration a separate IP address per interface (called Channels) and different user name and password (eight characters minimum). Note that the user name and password for LOM are in no way related to any system users you have. Remember, be careful that the IP address you configure for the LOM is not the same as the IP address you have previously given any of the interfaces. Refer to the Xserve documentation for more information on Lights-Out Management.

Network Names

After setting the initial administrator account and network settings, you are prompted to provide unique names for your computer.

▶ The *Primary DNS Name* is a unique name for a server, historically referred to as the fully qualified domain name, or FQDN. Some services on Mac OS X Server either require a working FQDN or will work better if one is available. It relies on the DNS Service being present on your network, running from another server. If the server you are setting up will be running the DNS Service, you should read Lesson 2, "Providing DNS Service," after reading this lesson. (Lesson 2 instructs you how to set up the DNS Service on your Mac OS X Server.)

▶ The *Computer Name* is used by clients who use the Apple Filing Protocol (AFP) to access AFP share points and print services on the server.

▶ The *local hostname* (changed by clicking the Edit button) is the name Mac OS X users see for this server when viewing the computers listed in /Network/Local. Those computers on the same IP subnet can always access the server by entering the local hostname followed by *.local*.

▶   You can also choose to enable remote management if you chose the Advanced configuration, allowing Mac OS X Server to be controlled by Apple Remote Desktop.

NOTE ▶ The computer name can include spaces but the local hostname cannot.

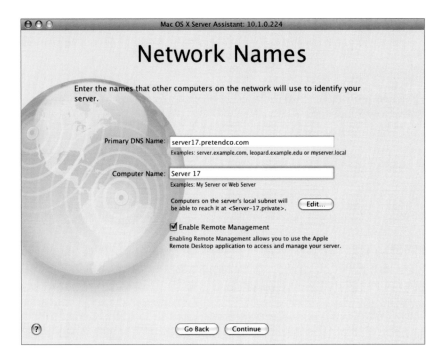

Time and Time Zone Information

Regardless of the configuration you choose, you are asked to specify the time zone where the server will be located and choose whether or not this server will use another server running the Network Time Service Protocol (NTP). It is important to note that if you are planning to handle authentication through Kerberos or connecting this server to another server running Kerberos, synchronizing time to avoid time drift is paramount. This is because by default, a Kerberos authentication scheme does not permit time skew greater than five minutes between itself and computers requesting authentication.

Server Backup (Standard and Workgroup Configuration)

You can choose to back up your server to another partition or a connected device. In a later screen you will decide if you wish to back up Mac OS X computers to your server.

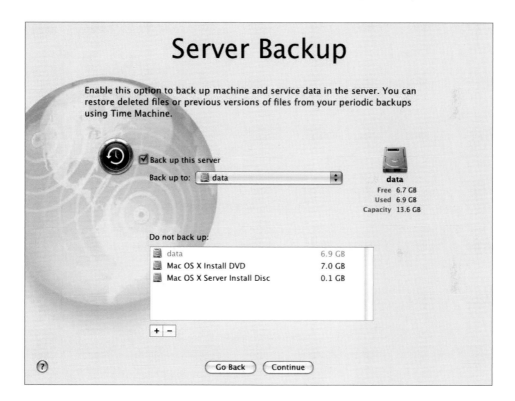

Mail and VPN Services (Standard Configuration)

At this point, the windows you see vary based on the configuration you chose earlier in the setup process. If you chose the Standard configuration, you will be presented with a Mail Service screen, which allows you to set up mail for all your users, enable a relay, and present the users with a welcome message the first time they log in to receive their mail.

You are also presented with a Remote Access screen in the Standard configuration setup that has a single checkbox, allowing users to use Virtual Private Networking services (VPN).

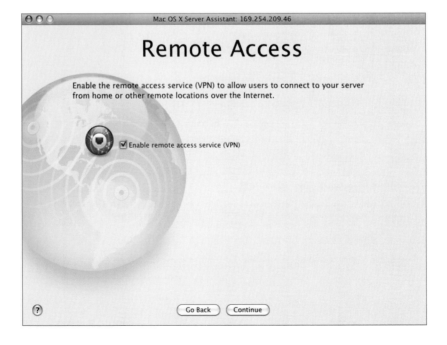

Select Services (Workgroup Configuration)

If you chose the Workgroup configuration, you will not see the previous two windows. Instead, you will be presented with a Select Services screen, which allows you to select the following services to be started:

▶ File Sharing (selected by default)

▶ Calendaring (selected by default)

▶ Instant Messaging (selected by default)

▶ Web (selected by default)

▶ Backup (selected by default)

▶ Mail (*not* selected by default)

> **NOTE** ▶ If you select Mail, you are next presented with the Mail Service screen.

▶ Remote Access (VPN) (*not* selected by default)

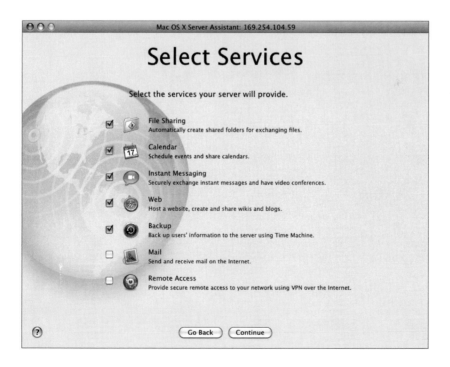

Directory Usage (Advanced Configuration)

If you chose the Advanced configuration, then you will not see the Mail Service, Remote Access, or Select Services windows. Instead, the Server Assistant requires you to choose one of two directory configurations for your server: Standalone Server or "Connected to a Directory System." If you choose the second option, you will be prompted to provide further information.

Choosing Standalone Server means that user information is stored locally and can be connected only by services on the local machine. Remote users can still connect to services via AFP, Service Message Block (SMB), and so forth, but remote clients cannot sign in to user accounts via the login window on their local machines using account information stored on the server. This is a typical configuration for file servers.

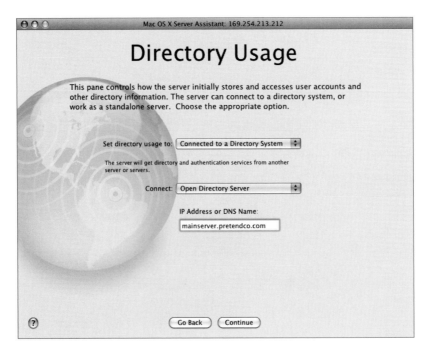

If you already have a Lightweight Directory Access Protocol (LDAP) server configured to permit user, group, and computer information to be used for authentication purposes on your network, select "Connected to a Directory System." You are then prompted to select how you will connect to the directory system. This option makes the server a "child" to some other authentication server. The default setting is to use another Apple Open Directory server by providing the fully qualified domain name or IP address of that server.

A common best practice, however, is to configure your server as a standalone system during the initial configuration. Once you've logged in to your server and ensured that networking, DNS, and other services are available, then use the Directory Access utility to connect another directory service.

Secondly, you can choose to join some other type of directory system by entering the appropriate IP or DNS information about that directory server. Lastly, you can allow the directory system to be used that is specified by a DHCP server. This option allows you to use the directory system information delivered by the DHCP lease. This would assume you are obtaining an IP address from a DHCP server, something that generally should be avoided for reasons given earlier in this lesson.

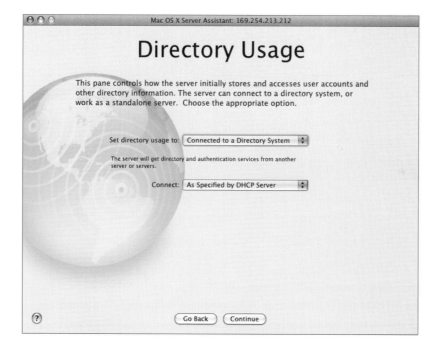

NOTE ► All subsequent windows apply to either the Standard or Workgroup configurations (or both). The next screen to appear for the Advanced configuration is the Confirm Settings screen, discussed later in this lesson.

Client Computer Backup (Standard or Workgroup Configuration)

New to Mac OS X Server v10.5 is the ability to back up client computers to your server, using a process called Time Machine. However, this option is available during setup only when choosing either the Standard or Workgroup configurations.

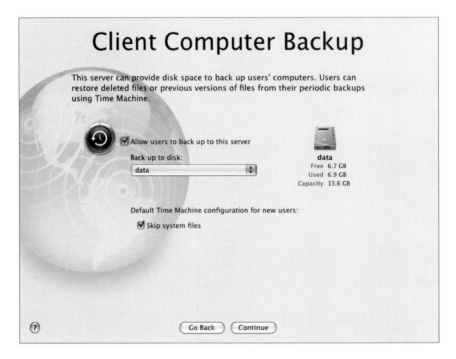

You have the option to back up the Mac OS X client computer's system files.

Account Authentication (Workgroup Configuration)

If you chose the Workgroup configuration, you are presented with a Users and Authentication screen. This screen only contains two options, to use the Mac OS X Server alone for authentication or to use another server and possibly the Mac OS X Server itself for authentication.

Choosing another server allows you to select (from the pop-up menu) or populate the entry field with the other server's fully qualified domain name or IP address. You would select this option if you already had a directory server and your server would implicitly trust that server. If you chose "This server provides all user accounts and authentication," you are presented with a subsequent screen to allow you to enter user account information, which will be shown in the following section.

Adding User Accounts (Standard or Workgroup Configuration)

The next screen to appear using either the Standard or Workgroup configuration is the option to add user accounts now or later.

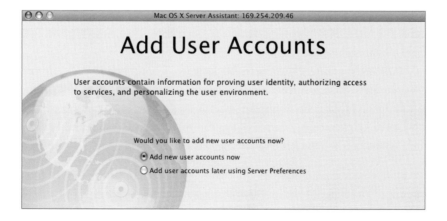

If you choose to add users now, you are presented with another screen, allowing you to enter the long name, short name, and password for each user. Tabbing through to the password field will also autogenerate a random password for each user. To add more than one user, click the add button ⊞ located in the lower left of the screen.

Confirm Settings (Advanced Configuration)

If you chose the Advanced configuration, after clicking the Continue button, setup concludes with the Confirm Settings screen. At this screen, you review your information by scrolling through the window. You *can* apply the settings you have just configured; however, for this book we will be saving our configuration first, so do *not* click the Apply button immediately when finished with the following exercise.

After you have finished adding users for Standard and Workgroup configurations or confirmed your settings for the Advanced configuration, your server begins to configure itself based on your previous choices throughout the setup process and subsequently restarts.

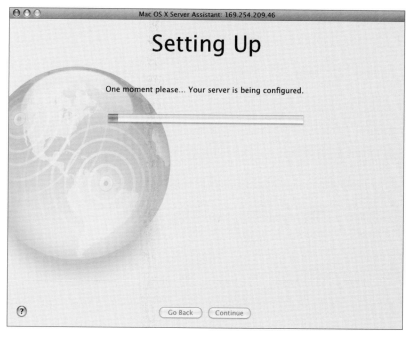

Upgrading Mac OS X Server

Upgrading a Mac OS X Server from Mac OS X Server v10.4 to Mac OS X Server v10.5 involves careful planning and testing, and it should not be undertaken lightly. Nor should it be done to a production server. If, after careful planning and testing you decide to upgrade, you are asked to upgrade at the install screen, not to wipe your volume, and to install the software. Secondly, you have the option to back up your existing configuration using Time Machine to another mounted volume before the actual upgrade occurs.

This permits you to return to your initial configuration should the update not work as planned.

Configuring Your Server Using Server Assistant

You can use the Server Assistant application to perform remote installations and configurations. You can do remote configuration by connecting to the server over the network and running the Server Assistant remotely.

1 Launch Server Assistant on your Mac OS X computer (located in the Applications/Server folder), choose the "Set up a remote server" option, and click Continue.

2 Place a checkmark next to your server in the Destination screen, click in the Password field, and again enter the first eight digits (case sensitive) of the hardware serial number (or 12345678 if necessary for older Macs) and click Continue.

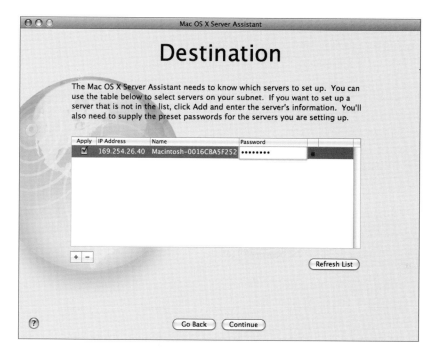

3 On the following four windows, choose a configuration (for this book you will use Advanced), a language, and a keyboard layout, and enter the Mac OS X Server software serial number, clicking Continue after each screen. Once the serial number is entered, you can drag the small text box in the lower-right corner of the screen to your desktop for later use.

4 Enter Registration information to your liking. Because you should not be connected to the Internet for the exercises in this book, this information will not be sent to Apple. Click Continue.

5   Set your local administrator long name, short name, and password. Reenter your password and click Continue.

Use *Local Administrator* as the long name, *ladmin* as the short name, and *ladmin* as the password. It is good practice to choose a strong password for your local administrator account. If you choose a different password, please write it down here for reference.

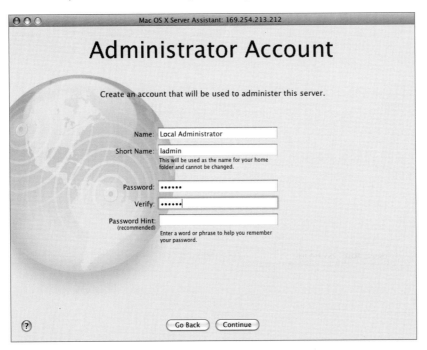

6   In the next screen, choose the option "No, configure network settings manually" and click Continue. In the following screen, choose only the Built-in Ethernet interface for TCP/IP and deselect any other interfaces. If you are using an Xserve, choose Built-in Ethernet 1. Click Continue.

7   In the TCP/IP connection screen for Built-in Ethernet, choose Manually from the Configure pop-up menu, and then enter the following information, after which you will click Continue:

▶   IP Address: *10.1.17.1*

▶   Subnet Mask: *255.255.0.0*

▶   Router: *10.1.0.1*

▶   DNS Servers: None at this time

▶   Search Domain: None at this time

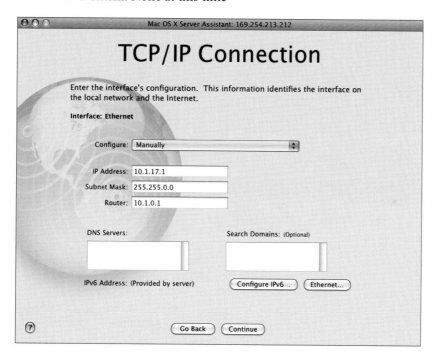

8   Use *server17.pretendco.com* for the Primary DNS Name and *Server 17* for the Computer Name. Click the Edit button to view the local host name. There is no need to change this name. If you own Apple Remote Desktop software and wish to enable that ability to use ARD to manage your server, you can select that option as well. Click Cancel, and then click Continue.

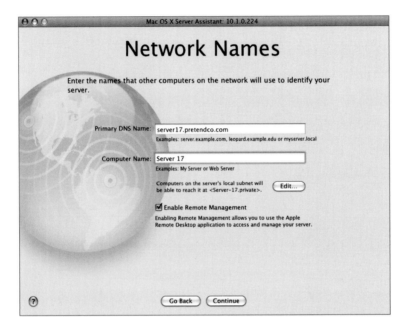

9   Enter the appropriate time zone information. Your server should not be connected to any outside network, so do not allow your server to look for a Network Time server by clicking the Edit button and deselecting the checkbox to do so. Click Continue.

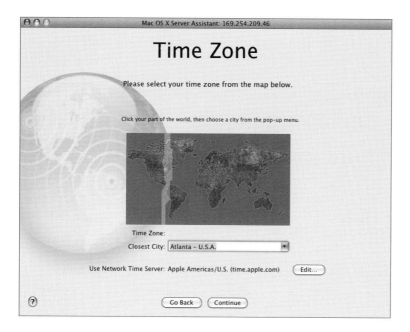

10 Choose the directory usage configuration—for this book, Standalone Server—and click Continue.

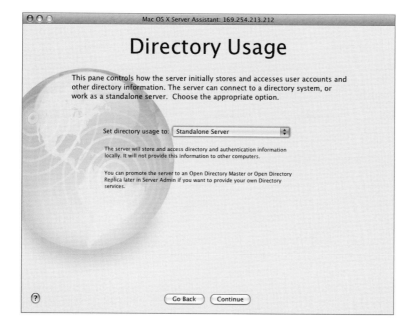

11 You are now at the Confirm Settings screen. Do *not* click the Apply button. Instead, leave your Mac OS X server unconfigured at this point. You will configure it in a later exercise.

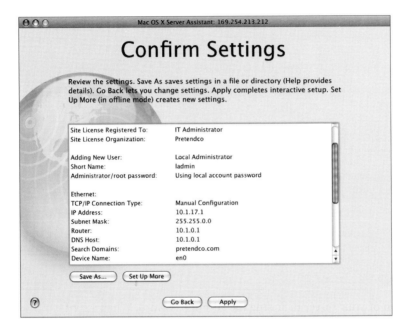

Generating Configuration Data

You can also generate and save the configuration data for later use.

To create server configurations that can be used later, run Server Assistant and choose "Save advanced setup information in a file or directory record." Then proceed to choose the configuration options for the target server in the subsequent windows.

There are three ways to save this information. The first way is to save it as a simple text file. By choosing the first option, Text File, you are saving this file to any location you choose, perhaps to be printed later or saved offline for others to view.

You can also create records to be used by any server, or you can create specific files or records, based on the Ethernet, or MAC, addresses of the target server. If you choose to create generic settings, you will need to leave the Network Names screen blank and configure TCP/IP to use generic settings, such as DHCP. After you have finished the configuration, you are given the option to save the configuration as an XML file, a text file (which can only be used as a description), or a directory record.

The XML file should be placed in a folder named "Auto Server Setup" on any volume mounted on the target server. When the Server Assistant starts, it looks for such a file and automatically configures the server. If you choose to save a configuration as a directory record, you must save it to an existing and fully functional directory server, so you'll need more than just the server you are setting up. If you've done a generic configuration, name the record *generic*. Otherwise, use the MAC address of the target server as the record name. When the Server Assistant starts, if the target server is connected to a network that includes the directory server, the assistant will look for the directory entry and automatically configure the target server.

When saving the configuration record, you have the option of encrypting the file with a passphrase. This is important if you cannot ensure the security of this file, because without a passphrase, the file is stored as clear text, permitting any user to view its contents—the exact configuration of your server including the admin password. When a configuration record is read by a server that is configuring itself, the passphrase is required and must be entered by choosing File > Supply Passphrase in Server Assistant before automatic configuration can take place.

Because you have not configured your server yet, you will save this file for later use in case you want to try this lesson again. Saving the file enables you to manually install a fresh copy of Mac OS X Server, and then have it automatically configured based on the settings we have stated here.

Save Your Settings and Automatically Configure Your Server
You will now save all the settings from all the steps you just completed as a single file, enabling you to configure this server identically should you want to reformat or reinstall the server software.

1   From the Confirm Settings screen, click Save As.

2   Select the Configuration File option and ensure the "Save in Encrypted Format" checkbox is selected and enter *apple* as the passphrase. Click OK.

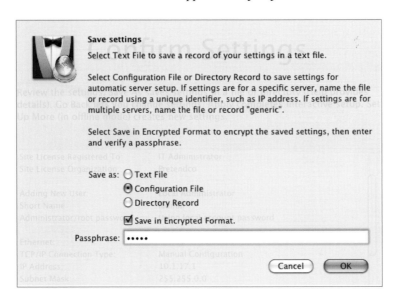

At the Save As dialog, you'll be creating a new folder called Auto Server Setup. Because you are doing this remotely, you will be saving the configuration file to your local Mac OS X computer or attached USB or FireWire device. Notice the name of the file is the 12-digit MAC address of your server, with "plist" as its extension.

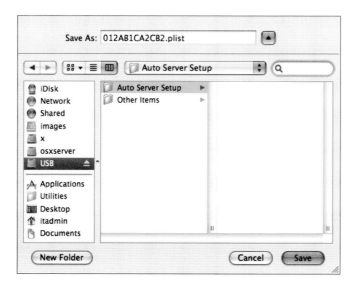

3 Save the file as the default name inside a newly created folder on any USB or FireWire device called Auto Server Setup.

4 Do *not* click the Apply button to apply the settings in Server Assistant.

5 Unmount and remove the USB or FireWire device from your Mac OS X v10.5 computer and plug it into your server.

6 Choose Supply Passphrase under the File menu of Server Assistant and enter the appropriate information and click Send.

Automatic configuration should begin within 30 seconds.

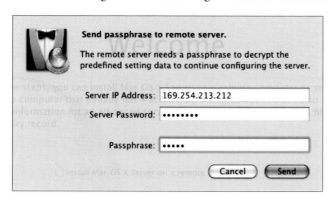

Using Tools

After you have installed Mac OS X Server and performed the basic configuration, you will use a few utilities to perform additional configuration and maintenance of your server. This section introduces eight key utilities:

▶ Network preferences pane

▶ Software Update

▶ Server Admin

▶ Workgroup Manager

▶ Server Preferences

▶ Server Monitor

▶ Server Status Dashboard Widget

▶ System Image Utility

▶ Xgrid Admin (not covered in this book)

Later lessons will introduce additional utilities, such as Directory Utility.

NOTE ▶ You can run Mac OS X Server Admin Tools v10.5 only on Mac OS X v10.5 or later.

Network Preferences Pane

When you are hosting a heavily used server, such as a high-demand file server, you may find that the amount of data that the server can send or receive is limited not by the speed of the server but by the speed of the network interface. Simply adding a second interface does not solve the problem, because the network traffic is targeted toward a specific network address, which is tied to a single interface.

Mac OS X v10.5 supports the 802.3ad specification, or *network link aggregation,* the ability to link two or more Ethernet interfaces together with the same IP address and have them appear as a single interface on the network. This allows network traffic to be shared between the two interfaces, in essence doubling the server's network throughput. Keep in mind that no single client will get more than the speed of one single interface. However, the total aggregate throughput will be the sum total of all interfaces that you have configured in this fashion.

To take advantage of link aggregation, you must have two or more Ethernet interfaces installed on the server. Each of these interfaces must be connected to a network switch that supports link aggregation control protocol (LACP).

To combine the interfaces, create a new network link aggregation configuration in the Network pane of System Preferences.

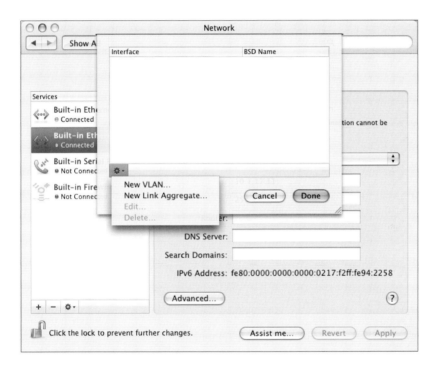

When you choose New Link Aggregate for the new interface, a sheet appears asking you to specify which interfaces should be combined. (In the illustrated example, the server is being configured to use the Xserve's two Built-in Ethernet interfaces). After you create the link aggregate configuration, you add it as a regular interface and configure the interface as if it were a regular Ethernet interface.

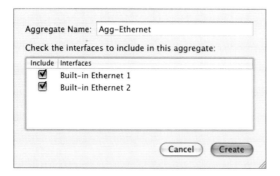

As with any network interface, there will be times when you need to troubleshoot issues related to the linked interfaces. To learn the status of the linked interface, choose the link aggregate configuration from the Services pane in the Network pane of System Preferences. The Status pane lists the information on the aggregate interface along with its speed, duplex setting, and status.

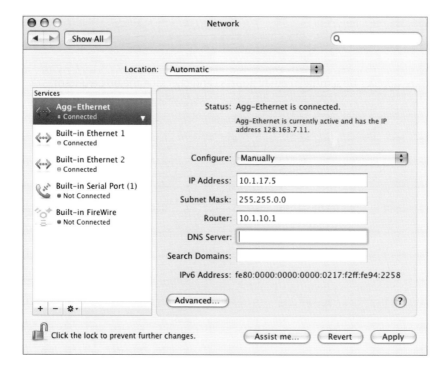

Software Update

After installation and setup are complete, you can update your server locally or remotely. Locally, you would use the Software Update preferences pane of System Preferences or select Software Update from the Apple menu. You should choose to show the details of the updates and select which updates you wish to install, or you can choose to install all updates. Next, authenticate as your local administrator to begin the update process.

Alternately, you can run Software Update remotely by using the Server Admin tool to update your Mac OS X Server. Software Update uses the server's Internet connection to check for the latest software updates for the server. You can also have Server Admin alert you to the presence of software updates by setting an email address and checking the box requesting notification of such updates. This is done under the Settings tab of Server Admin. Regardless of the method, Software Update provides updates for both the base Mac OS X operating system and Mac OS X Server.

> **NOTE** ▶ Plan for software updates. As updates to the server software become available from Apple, you will want to apply them to your servers. This should be done carefully. Your installation may contain third-party software or custom installations that have not been fully qualified with the updated software. Always preflight updates on nonproduction servers before rolling out the changes. Updates from Apple are important and will add value to your implementation. You need to evaluate the updates according to your customer's needs and apply the updates when appropriate—not just because they are available.

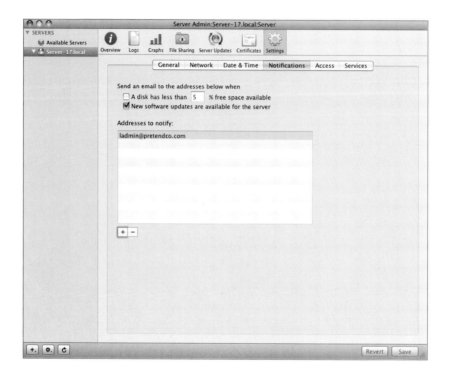

Server Admin

With Server Admin you can configure and monitor services running on Mac OS X Server systems. You also use Server Admin to set up and manage share points, such as folders, or other volumes.

> **NOTE ▶** We cover Server Admin only briefly in this lesson; it is covered in greater detail throughout the book.

Selecting a Server

1   From your server, click the Server Admin icon in the Dock. Or, from your Mac OS X v10.5 computer, launch Server Admin, which is located in the Applications/Server folder (you previously installed the Server Admin Tools on your Mac OS X v10.5 computer).

2   In the Address field, enter the IP address or use the existing local host name (or DNS name if the network is set up for DNS in a production environment) of the server.

Use 10.1.17.1 for now.

3   Authenticate as your local administrator. In this case, use the user name and password (ladmin) you supplied earlier in the Server Assistant.

4   Click Connect.

The All Servers list on the left contains a list of all the servers you're connected to (in this case, just your server at the moment) and the services available on each. To add a server to the window, click the add button in the bar at the bottom of the window and log in to the server. To remove a server from the list, select it, click the gear button, and choose Remove Server.

5   If you did not choose to start any services earlier in the setup process, you will be presented with a window alerting you that there are no services running. Click the Cancel button.

If you select your server from the All Servers list on the left, you will be able to interact with your server directly. If, however, you click directly on the All Servers text in the list, you will be able to view statistics on all the connected servers, such as the name, operating system, CPU usage, network throughput, disk usage, uptime, and number of connected users. Double-clicking the disk usage icon will bring up a window showing the percentage of CPU usage, network traffic, and disk space being used for all mounted volumes.

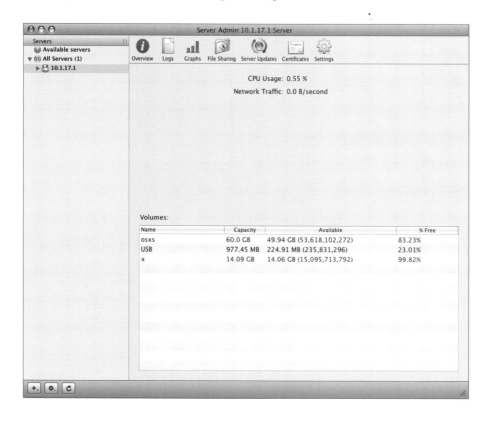

Working with General Settings

To work with the general settings for a server, select the server in the All Servers list and use the buttons at the top of the window:

1   Click Overview to view information about the server. You can view hardware information, server software version information, services running, and disk usage, network throughput, and CPU usage (all located in the Status portion of the Overview window).

2   Click Logs to view the system log, security log, or software update log.

3   Click Graphs to view a graphical history of server CPU and network activity.

Once Graphs are selected, you can choose to view both network traffic and CPU usage over varying lengths of time (past day, 1, 2, 4, 6, 12, and 24 hours; 2, 3, 5, 7 days and the past week) by selecting either option from the pop-up menu at the bottom of the window.

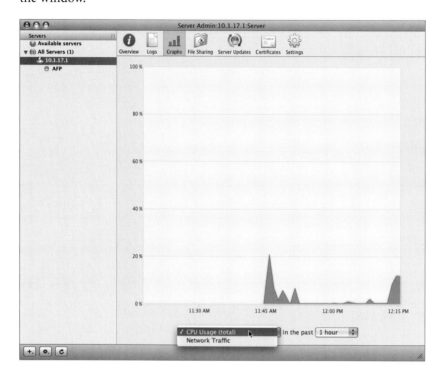

4   Click File Sharing to view all mounted volumes, preset share points, user and group permissions, and quotas on share points. You can also browse a volume hierarchy and set up new share points.

5   Click Server Update to use Software Update to remotely update the server's software.

6   Click Certificates to view the default certificate generated when Mac OS X Server v10.5 is set up or create and manage your own certificates.

7   Click Settings and the subsequent tabs to edit information such as the date and time, the server's computer name and serial number, to configure services, and to enable Simple Network Management Protocol (SNMP), NTP, Secure Shell (ssh), Apple Remote Desktop (ARD), and the FileSync Agent Protocol.

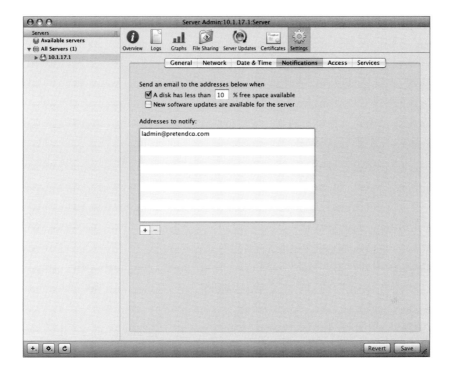

8   Click Notifications to configure the sending of an email to a specified address when one of two criteria are met:

▶   A disk has less than x% of free space, where x is determined by you.

▶   New software updates are available for the server.

9   Click Access to restrict who can connect to the server over various services and who can administer those services.

10   Click Services to select various services to be offered by your server.

Working with Services

To work with a particular service on a server, select that service and check the box next to the service, then click the Save button at the bottom of the window. Next, click the disclosure triangle beside the server, then click the service. Use the buttons at the top of the window to manage the service's settings and display status information, including logs and graphs.

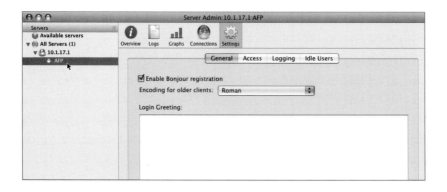

To start or stop a service, select it in the All Servers list under your server, then click the Start Service Name ▶ or Stop Service Name ✕ button at the bottom of the window. Server Admin can have several windows open at once by selecting New Server Admin Window under the Servers menu, and you can be connected to several servers simultaneously by clicking the Add Server button at the bottom of the window. Table 1.4 defines the Mac OS X Server services.

Table 1.4 Mac OS X Server services list

Service	Function
AFP	File sharing for Macs
DHCP	Distributes IP address and associated information
DNS	Maps IP addresses to names
Firewall	Protects ports against attacks
FTP	File sharing for most computers
iCal	Calendar service for users and groups
iChat	iChat service for user and groups
Mail	Mail service
MySQL	Database service using MySQL
NAT	Network Address Translation
NetBoot	Network booting and installing service
NFS	File sharing for most computers
Open Directory	Shared directory and authentication service
Podcast Producer	Automates and shares processing of podcast creation
Print	Offers print services
QuickTime Streaming	Streams media for access via web page or QuickTime Player
RADIUS	Strict authentication for remote access to server

Table 1.4 Mac OS X Server services list (continued)

Service	Function
SMB	File sharing for Windows and Macs
Software Update	Offers Apple software updates stored locally
VPN	Virtual Private Network service
Web	Create and manage multiple web sites
WebObjects	Hosts WebObjects applications
Xgrid	Manages processing jobs across a grid of Macs

When you select certain services, such as RADIUS, you may be presented with a dialog asking if you would prefer assistance in setting up that particular service that, when clicked, opens a new window and presents a step-by-step assistant helping you through the setup of that service.

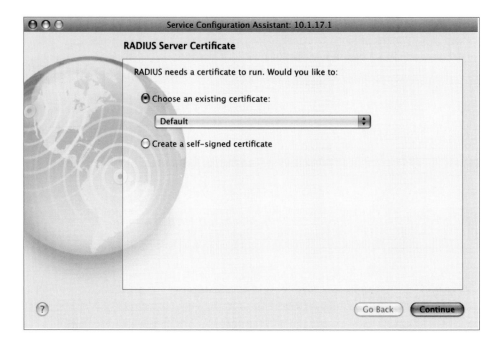

Exporting and Importing Settings

You can export (and subsequently import) both service settings and your server settings by choosing Export > Service Settings and/or Export > Server Admin Preferences. When exporting your Server Admin preferences, you can save the single file anywhere you choose. When saving service settings, you are presented with a dialog showing all the currently running services. You simply select the checkbox next to the services whose settings you want to save and click OK. Find a location suitable for saving those preferences and save them.

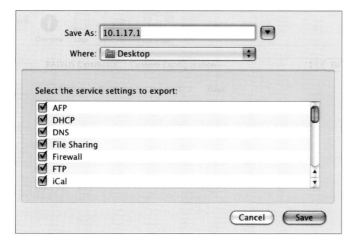

Conversely, when you are ready to import a service setting, simply locate the appropriate file and choose Server > Import in Server Admin.

Enabling Screen Sharing

Using Server Admin, you can control the screen of a Mac OS X Server v10.5. You must first connect and authenticate to the server, so you can see the Overview window and other various services windows. With the server selected from the All Servers list on the left, choose "Share Server's Screen" under the gear button  .

An authentication window appears, asking you for your local administrator user name and password. Once you enter the information requested and click Connect, a new window appears, allowing you to take control of the keyboard and mouse of your server.

Workgroup Manager

With Workgroup Manager you can administer users, groups, computers and computer groups, and perform client management. Account information can be entered individually or imported from a compatible file. There are two ways to use Workgroup Manager, depending on whether you spend most of your time working with one server or several. If you work with a single server most of the time, authenticate when you open Workgroup Manager.

> **NOTE ▶** We cover Workgroup Manager only briefly in this lesson; it is covered in greater detail throughout the book.

To work with Workgroup Manager:

1   From your server, click the Workgroup Manager icon in the Dock. Or, from your Mac OS X computer, launch Workgroup Manager, which is located in the Applications/Server folder.

2   In the Address field, enter the IP address or use the existing local name (or DNS name if the network is set up for DNS in a production environment) of the server or click Browse to select from a list of servers on your local network. You will use 10.1.17.1 for this book.

NOTE ▶ If you administer several different servers and work with different directory domains (directories will be discussed in Lesson 4, "Using Open Directory"), open Workgroup Manager without authenticating. To do so, click Cancel in the Workgroup Manager Connect window and choose View Directories from the Server menu. You will have read-only access to information displayed in Workgroup Manager for directories you have access to. To make changes, click the lock icon to authenticate as an administrator.

3 After you authenticate, a dialog appears notifying you that you will be working in the local directory, one that is not visible to others in your network. Click OK, and the Accounts window appears with lists of user, user groups, computers, and computer groups in the server's local directory domain. The following options are available:

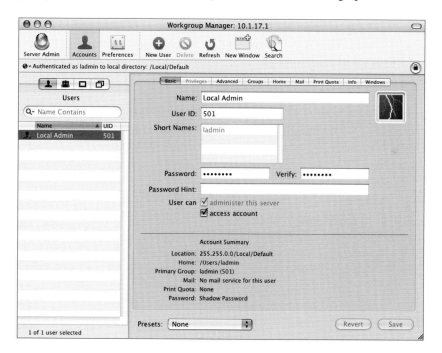

▶ Click the Server Admin icon in the toolbar to launch Server Admin.

▶ Click the Accounts icon in the toolbar to administer user, user groups, computers, or computer groups.

▶ Click the Preferences icon in the toolbar to work with preferences for managed accounts.

Server Preferences

Server Preferences is similar to System Preferences in look and feel. It appears when you initially set up your server with either a Standard or Workgroup configuration. You will not be able to use this application if you specified an Advanced configuration when setting up your server.

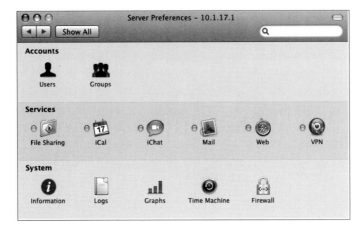

Server Preferences is used instead of Server Admin and Workgroup Manager to manage local user and group accounts and just a few of Mac OS X Server's v10.5 services. They are:

▶ File sharing

▶ Calendaring service

▶ iChat service

▶ Mail service

▶ Web service

▶ Virtual Private Networking (VPN) services

▶ Firewall service

You can also view server information and system and secure log files, show usage graphs, and manage Time Machine settings. If you choose to alter a Standard or Workgroup configuration during setup by not selecting more services than the Server Assistant suggests (or if you do an Advanced configuration), you will receive an error when attempting to use Server Preferences for management of your server.

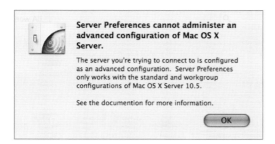

Server Monitor

Server Monitor is used to monitor various statistics of your server:

▶ General server information

▶ Drive status

▶ Power information

▶ Network activity

▶ Temperature and blower statistics

▶ Memory configuration and health

▶ Security lock information

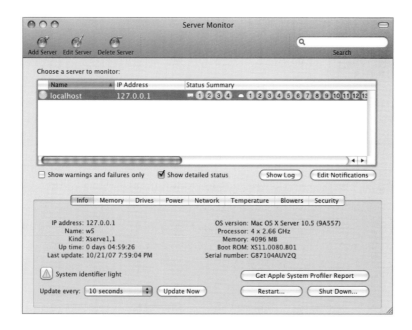

When using Server Monitor on an Intel-based Xserve, it is important to enter the Lights-Out Management (LOM) IP address and administrative information.

Server Status Dashboard Widget

The Server Status Dashboard Widget permits an administrator to monitor several aspects of your server. It is installed on Mac OS X Server and on any Mac OS X v10.5 Mac that has Server Admin Tools v10.5 installed. The Server Status widget will monitor:

▶ Various services and their status

▶ CPU utilization

▶ Network load

▶ Disk usage

The Server Status Dashboard widget is installed along with all other Server Admin tools although it does not appear in the /Applications/Server/ folder.

To use the Server Status Dashboard widget, first activate the Dashboard by clicking the F12 button on your Mac OS X v10.5 Mac, clicking the plus button in the lower-left corner, and selecting the Server Status widget from the list at the bottom of the screen.

Once the Server Status widget appears, enter your server's IP address (or fully qualified domain name if your server is set up within a working DNS environment) and local administrator's short name and password, and click the Done button.

Once you are connected, you will see three icons across the middle of the widget, and clicking each one will reveal (in order from left to right) CPU utilization, network activity, and free disk space. Clicking each icon will update the graphic above the icons with the relevant information for your server. Moving your mouse over the graphic will show used and free totals for disk usage and permits you to change the view of network activity and CPU usage over time (last hour, last day, last week).

You can also open a second widget and connect to the same server should you want to monitor more than one item simultaneously, such as the percentage of disk space (used and free) and network activity.

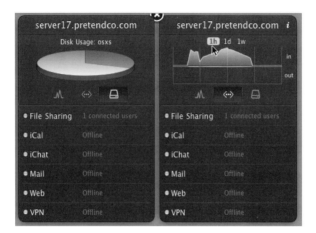

Troubleshooting

For troubleshooting during installation, you can display the installer log, as discussed earlier in this lesson. This is most useful when an installation does not complete correctly. In that case, rerun the installation with the log file showing, so that you can identify where the problem occurred and compare it to a successful installation's log file.

If you use Server Assistant to create an automatic configuration file, as we did in this lesson, be sure to delete the file from the drives attached to the server after the server has been set up. Otherwise, if you need to repurpose the server after you reinstall the server software, the server will be automatically configured using the old configuration data.

> **NOTE** ▶ One common problem found in server installations is incompatibility with third-party hardware and software configurations. Many times bad third-party RAM has caused problems. Isolate the changes to your system when you run into problems. Keep the variables to a minimum.

What You've Learned

▶ Mac OS X Server requires a desktop computer with a PowerPC G4 (867 MHz or faster), G5, or Intel processor, at least 1 GB of RAM, and 20 GB of available disk space.

▶ The Mac OS X Server Assistant guides you through the initial configuration of your server.

▶ You can install and configure Mac OS X Server v10.5 remotely using a variety of tools such as Server Assistant and Server Admin.

▶ Link aggregation enables you to improve performance by combining two or more Ethernet ports and having them act as one.

▶ Apple provides updates to Mac OS X Server through the Software Update service. To ensure that your system is up-to-date, run Software Update on a regular basis.

▶ You use Server Admin to configure and monitor Mac OS X Server services and share points.

▶ You use Workgroup Manager to manage user, user groups, computer and computer groups, and managed preferences.

▶ You can use the Server Status widget to monitor the state of various services, disk usage, and CPU and network use over time.

References

The following documents provide more information about installing Mac OS X Server. (All of these and more are available at www.apple.com/server/documentation.)

Administration Guides

Mac OS X Server Getting Started (http://images.apple.com/server/pdfs/Getting_Started_v10.5.pdf)

Upgrading and Migrating to Mac OS X Server v10.5 Tiger (http://images.apple.com/server/pdfs/Migration_v10.5.pdf)

Mac OS X Server Command-Line Administration (http://images.apple.com/server/pdfs/Command_Line_v10.5.pdf)

Apple Knowledge Base Documents

You can check for new and updated Knowledge Base documents at www.apple.com/support.

Document 301590, "Mac OS X Server: Admin Tools compatibility information"

Review Quiz

1. What are the minimum hardware requirements for installing Mac OS X Server v10.5?

2. What information must you collect before installing Mac OS X Server?

3. What are three things that the Server Assistant application can be used to do?

4. In what formats can Server Assistant save setup information, and what is each format used for?

5. What tool should be used to keep Mac OS X Server up-to-date with the latest versions of software?

Answers

1. The minimum requirements are:

   ▶ A desktop Macintosh computer with a PowerPC G4 (867 MHz or faster), G5, or Intel processor

   ▶ 1 GB of RAM (at least 1.5 GB of RAM for high-demand servers running multiple services)

   ▶ 20 GB of available disk space

2. Hardware serial number and MAC address(es) of the computer, administrator name and password, computer name, TCP/IP configuration, and directory service usage.

3. Server Assistant can be used to install Mac OS X Server v10.5 on a remote server, to set up a remote Mac OS X Server v10.5 system, and to save and encrypt setup information for a Mac OS X Server v10.5 server in a file or directory record.

4. Server Assistant can save setup information in the following formats:

   ▶ Text file: Used as a description of the setup (just a reference).

   ▶ XML file: Can be placed on any volume mounted on the target server to automatically configure that server.

   ▶ Directory record: Can be saved in the directory service master to be discovered by a target server for automatic configuration of that server.

5. Software Update (in System Preferences) or the Software Update window of Server Admin.

2

Time   This lesson takes approximately 1 hour to complete.

Goals   Describe how the Domain Name System associates computer names with IP addresses

Create a new zone using the Server Admin tool

Add Mail Exchange records to a DNS zone

Verify the DNS service is functioning properly

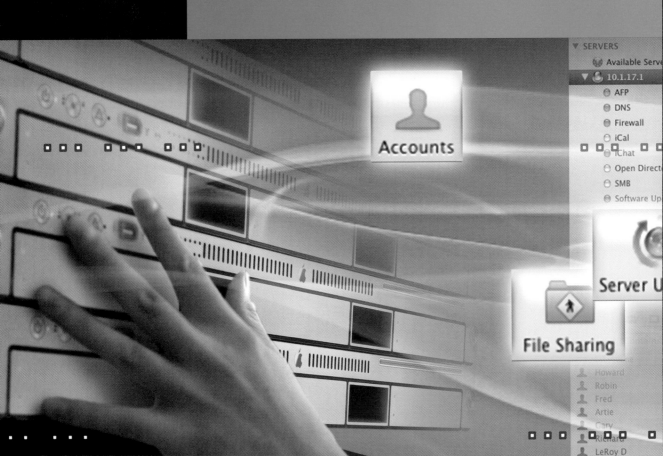

Providing Basic DNS Service

DNS is the method computers use to map IP addresses to domain names. Computers use IP addresses to locate one another, but they are not easy for people to commit to memory. Domain names, such as www.apple.com or train.apple.com, are much easier to remember, but they need to be translated into the IP addresses that computers use. In essence and at its most basic level, DNS performs this translation.

A DNS service is also used to cache information, reducing the amount of traffic necessary to resolve names that are accessed frequently. For example, a DNS service running on a Mac OS X Server can cache requests for other servers it already knows about, returning subsequent requests from the cache without looking up the information again. The cache has a parameter that can be set to expire the cache's data after a given amount of time.

If more than one DNS service server is used, information on one server may not be the same as information on another. If requests for information come into your DNS service server and your server does not know the answer, it may relay the request to another DNS server. Relaying requests is common for DNS service servers that do not contain information about a certain server in either its own files or the cache.

DNS Basics

Here's a simple example for understanding DNS. Imagine a user who wants to access a website such as Apple's training site. That user is connected to the correct server for Apple's training department by entering *http://train.apple.com* in a browser. The following graphic depicts what is actually happening behind the scenes on the Internet to make this connection occur.

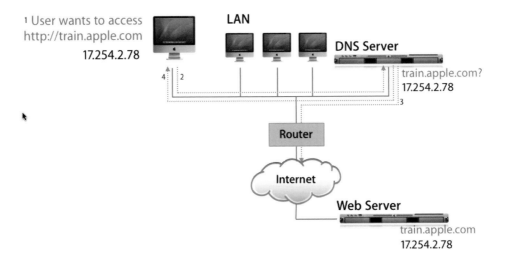

1. A user enters *http://train.apple.com*.

2. The user's computer checks with a DNS server to find the IP address associated with the domain name train.apple.com. The computer uses the DNS server configured in Network preferences to look up this information. This is referred to as a *forward lookup* or just *lookup.*

3. The DNS server determines the IP address that corresponds to the domain name requested in the lookup. It returns this information to the user's computer.

4. The user's computer then uses the IP address to request the training webpage by sending this IP address to its default Internet router.

This DNS scenario oversimplifies the true capabilities of DNS. The real power of DNS is that any valid IP address in the world can be found quickly and easily, yet easily maintained. This is due to the global design of DNS.

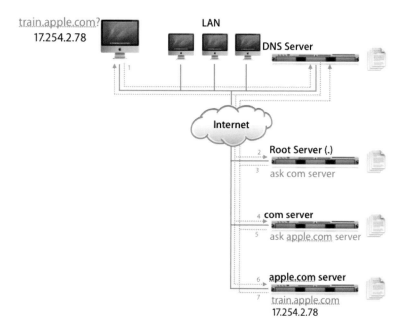

DNS combines a global search space with a local, relatively easy way to maintain the search space. It does this through a hierarchical structure in which each organization is responsible for maintaining its own DNS information.

1. Again, we have a user who enters *http://train.apple.com*, perhaps from Japan.

2. The Japanese company most certainly maintains its own DNS service running locally on a server there, but this server may not know how the DNS structure is handled across the Pacific and must therefore contact one of the 13 root servers across the globe.

3. These servers return the information concerning how to contact one of the .com DNS servers to the requestor—in this case the Japanese company's DNS server.

4. The Japanese DNS server subsequently contacts one of the .com servers asking for apple.com.

5. The .com server locates the appropriate record (possibly by contacting other .com DNS servers or redirecting the request) and returns the information concerning how to contact apple.com.

6. The Japanese DNS server subsequently contacts apple.com asking for train.apple.com.

7. The DNS service handling all of apple.com's servers returns the information concerning how to contact train.apple.com, and the Japanese DNS server hands over that information—in the form of an IP address—to the client that originally made the request.

All valid DNS servers on the Internet can eventually find DNS information on any address by following the hierarchical lookup through this top-level approach. In this case, the computer in Japan finds the correct DNS mapping by following the lookup process and eventually finding a DNS server in the United States that is responsible for mapping the address train.apple.com to the IP address 17.254.2.78.

This process highlights the other key aspect of DNS—locally maintained DNS servers. For example, Apple maintains a list of computers for various web services. Apple can reassign IP addresses internally to meet its server needs, as long as Apple maintains a correct set of DNS files on its local DNS servers and has the DNS servers configured appropriately to be available to higher-level DNS servers that contact them.

The key to these DNS servers is correctly configured files containing the DNS information. These files are typically referred to as *DNS configuration* and *zone* files.

DNS Setup

Mac OS X Server includes DNS server functionality based on the standard UNIX-based implementation of BIND (Berkeley Internet Name Domain). BIND is the most common implementation of DNS in use on the Internet today, and Mac OS X and Mac OS X Server currently include BIND version 9.4.1.

Most companies that use Mac OS X Server for services such as file, print, and web serving have already established appropriate DNS service. This service could be provided by dedicated DNS departments in their organizations or by an Internet service provider (ISP). Companies running their own mail services would also want to ensure DNS service correctly maps their IP addresses to their mail domains. If a company has not established DNS service yet, the following steps are required to configure DNS for Mac OS X Server:

1 Register your domain name via any valid registrar, such as VeriSign.

2 Use Server Admin to enable the DNS service.

3 Configure BIND on Mac OS X Server by modifying the DNS configuration and zone files.

4   Set up mail exchange (MX) records (optional).

5   Start DNS service.

> **NOTE ▶** DNS is a complicated topic that covers a wide range of configuration options and settings. This lesson does not cover in-depth DNS configuration. You will add information to your DNS configuration that will enable you to associate a friendly name with your computer and see the effects of that change.

With Mac OS X Server, you can configure DNS zone files with Server Admin.

> **NOTE ▶** This lesson covers the setup of basic DNS records. To find detailed information on configuring DNS files, refer to the "References" section at the end of this lesson.

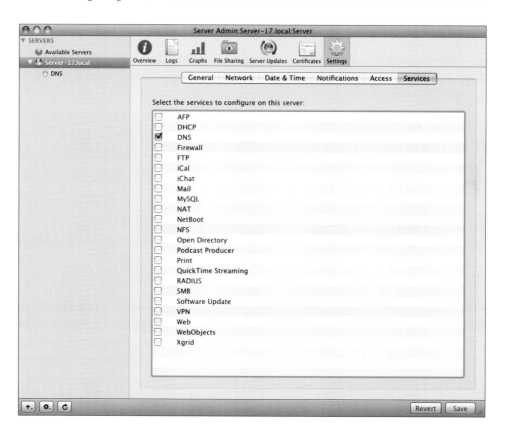

DNS Zones

Zones are the basic organizational unit of the DNS. Zones contain records, and are defined by how they acquire those records and how they respond to DNS requests. There are three kinds of zones:

- ▶ A *master zone* has the master copy of the zone's records and provides authoritative answers to lookup requests.

- ▶ A *slave zone* is a copy of a master zone stored on a slave or secondary name server. Each slave zone keeps a list of masters that it contacts to receive updates to records in the master zone. Slaves must be configured to request the copy of the master zone's data. Slave zones use zone transfers to get copies of the master zone data. Slave name servers can take lookup requests like master servers. By using several slave zones linked to one master, you can distribute DNS query loads across several computers and ensure that lookup requests are answered when the master name server is down.

  Slave zones also have a refresh interval that determines how often slave zones check for changes from the master zone. You can change this interval by using the BIND configuration file. See the BIND documentation for more information.

- ▶ A DNS *forward zone* directs all lookup requests for that zone to other DNS servers. Forward zones don't do zone transfers. Often, forward zone servers are used to provide DNS services to a private network behind a firewall. In this case, the DNS server must have access to the Internet and a DNS server outside the firewall. Finally, forward zones cache responses to the queries that they pass on. This can improve the performance of lookups by clients that use the forward zone.

Add a Zone to a DNS Server

Before you can add a zone, you must first enable the DNS service on your server. To do so, launch Server Admin and authenticate as your local administrator. Select your server from the Available Servers list, click the Settings icon in the toolbar, and click the Services tab. Enable DNS and save the changes. You can now select the DNS service under your server on the left side of Server Admin and create a new zone.

You manage zones using Server Admin. For each zone, you can add, edit, delete, and duplicate records. When you add a record, you are prompted for the type of record you want to add. After you add a record, it is displayed in the Records list for that zone.

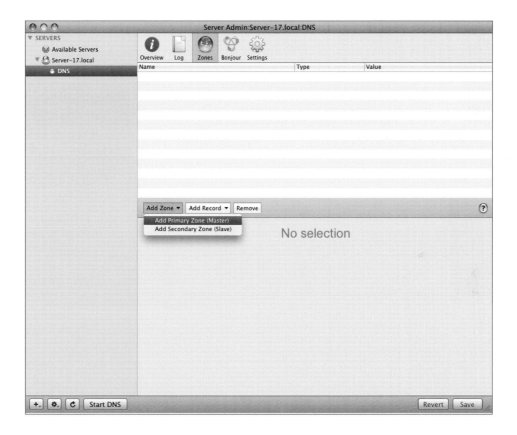

1   Select the DNS service and click the Zones icon in the toolbar.

2   Click the Add Zone button and choose Add Primary Zone (Master).

3   Select the example zone from the list and edit the Primary Zone and Machine name to represent your domain and your computer name. In this case, we are using pretendco.com. and server17, respectively. Save the changes.

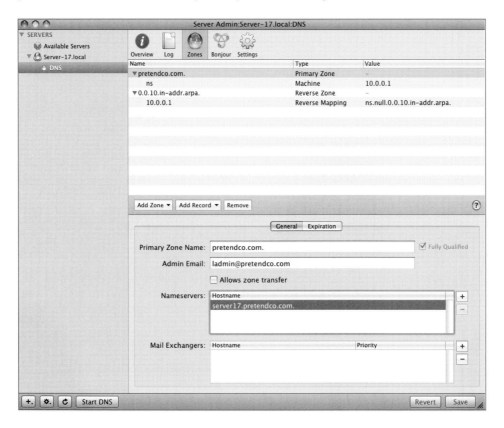

4   Click the disclosure triangle next to your zone and choose the machine record in the list. Edit your machine name and IP address to correctly reflect the IP address of your server. Save the changes. A new record, a reverse record, is now created and correctly updated with the information you provided. The reverse record simply resolves the IP address back to the server, just as the forward record resolved the name to the IP address.

5   Start the DNS service by clicking the Start DNS button. Then open the Network preferences pane on your Mac OS X Server and enter the IP address and domain name of your server. Apply the changes. Your server is now running DNS and looking at itself to ensure that any other service—such as Lightweight Directory Access Protocol (LDAP)—will respond to either the IP address or the computer's fully qualified domain name.

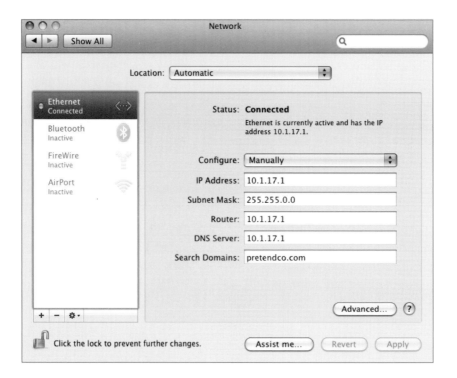

DNS Zone Records

Each zone contains a number of records. These records are requested when a client computer needs to translate a domain name (like www.pretendco.com) to an IP number. Web browsers, email clients, and other network applications rely on zone records to contact the appropriate server. You create records by adding machines to a zone in Server Admin. In some cases, you are adding secondary names for the same machine. For example, server17.pretendco.com can also be www.pretendco.com and/or smtp.pretendco.com.

Your master zone's records will be queried by other computers across the Internet so they can connect to your network services. There are several kinds of DNS records. The following are the records that are available for configuration by Server Admin's user interface:

▶ Address (A): Also known as a machine record. Stores the IP address associated with a domain name. An A record is created for each machine entry added to a zone.

▶ Canonical name (CNAME): Stores the "real name" of a server when given a nickname or alias. For example, mail.pretendco.com might have a canonical name of mailsrvr1.pretendco.com. A CNAME record is created for each entry in the Alias field when adding a machine to a zone.

▶ Mail exchange (MX): Stores the name of the computer that is used for email for a domain. An MX record is created when you specify that a machine is a mail server. You can have more than one MX record for your domain pointing to different servers. Lower numbers are given priority over higher numbers when users attempt to use the mail servers on your network.

▶ Service (SRV): Service records store the information about various services, such as LDAP, Jabber, and Simple Mail Transfer Protocol (SMTP). These services are then mapped to the proper IP address and resolved to their respective domain name.

▶ Pointer (PTR): Automatically created. Stores the domain name of a given IP address (reverse lookup). A PTR record maps an IP address to a computer's DNS name. The pointer record contains the four octets of the IP address in reverse order followed by in-addr.arpa. (For example, 10.1.17.1 becomes 1.17.1.10.in-addr.arpa.)

Mac OS X Server simplifies the creation of these records by focusing on the computer name being added to the zone rather than the records themselves. As you add a computer record to a zone, Mac OS X Server creates the proper pointer zone record that resolves to a certain computer address.

> **NOTE** ▶ The term fully qualified domain name (FQDN) refers to the entire address of a host computer. For example, "sales.apple.com" is an FQDN, whereas "sales" is a relative domain name. To indicate that a domain name is fully qualified, add a trailing dot to it (which Mac OS X Server v10.5 automatically does when selecting the checkbox for Fully Qualified). For example, "sales.apple.com." indicates that this is not a relative domain name.

Add Records to a DNS Server

DNS is a complicated topic that covers a wide range of configuration options and settings. This lesson does not cover in-depth DNS configuration. You will add information to your DNS configuration that will enable you to associate a friendly name with your computer and see the effects of that change. You will be adding several types of records to permit the server to respond to additional names—such as www.pretendco.com—that will be used in later lessons. You will also be adding a record for your Mac OS X computer, so it can also resolve to a name.

1 Within Server Admin, select the DNS service if it's not already selected and click the Zones icon in the toolbar. Select the Primary Zone for your server. Click the disclosure triangle to view the machine record, but do not click the machine record yet.

2 Click the add button adjacent to the Mail Exchangers entry box and enter the word *mail* in the Hostname list. Then enter the number *10* in the Priority list and click Save. The FQDN will appear in the list along with the priority value for that MX record.

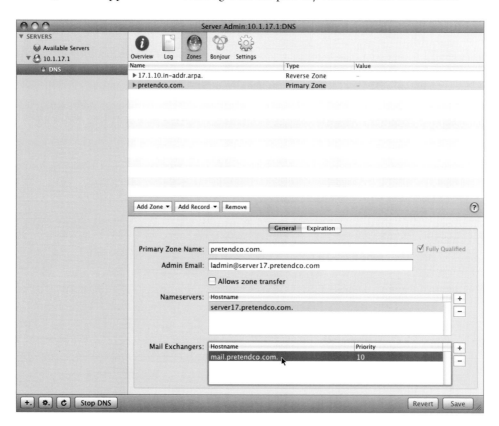

3 Select the machine record from the list, click the Add Record button, and choose Add Machine (A).

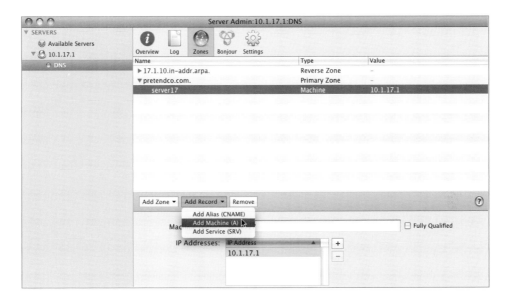

4 Click the add button to create a machine record and edit the IP address accordingly. Click Save.

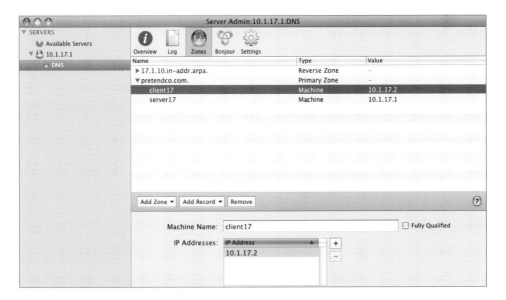

5 Repeat the process of adding a record, but this time, choose Add Alias (CNAME) record.

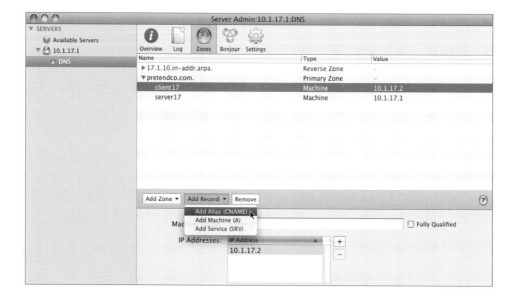

6 Select the line "newAlias" from the list of records in the zone. When you do so, the bottom pane of the window changes to reflect what you have chosen.

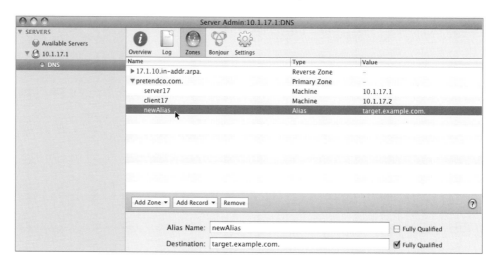

7 Enter *www* in the Alias Name field and *server17* in the Destination field. It is not necessary to check the Fully Qualified boxes because they will uncheck themselves when
you enter the data.

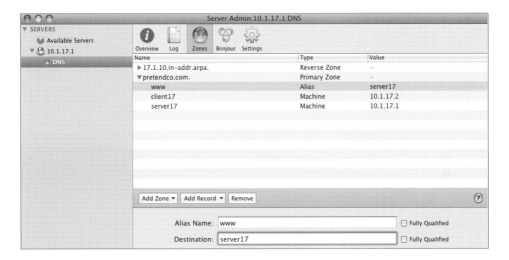

After you click Save and look at the Alias record in the list above (under the pretendco.
com zone) within Server Admin, you will notice that the Fully Qualified box is now
selected. This box refers to how the name is shown, where server17 is just the name,
but server17.pretendco.com is the FQDN.

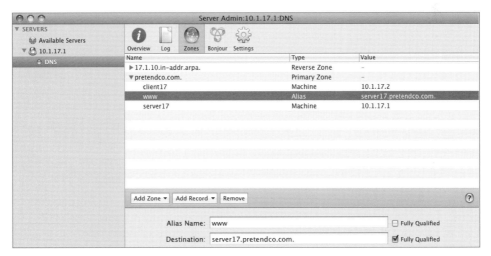

You have now added a mail exchange record and set its priority, added a machine record for your Mac OS X computer, and added an alias record for using www.pretendco.com and having it resolve to the same IP address as server17.pretendco.com.

Enter the DNS Search Information

You must now change the IP configuration information and enter DNS search information inside the Network preferences pane of your Mac OS X computer.

1   On your Mac OS X computer, open System Preferences, navigate to the Network preferences pane, and configure your network settings as follows:

▶   IP Address: *10.1.17.2*

▶   Subnet: *255.255.0.0*

▶   Router: *10.1.17.1*

▶   DNS Servers: *10.1.17.1*

▶   Search Domains: *pretendco.com*

2   Click the Apply button and quit System Preferences.

Troubleshooting

DNS issues take many forms. You may have problems related to end users who misunderstand your DNS hierarchy, or typographic problems in your DNS aliases. A system administrator must be able to determine where a DNS entry is being resolved.

Isolate and Resolve DNS Issues

DNS is a complicated and subtle protocol. Its distributed nature often makes it difficult to discern where a problem lies: Is it the client, the local DNS server, or some remote DNS server on the Internet? Advanced DNS issues will likely require an experienced system administrator. However, a few quick checks can help you isolate a problem.

Perform DNS Lookups

The best graphical tool for troubleshooting DNS issues is Network Utility. The real test of any DNS change is when your DNS clients can use the new entry. Because of the limited number of services available (we have used only a fraction of what can be set up with DNS), you will use both ping and lookup from your client computer to see if DNS is configured properly. There are a variety of ways to ensure DNS is working. Using both the Ping and the Lookup panes of Network Utility allows for testing of the DNS service on your server.

Perform the following checks when you troubleshoot DNS problems:

▶   Check hardware and network issues.

▶   Verify that network settings are correct in the Network pane of System Preferences.

▶   Use Network Utility's Lookup pane to test your DNS server.

▶   Use Network Utility's Ping pane to test direct IP connectivity, bypassing DNS.

▶   Ping another computer on your subnet to test for basic IP connectivity, but also be sure to test the IP address that is listed as the DNS server in Network preferences.

▶   Check with a network administrator to ensure that DNS servers are configured properly.

   NOTE ▶ In most cases, DNS problems stem from a local configuration issue (hardware, network, or software) or from a recently installed DNS server. DNS servers that have been in place for some time are typically not the source of problems.

1   On your client computer, open /Utilities/Network Utility and click the Ping tab.

2 In the address field, type *server17* and click the Ping button.

The ping command should execute properly and resolve to 10.1.17.1.

This confirms you successfully created the zone record and initial machine record.

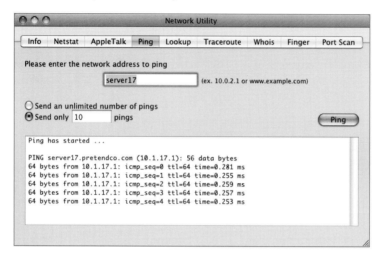

3 In the address field, type *client17* and click Ping.

The ping command should execute properly and resolve to 10.1.17.2.

This confirms you successfully created the secondary machine record.

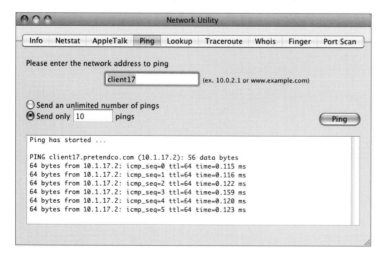

4   In the address field, type *www* and click Ping.

The ping command should execute properly and resolve to 10.1.17.1.

This confirms you successfully created the alias record.

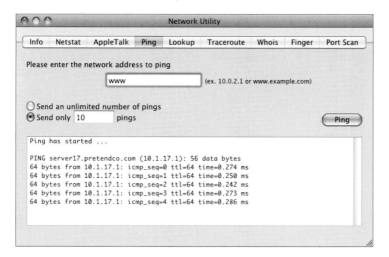

5   Click the Lookup tab of Network Utility and enter the same information you entered in the Ping field.

Entering *server17* should return a machine (A) record of 10.1.17.1.

Entering *client17* should return a machine (A) record for 10.1.17.2.

Entering *www* should return an alias (CNAME) record for 10.1.17.1.

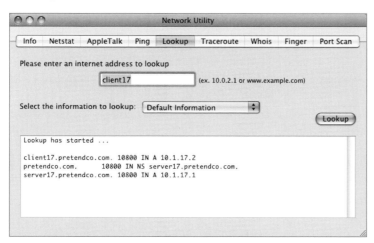

DNS Activity Monitor

Within Server Admin, you can monitor DNS activity on Mac OS X Server using the Overview, Activity, and Log panes for DNS.

▶ The Overview pane displays information such as DNS server status (Running/Stopped), start time, and number of Primary and Secondary zones allocated.

▶ The Log pane displays current information about start time and DNS queries (lookups). The level of logging can be changed under the Settings pane.

▶ The Bonjour pane permits management of automatic discovery of DNS records by all clients on the local subnet and permits the restriction of advertised Bonjour services, such as iTunes or iPhoto, on the local subnet without the appropriate user name and password.

▶ The Settings pane enables recursive queries and DNS forwarding to specific networks, along with changing the level of DNS logging.

DNS is an essential function in any running version of Mac OS X. Many services look for DNS information to find critical information. Examples of these services are the login window, server administration tools, directory services, Internet communications, and any direct web access. Incorrectly configured DNS could result in a long delay in these services completing their associated tasks.

What You've Learned

▶ Typically, when you think of setting up a server, you think of configuring a file, mail, or web server. However, Mac OS X Server can provide even more fundamental network services, such as DNS.

▶ DNS provides the ability for domain names to be converted to IP addresses. DNS is turned on using Server Admin.

▶ An alias (CNAME) record maps another name for your server to the same IP address.

▶ MX records are used when telling DNS where to locate the mail servers on the network and in what order they should be used.

▶ Network Utility is used to troubleshoot DNS server records.

References

The following documents provide more information about installing Mac OS X Server. (All of these and more are available at www.apple.com/server/documentation.)

Administration Guides

Managing the DNS Service (http://images.apple.com/server/macosx/docs/ Network_Services_Admin_v10.5.pdf)

Books

Albitz, Paul, and Liu, Cricket. *DNS and BIND* (O'Reilly, 2001).

Apple Knowledge Base Documents

You can check for new and updated Knowledge Base documents at www.apple.com/support.

Review Quiz

1. What are the global and local aspects of DNS architecture?

2. What is an alias record?

3. What are three types of records that can be added using Server Admin to Mac OS X Server's DNS zone files?

4. What are three possible steps you can take when investigating a DNS problem?

Answers

1. DNS is a distributed system. It is local in that each separate domain is responsible for its own configuration, so that domain configuration files are located on multiple DNS servers across the Internet. It is global in that all the separate domains are integrated into one unified system in which queries are handled by the responsible name server and all clients can obtain correct name resolution from anywhere on the Internet.

2. Canonical name (CNAME): Stores the "real name" of a server when given a nick-name or alias. For example, mail.pretendco.com might have a canonical name of mailsrvr1.pretendco.com. A CNAME record is created for each entry in the Alias field when adding a machine to a zone.

3. Alias (CNAME), machine (A), and service (SRV) records.

4. You can:

   a. Verify network settings.

   b. Use Network Utility to test for forward and reverse lookups.

   c. Use Network Utility to ping the DNS server.

   Use Network Utility to test for basic IP connectivity by pinging another device on the subnet.

3

Lesson Files   Server Essentials > Lesson_03 > 01employees

Time   This lesson takes approximately 3 hours to complete.

Goals   Configure Mac OS X Server to control access to an account

Configure Mac OS X Server to control access to files and folders based on user and group accounts

Define authentication and authorization as they are used in Mac OS X Server

Use Server Admin to configure share points and permissions

Use Workgroup Manager to create local user accounts and groups

Use Server Admin and Workgroup Manager to create administrators

Understand and implement file system and service ACLs in Mac OS X Server

Authenticating and Authorizing Accounts

Authentication is the process by which a person identifies which user account he or she will use on the system. This is similar to, but slightly different from, saying that authentication is how a person proves his or her identity to a system. This distinction is useful because multiple people may share the same user name and password, or one person may have multiple user accounts on the same system. In each case, the name and password identify which user account the person wants to use, assuming the name and password are entered correctly. While there are other methods of authenticating a user account, such as smart cards or voice print, a name and password are the most common (and are assumed for this lesson).

Authorization is the process that determines what a person with an authenticated user account is allowed to do on the system. Authorization is associated with user account file-access permissions that are set through Mac OS X, or through the Mac OS X Server administration tools for service access.

This lesson will cover creating and maintaining user and group accounts on your server. You'll learn how to configure user and group accounts as well as how these accounts are used for controlling access to both files and services. Access is based on authentication, therefore it is important that you understand how authorization is handled.

Managing Server Access

When configuring any server for access by users, you'll need to determine what services the server will provide and what levels of user access to assign. So far, we have discussed only network services, which do not require any specific user access to the server once the service is enabled. For many of the other services this book will cover, such as file sharing, you will need to create specific user accounts on your server.

When considering the creation of user accounts, you'll want to determine how to best set up your users, how to organize them into groups that match the needs of your organization, and how to best maintain this information over time. As with any service or information technology (IT) task, the best approach is to thoroughly plan your requirements and approach before starting to implement a solution.

Creating and Administering User and Administrator Server Accounts

Authentication occurs in many different contexts in Mac OS X and Mac OS X Server, but it most commonly involves using a login window. For example, when you start up a Mac OS X computer, you may have to enter a user name and password in an initial login window before being allowed to use the system at all. (By default, Mac OS X is set to automatically log in with the first account that was set up on the system, without asking for a password. Unless you change this default setting using the Accounts pane of System Preferences, you will not see the initial login window when you start up the system.) While the login example might seem to apply only to Mac OS X, it could be that you are authenticating to a user account that lives across the network on Mac OS X Server.

Another example occurs when you connect to a network server, whether via AFP or SMB. A user must authenticate before accessing these services, even if logging in just as a guest user. If a login name and password are not entered correctly, a "Login failed" alert appears, indicating a failed attempt at authentication.

To administer a server through Server Admin or Workgroup Manager, an administrator must authenticate using those applications. This is required whether the server is being administered locally or remotely.

Using Server Preferences for User Accounts

If you configured Mac OS X Server as a Standard or Workgroup server, you can use the Server Preferences application for configuring user accounts. This application manages users and groups using an interface very similar to the Accounts preferences pane on Mac OS X.

Server Preferences gives you the basic options for account management, including the account details, contact information, services that user is authorized to use, and groups to which a user belongs. As mentioned in Lesson 1, if you've configured your server as an Advanced server, you won't be able to use the Server Preferences application. Because the user-related options are generally self-explanatory when using Server Preferences, we'll focus on the Advanced server management methods for the remainder of this lesson.

Using Workgroup Manager for Configuring User Accounts

Workgroup Manager is the primary tool for creating and configuring user accounts on Mac OS X Server. To grant a person specific permissions on Mac OS X Server, you must set up a user account for that person. User accounts on Mac OS X Server are the same as on Mac OS X, although accounts created with Workgroup Manager provide more complex options and settings. They also enable you to create network-visible accounts, accounts that can be used to log in remotely.

On Mac OS X Server, you can have local user accounts and network accounts. Standard user accounts on Mac OS X enable a person to access files and applications local to that computer. Similarly, user accounts on Mac OS X Server permit users who log in locally to access files or services (such as mail and print services) that are located on the server, but they also give remote users access to server volumes and associated files if the users are created in a network-visible directory service. Local users can connect to servers remotely, but can log in only locally.

Here are some examples of Mac OS X Server user account settings:

- ▶ Name
- ▶ UNIX user ID (UID)
- ▶ Short names
- ▶ User password type (shadow hash, crypt, open directory)
- ▶ Home folder location
- ▶ User address information
- ▶ Mail settings
- ▶ Print settings

When using Workgroup Manager with Mac OS X Server, you can assign multiple short names to a single user account. The first short name cannot be longer than 31 characters, but additional short names can contain up to 255 characters. This could allow a user to have a different email name, without having to change the previous short-name entry. The initial short name is the one used to create the home directory for that particular user.

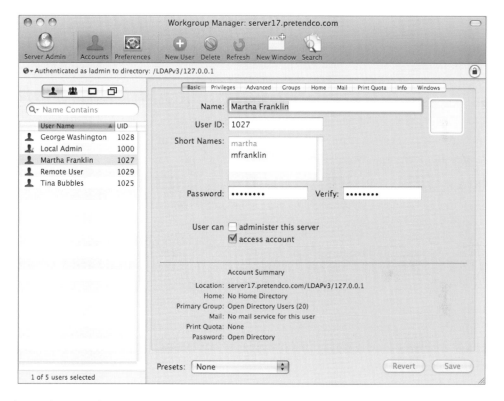

In the Basic pane, the user ID is a numerical value that the system uses to differentiate one user from another. Though users gain access to the system with a user name, each name is associated with a UID, and that's what the computer primarily cares about.

Note that when two users log in with different names and passwords but with the same UID access documents and folders, the system will consider them to be the same owner. If you attempt to create two users with the same UID in Workgroup Manager, you'll have to confirm that you really want to do that.

Workgroup Manager has other uses besides managing user accounts. It is also used to manage group accounts, which consist of a collection of users. Additionally, it manages computer accounts, which control features available to a given computer, and computer groups, which, as you might guess, are just collections of computer accounts. Workgroup Manager is also the application used to control certain default settings for users and computers. This topic will be covered more in Lesson 10, "Managing Accounts."

Using Workgroup Manager for Configuring Administrator Accounts

An administrator account is a special type of user account on Mac OS X Server that enables the user to administer the server. A user with an administrator account can create, edit, and delete user accounts, as well as modify the settings of various running services on the Mac OS X server where the administrator account exists. The administrator uses the Server Admin application to configure most service settings, and Workgroup Manager to edit users, groups, and account preferences.

To give a user an administrator account, select the "User can administer this server" checkbox (shown in the previous figure) in the Basic pane in Workgroup Manager.

If the Open Directory service on the server is configured as an Open Directory Master, there will be a second administrator option, found in the Privileges pane, named "Administration capabilities." Setting the "User can administer this server" option permits the user to manipulate file access on the server and manage the server using the Server Admin application, while the "Administration capabilities" option pertains to directory data only, such as user and group management. This means you could create an administrator that can add a user home directory but cannot add a user account to the directory. The inverse is not true, however. When a server is configured as an Open Directory server, a user must be set as both a server administrator and be given Workgroup Manager privileges to make changes using Workgroup Manager, even to work on the local directory domain. New in Mac OS X Server v10.5 is the ability to create a Limited Administrator. This functionality gives you the ability to allow a given administrator authorization to modify certain users or members of certain groups. If the Open Directory service is configured as a Standalone server, these options will not be available to you. Such servers are limited to specifying only whether someone is an administrator, rather than providing the ability to control who can manage which accounts, as you can do with an Open Directory server.

NOTE ▶ Open Directory and management of directory domains is covered in Lesson 4, "Using Open Directory."

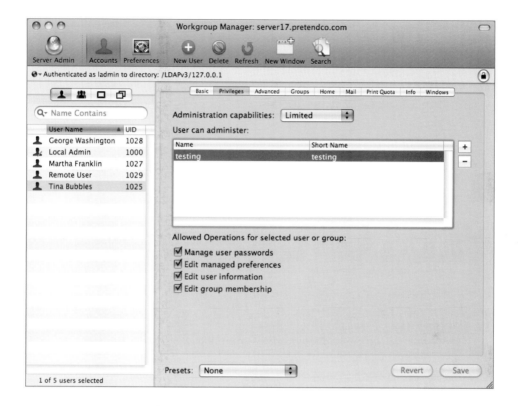

Configuring Local User Accounts

Mac OS X Server creates a list of local accounts for managing access to resources, such as files when running as a file server. You will use the Workgroup Manager utility to add two sample local users to your server computer, and then import a file containing additional users.

NOTE ▶ During this entire lesson, you will be using your Mac OS X computer to configure your Mac OS X Server computer. This demonstrates that you can perform server configuration from any Mac OS X computer that has network access to your server computer. You will also be authenticating Workgroup Manager as your Local Admin account.

Add Users

Follow these steps to add two users to your Mac OS X server:

1   On your Mac OS X client computer, open Workgroup Manager and connect to your Mac OS X server as Local Administrator.

    Because the Local node can only be used for authentication to resources resident on the server, you will be notified that your directory node is not visible on the network. You will learn about directory services in Lesson 4.

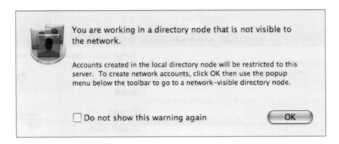

2   Click OK.

3   Ensure that the Accounts button is selected in the toolbar, the list of users is displayed, and the current administrator account is selected and visible.

4   Click the New User button in the toolbar.

    If the button is dimmed, click in the list of users to activate the button.

5   In the Basic pane, enter the following information for the first new user:

    ▶   Name: *Tina Bubbles*

    ▶   Short Names: *tinabubbles*

    ▶   Password: *tina*

    ▶   Verify: *tina*

6 Leave the other settings at their default values (including leaving Presets, at the bottom of the window, set to None), and be sure you don't select "User can administer this server."

7 Double-click the second line (the empty one below "tinabubbles") in the Short Names field to add another short name.

8 Type *bubbles,* then click Save.

The new user name appears in the list of users on the left side of Workgroup Manager window. You should also see that the first short name is now dimmed, indicating that it cannot be changed. Notice that the name and alternate short names can be edited after this point.

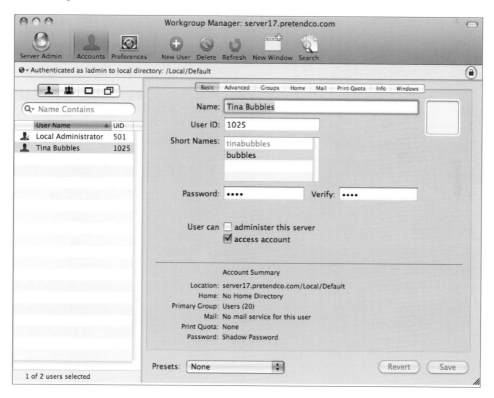

9   Add a second user, Warren Peece, by clicking the New User button and entering the following values:

  ▶   Name: *Warren Peece*

  ▶   Short Names: *warren*

  ▶   Password: *warren*

  ▶   Verify: *warren*

  ▶   Leave the other settings at their default values.

10   Click Save.

11   Select the existing Local Administrator account from the list of current users.

Notice that the administrator account has the "User can administer this server" option selected.

Now compare the two new accounts with the administrator account. What are the differences between the three accounts? The "User can administer this server" is selected on Local Administrator and not on the others. When you create new users, they are not automatically administrators. You must check the appropriate box to allow them to be administrators.

Configure Comments and Keywords

During the setup of accounts, you can configure advanced features such as comments and keywords in each account. These features are useful for organizing users or searching for particular users based on something other than name or user ID. This provides for a more realistic search pattern should you need to specify a range of users without actually adding them to a specific group.

1   Select Tina Bubbles from the list of users.

2   Click Advanced.

3   In the Comment field, type *Employee# 408081.*

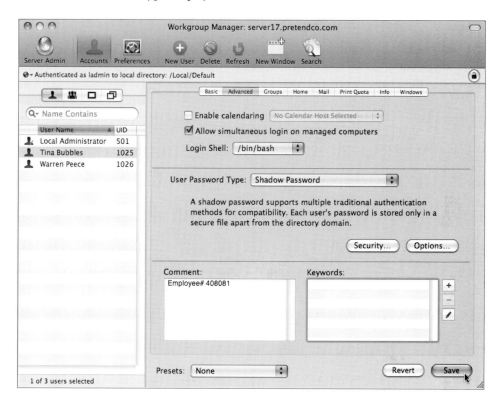

4   Click the Add (+) button next to the Keywords field.

5   In the sheet that appears, click Edit Keywords button.

6   In the "Manage available keywords" sheet that appears next, click the Add (+) button.

7   In the text field, type *Manager.*

8   Click the Add (+) button again.

9   In the second text field, type *Marketing.*

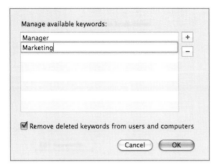

10 Click the Add (+) button again to add a third keyword: *Engineering*.

11 Click OK to save the new keywords and return to the "Select the keywords to add to tinabubbles" sheet.

12 Select Manager and click OK to add the *Manager* keyword to Tina's user account.

13 Click Save.

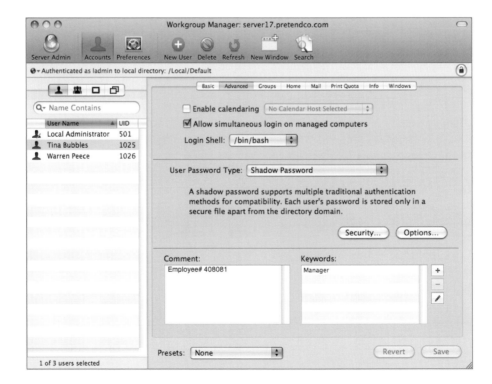

14 Click the Add (+) button again and add the *Marketing* keyword to Tina's account. Click Save.

15 Select Warren from the user list, click the Add (+) button, and add the *Manager* and *Engineering* keywords to Warren Peece's user account.

16 Add *Employee# 410103* to the Comment field for Warren's user account, and click Save.

17 In the search field above the list of users, choose Keyword Contains from the menu next to the magnifying glass icon and type *Manager*.

Only Tina Bubbles and Warren Peece's accounts should appear in the user list.

18 In the search field above the list of users , choose Keyword Contains and type *Eng*.

Warren Peece is now the only user listed, because you added the Engineering keyword to only Warren's account.

19 In the search field, choose Comment Contains and type *41*.

Only Warren Peece should be listed in the user list because his account's comment contains "41" in his employee number.

Exporting and Importing Users and Groups

You can create user accounts individually, or you can import them from a properly formatted file. The file could be created on your own, created with a third-party tool, restored from another server, or restored from a backup of the current server. To back up and restore user and group accounts (discussed in the next section) from a Mac OS X Server computer, use the Export and Import commands in Workgroup Manager.

To back up user and group accounts defined in Workgroup Manager, first select the accounts you wish to export, choose the Export command from the Server menu, and specify a name and location for the resulting file.

NOTE ▶ You must export users, user groups, computers, and computer groups separately if you wish to export all of your accounts. The export function saves only the accounts selected in the current Workgroup Manager view. It's also important to note that user passwords are never exported, so anytime you import users from a file, they will need to set new passwords.

To restore user or group accounts using Workgroup Manager, use the Import command from the Server menu. In the Import dialog, choose "Ignore new record" from the Duplicate Handling pop-up menu. This setting will skip any records if a user with that UID already exists on your server.

TIP ▶ You can import files containing user and group accounts using the Import command.

When you are setting up a new server and will be supporting more than just a few users, you will probably import the users from a configured text file instead of adding each of them individually. In this section, another system administrator has provided you with a file containing formatted user records to use with your server.

TIP ▶ When importing user and group accounts with the Import command, try to limit the number of accounts in each file to 10,000 users. Although importing a larger number of accounts for a single file is supported, you will find that keeping the number of accounts smaller is more manageable.

1   In Workgroup Manager on your Mac OS X computer, choose Server > Import.

2   In the import users sheet, navigate to and select the Users > Shared > Student_Materials > Lesson_03 > **01employees** file.

Leave all the settings at their default values.

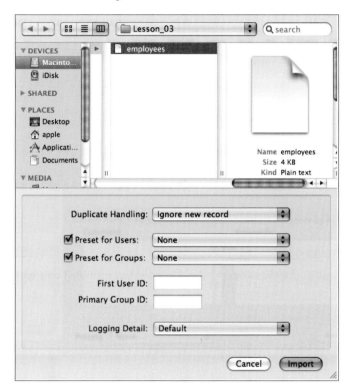

3   Click Import.

An additional seven users are imported. Because passwords are not included in the users' import files, you need to set a password for each new account. For now, you will set all of the accounts to use the same password.

4   In the list of users, select all the newly imported accounts.

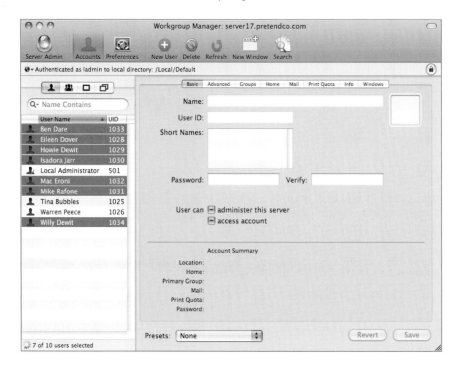

5   In the Advanced pane, choose Shadow Password from the User Password Type pop-up menu.

This option appears if multiple accounts are selected.

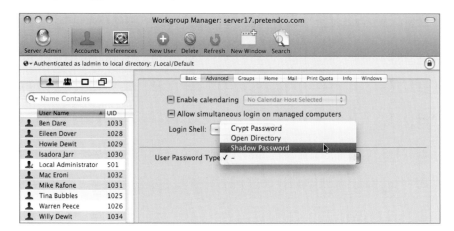

6 In the dialog that appears after selecting Shadow Password, in both the Password and Verify fields, type *changeme*. Click OK.

7 Click Save.

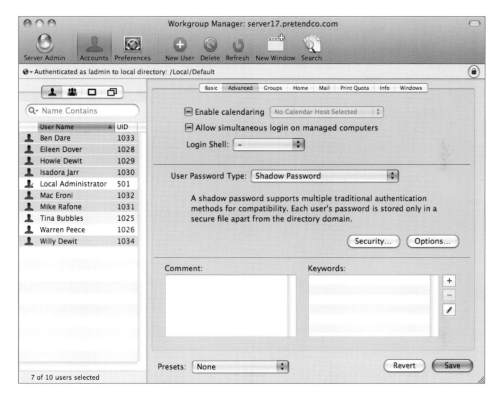

You have set all the new accounts to use the same password. In Lesson 4, you will learn how to use Workgroup Manager's password policies to force users to set a new password.

Working with Group Accounts in Workgroup Manager

Group accounts are closely associated with user accounts on Mac OS X Server. Group accounts enable administrators to quickly assign a set of permissions to multiple users. Mac OS X allows an easy way to change group assignments and permissions through the Get Info command, and also provides a simple interface for creating small groups using the Accounts preferences pane. With servers, however, you usually want to have many more groups with many more members.

To create a group on Mac OS X Server, open Workgroup Manager, simply click the New Group button in the toolbar, and enter a name for the group. There are additional options for the group, but they are not required for the group to be functional.

Long user and group names can contain non-Roman characters. Depending on the character set, you may have as few as 85 characters available for the long name. If you are using exclusively Roman characters in your user names, you can safely use 255 characters. Short user and group names must consist of no more than 255 Roman characters.

Mac OS X Server v10.4 addressed a number of limitations about how groups were used in previous versions of Mac OS X Server. For example, the restriction of users having membership in only up to 16 groups has been removed. Groups can also be nested in other groups, which allows a more natural way to represent users in an organization.

Working with User Accounts and Group IDs

Every user has a single primary group ID (GID). The system stores the user's primary GID in the underlying user account record. All other group membership information is stored in the underlying group records. When a user creates a file, the default group is used for read permissions.

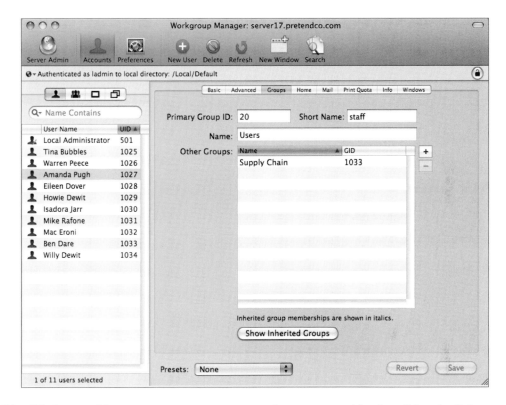

Using Workgroup Manager, you can remove a user from a group either by editing the Other Groups field in the user account or by editing the group account. However, you cannot change a user's primary group ID by these methods. Users who are members of a group by virtue of their primary group ID appear in italics in the group membership list. This is your indication that you can't remove them from the group account as you normally would—by selecting the user and clicking the remove user (–) button. Instead, you have to edit the primary GID in the user account.

Creating Groups with Workgroup Manager

You'll use Workgroup Manager to create and manage local groups.

1   In Workgroup Manager on your Mac OS X computer, click Accounts in the toolbar.

2   In the left pane of the window, click the Groups button.

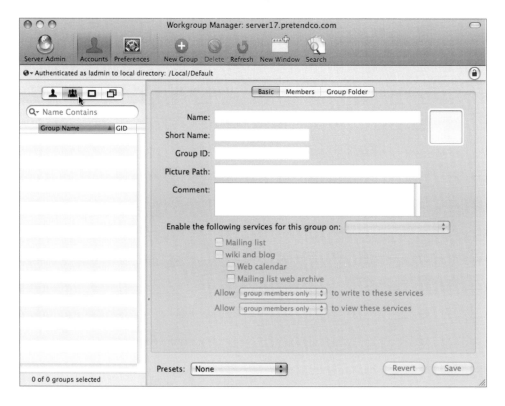

3   In the toolbar, click the New Group button to create a new group.

4   Enter the following information for the first new group:

  ▶   Name: *Engineering*

  ▶   Short Name: *engr*

5   Leave all other fields at their default values and click Save.

6   Create a second group:

  ▶   Name: *Marketing*

  ▶   Short Name: *mktg*

7 Leave all other fields at their default values and click Save.

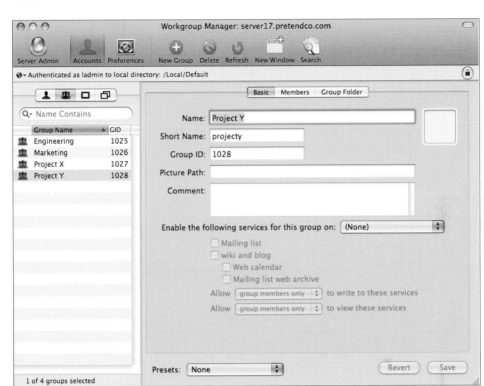

Now create two more groups: Project X and Project Y:

8 Create a group for the Project X team:

▶ Name: *Project X*

▶ Short Name: *projectx*

9 Leave all other fields at their default values and click Save.

10 Create another group for the Project Y team:

▶ Name: *Project Y*

▶ Short Name: *projecty*

11 Leave all other fields at their default values and click Save.

Associating Users with Groups

Now that you have created four groups, you need to assign to them the users you previously created. You will do this using two different methods: adding users to a group and adding group membership to a user account.

Adding Users to Groups

The most common approach for populating groups with users is to select a group and then add one or more users to it. On your server, you will select a group, and then add users to the group based on keywords.

1   Select the Marketing group from the list of groups.

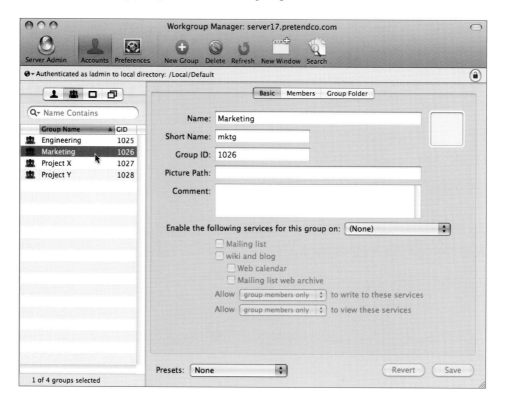

2   In the Members pane, click the Add (+) button to the right of the Members list.

The Users and Groups drawer appears.

3   From the pop-up menu in the search field in the Users and Groups drawer, choose Keyword Contains and type *Mar*.

This locates all of the users with the Marketing keyword.

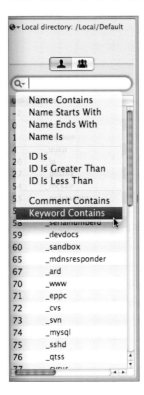

NOTE ▶ Searches are case-sensitive, and they search through the long names, not the short names.

4   Select all the displayed users and drag them to the Members list.

You should now see the users listed in the Members area for the Marketing group.

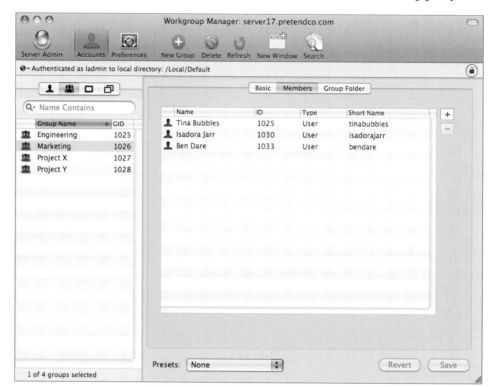

5   Click Save.

Adding Group Membership to a User Account

While you could easily use the process in the previous section to add Warren to the Project X and Project Y groups, try an alternate approach by adding the groups to Warren's account.

1   Click the Users button on the left side of the Workgroup Manager window and select Warren Peece from the list of users.

2   Click Groups on the right side of the pane.

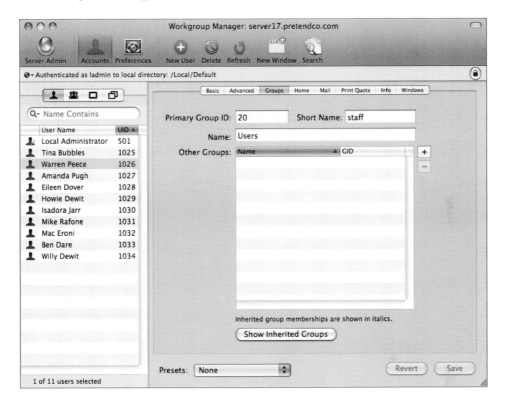

3   Click the Add (+) button.

The Groups drawer appears, displaying the list of groups that are currently defined on the system. This list includes both the groups that you created and the system-defined groups that Mac OS X Server created during installation.

4   Select the Project X group and drag it from the Groups drawer to the Other Groups list.

Notice that as you drag the group, the pointer changes to a plus sign. This means that you are adding this group to the text field.

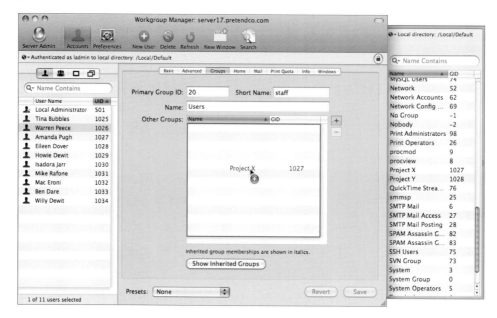

5 Click Save.

You have now successfully added the Project X group membership to Warren's account. However, Warren also needs access to Project Y.

6 Repeat steps 3, 4, and 5 to add the Project Y group to Warren's user account.

You have just added multiple groups—Project X and Project Y—to Warren's user account.

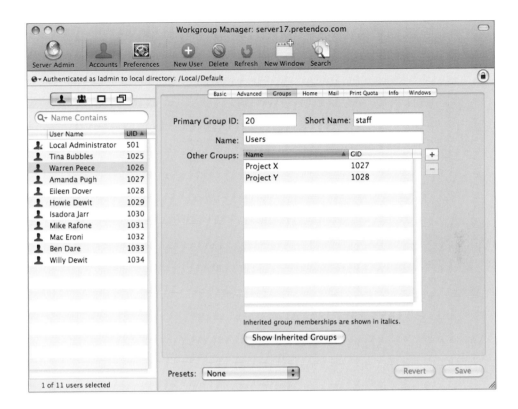

Adding Groups to Groups

Let's say that you need a group that enables you to control permissions for the entire Engineering department, which consists of two divisions, Project X and Project Y. You could populate the Engineering group with all of the individual engineering user accounts. However, an easier approach is to add the two project groups to the Engineering group. This effectively adds all members of those groups to the main group, which is a more effi-cient way to manage groups than in previous versions of Mac OS X Server.

1   Click the Groups button on the left side of the Workgroup Manager window and select the Engineering group from the list of groups.

2   In the Members pane, click the Add (+) button to the right of the Members list to open the Users and Groups drawer.

3   In the Users and Groups drawer, click the Groups button.

4   Drag the Project X and Project Y groups to the Members list.

All members of the Project X and Project Y groups now have access to anything that the Engineering group does.

5   Click Save.

You have now added both users and groups to your server, as well as groups to groups.

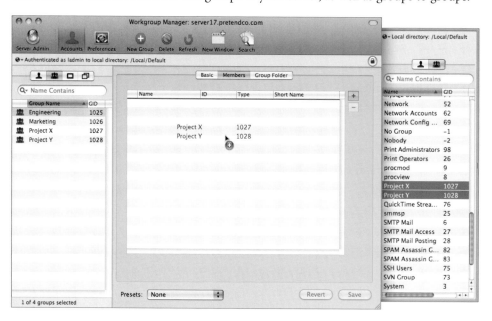

Controlling Access Through Server Accounts

Authorization is used throughout Mac OS X and Mac OS X Server. The most common example is usually transparent to the user: Every time a user accesses a file, the computer checks file permissions against the user's account information to see if the user is authorized to use the file. In Mac OS X and Mac OS X Server, owner and group permissions are associated with every file, folder, and application.

When accessing a file server, you typically have to authenticate and then you see a choice of valid share points available to mount. When you navigate inside a mounted share point, folders' badges (small icons displayed on or under the folder icon) show whether you are authorized for read-write, read-only, write-only, or no access for that folder.

When connecting to a server with Server Admin or Workgroup Manager, after you authenticate, your user name will be checked to see if it is authorized to perform administrative functions. Additionally, authorization checks are made any time a user tries connecting to any service, such as the Podcast Producer, on your server to see if that user is allowed to use that service.

Using Authorization on Mac OS X Server

Portable Operating System Interface (POSIX) permissions are the permissions that have been used on Mac OS X and Mac OS X Server since day one. They are still used both on Mac OS X and Mac OS X Server, and they exist for every file system file or folder on the file system. POSIX permissions are the traditional UNIX-style permissions that enable you to apply read, write, and execute permission for three groups of users: the owner, the group, and all other users. The initial permissions that you see in the Get Info window of Mac OS X are POSIX permissions.

Before Mac OS X v10.4, POSIX permissions were the only way to control file access on Mac OS X Server. Mac OS X Server v10.4 built on the Mac OS X heritage of using POSIX permissions, but it added the ability to define complex access rules that are not possible with standard POSIX permissions. This was done with *access control lists* (ACLs). ACLs are supported on disks formatted as Mac OS Extended volumes. They are stored in the file system itself, using extended attributes that have always existed in Mac OS Extended file systems, but have been unused. This is how ACLs are supported without reformatting the volume to a new file-system format. In Mac OS X v10.5, ACL support is enabled by default.

For users accessing the server over the network, ACLs are supported for AFP and SMB protocol connections. ACLs are also compatible with ACLs from the Windows world, thus providing a better user experience when accessing Mac OS X Server from Windows clients, since users expect a more granular level of permissions settings than were previously available with Mac OS X Server. These access permissions can be set to support a rich organizational workflow where user permissions need to vary widely as a document gets passed among different authors and reviewers. If you use the Get Info window of Mac OS X to add additional users or groups to the permissions list, they will be added using ACLs.

It is important to understand that ACLs are familiar to Windows administrators yet are something of a new concept to Macintosh administrators. This makes the introduction of Mac OS X Server into a Windows environment easier to implement.

Reviewing POSIX Permissions

Every file and folder in Mac OS X has ownership and permissions information that define the privileges available for that file or folder. Ownership includes configuring both an owner and a group, while permissions includes setting specific access settings for the owner, the group, and everyone else, commonly referred to as "other." When set from the Finder, these permissions can be Read & Write, Read only, Write only (Drop Box), and No Access. When set from the command line, there are a few more possibilities. When you change the ownership or permissions of an item using a command-line interface, the changes are reflected in the Info (or Inspector) window for that item. Likewise, when you change the permissions in the Info window, the changes can be seen when displaying the item in a command-line interface.

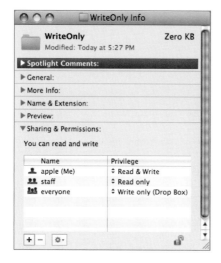

In the example figure, the d in front of the permissions indicates that the file is a folder (*d* for *directory*). The permissions for the owner, rwx, correspond to Read & Write in the Info window for that folder. The permissions for the group, r-x, correspond to Read only in the Info window, while the everyone permissions of -wx mean that everyone else can write to the folder, but can't read it. The x, or execute, permission on a file identifies a program that can be run. For a folder, the execute permission determines whether the folder can be searched. To access a file in a folder, you must have search permission for each folder from the root folder down to and including the folder containing the file.

> **NOTE ▸** Directories and files usually default to having the everyone/other permissions set to read-only. Although this sounds secure, keep in mind that your server may have Guest Access enabled, which may permit any computer that can reach your server the ability to read those files.

In POSIX, the user ID associated with the file or folder defines permissions ownership. If the numeric UID of the file or folder matches the UID defined in the user account, then that user is considered the owner of the file or folder. Group access is determined similarly: Each file or folder has a group ID associated with it. Each group account has a numeric GID. If the user is a member of a group with a GID that matches the GID of the file or folder, then the user has access as defined in the group permissions settings.

POSIX Permissions Limitations

As a simple example of setting access permissions, suppose you have a school district that is configuring a shared math folder (named Math Files) on its server. The district's administrators want to allow math teachers to read, write, and delete math files, and to allow any math student to read the same files. Ideally, they would like to set the Math Files folder so only math students, not all students, are allowed to see it. This example would be difficult to support with standard POSIX privileges, as you would be limited to a single group to control privileges.

There are a couple of approaches to this problem, yet each has its limitations. In the first method, you assign the Math_Teachers group to the folder and give the Math_Teachers group read and write access. Then you prevent math students from writing by assigning read-only access to Everyone. The problem with this scenario is that you have granted read access to everyone in the school for the Math Files folder.

Another approach is to consolidate the math users—teachers and students—into a group called Math Department. You can give this group access, and deny access to everyone else. This solves the problem of the entire school accessing the Math Files folder, but you have introduced a new problem: Since the students and teachers are combined into a single group, Math Department, students and teachers have identical access privileges, and you want students to read only, not to write. You've lost that granularity. You could probably create two subfolders with different group access permissions for math students and math teachers, but what if you wanted even finer control? Maybe non-math teachers should have read-only access similar to math students.

You get the point: You must work around limitations in the permissions system rather than using the permission system to naturally express the access and workflow that exists in the organization. Luckily, the access-control system in Mac OS X Server helps you find a natural way—ACLs—to set up and enforce access permissions.

Setting POSIX Permissions with Server Admin

To modify the POSIX permissions for a folder:

1   Using Server Admin on your Mac OS X computer, connect to your Mac OS X server.

    NOTE ▶ You must have your server configured for at least one file-sharing service, such as AFP, to use the File Sharing configuration features for setting permissions. The file-sharing service need not be started, but it must be present. If it is not present, you can select your.server.name > Settings > Services to add it.

2   Click File Sharing in the toolbar.

3   Click Browse just under the toolbar.

4   Select a folder in the file system for which to apply settings.

5   Select the user or group under the POSIX portion of the permissions.

6   Click Edit (the pencil button).

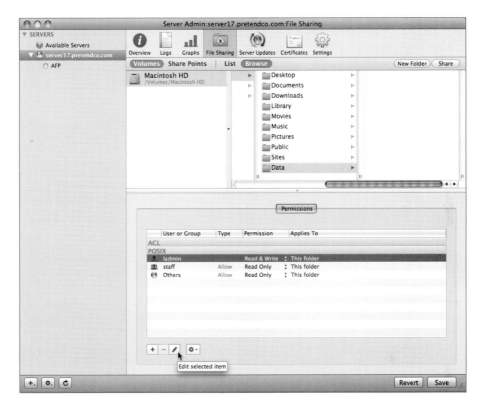

7   Type a different short name for the user or group and click the checkboxes to change the current settings, and then click OK.

8   Use the pop-up menus to assign permissions for owner, group, and everyone.

9   Click Save.

As in Mac OS X, when a user attempts to access a file or folder, the user account is compared with the file or folder's owner and group. If the user account is the owner, then the permissions assigned to the owner are enforced, and the permissions for the group and everyone are ignored for that account. If the user account is not the owner but is a member of the group, then group permissions are enforced. If the account is neither the owner nor a member of the group, everyone's permissions are enforced. In an "owner-only delete" scenario such as what may exist in a shared temporary scratch space, an authorized user has read-write access to the file but only the owner can delete it. This option, known as the sticky bit, can be set only at the command line via chmod +t.

Setting ACLs

In both the client and server versions of Mac OS X v10.5, ACLs are enabled by default, but if you find that you're unable to assign ACLs to a particular volume, it's possible that ACLs may need to be enabled using the fsaclctl command in the Terminal utility.

Setting ACLs with Server Admin

In Mac OS X Server v10.4, you used Workgroup Manager to set file-system ACLs, but in v10.5, you use Server Admin. Here are the generic steps to update the file-system access-control entries in the ACL (this is similar to POSIX permissions management, except for the location where you drag the users and groups from the Users and Groups drawer):

1   Using Server Admin on your Mac OS X computer, connect to your Mac OS X server.

    If you are already connected to your server, select the server's entry in the list of available servers on the right side of Server Admin.

2   Click File Sharing in the toolbar.

3   Click Browse just under the toolbar.

4   Select a folder in the file system for which to apply settings.

5   Click the Add (+) button to open the Users and Groups drawer.

6   Drag a specific user or group to the ACL list.

    If there are currently no entries in the ACL list, you'll just see a blue line appear between the ACL and POSIX lists as you're dragging the user or group.

7 For each permission entry, use the pop-up menus in the Permissions column on a user or group entry to select permissions from standard predefined sets. Alternatively, click the Edit (pencil) button to configure custom settings.

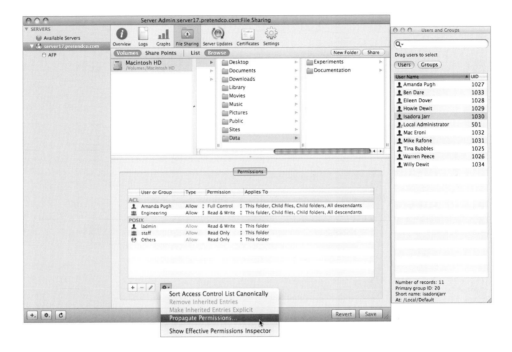

8 Configure additional users or groups as required.

9 If desired, modify the inheritance rules using the Applies To pop-up menus for each user or group entry.

10 Click Save.

11 If desired, use the Action (gear wheel) menu to propagate settings to enclosed files or folders.

Determining User Access to a Folder

ACLs can grow complex in a large organization. Judicious use of group membership should help clarify which users have access to which items, but you may still find yourself unsure of who has access to a given folder. The Effective Permissions Inspector will tell you exactly what access a particular user has to the selected folder. To use this tool, choose

Show Effective Permissions Inspector from the Action (gear wheel) menu. Once the inspector window opens, drag a user or group to the window; the inspector will display the precise access permissions for the given user or group and the selected file, folder, or volume.

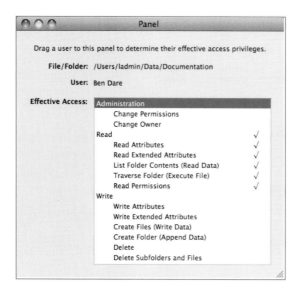

Distinguishing the Use of UID, GID, and GUID

You have learned that POSIX owners and groups are determined by user and group IDs. Because UIDs and GIDs are simple integers, it is possible that users can have duplicate user IDs. Usually this is an error, but sometimes an administrator will want the POSIX UID to be identical on two separate users.

ACLs are much more complex and require a unique identification of a user or group. For this purpose, every user and group has a globally unique ID (GUID). This is not exposed in the user interface (the GUI), because there should be no reason to change it. Every time a user is created, a new 128-bit number (example: 835E78F0-7808-4758-8C92-CF8AB428B99B) is generated, based upon the clock time, and other information, when the user is created. In this way, users and groups are virtually guaranteed unique identification in ACLs.

> **TIP** "I can't see the files I should see" can be a common complaint from users who access a complex server. The next time you hear this, use the Effective Permissions Inspector to investigate the permissions that user has.

ACL Workflow Examples

When working with ACLs, it is important that you plan your setup properly to avoid conflicting permission settings, such as having a user be a member of two groups, one with read permissions on a folder and one with no access permissions on the same folder. These types of conflicts can occur if you do not plan your ACL permissions models well.

Multiple Groups

The POSIX permissions work well in a single desktop mode such as Mac OS X client. Yet when the system becomes more complex, such as in corporate or enterprise environments, the POSIX model does not scale well.

Complex workflows might require more than just the Owner, Group, and Everyone classes available with POSIX. In particular, having a single group is very limiting. The POSIX owner must be an individual user account (it can't be a group), and granting permission to Everyone usually opens up the files to a wider audience than you want. ACLs permit multiple groups assigned to a folder, each with a unique permissions setting. This is a common requirement in any environment that has multiple groups collaborating on a single project. Imagine a production environment that has writers, graphics editors, copy editors, and production editors. Different groups work on the same file at different points during the project. Because ACLs can assign different permissions to multiple groups, you must carefully plan what your group structure is going to look like to avoid any confusion.

Each group would have specific permissions for each folder. For instance, a user in the Writers group can put a document in the Submissions folder and can read and write to that file while in that folder. However, the Copy Editors group can only read the files in the folder. Those users in the Production Staff and Graphics Editors groups are specifically denied any read or write access to the Submissions folder.

Also, users in the Writers group are allowed to move the document into the Editors folder, but are denied permission to read what is in the folder. Users in the Copy Editors group have read permissions and are allowed the specific write permissions of creating folders or files within the Editors folder, so they can make a copy of the document within the folder. Users in the Graphics Editors group have read permissions as well, but are allowed only write attributes to the document; they cannot create new files within the Editors folder. Users in the Production Staff group can read the files.

Finally, users in the Production Staff group can copy the document into the Production folder, and can read and modify any documents in that folder. Users in the Writers group are specifically denied permission to read or write to the Production folder or any documents in the folder. Users in the two editor groups have all the read permissions, but can write only extended attributes.

Nested Groups

In addition to assigning multiple groups to a single folder, Mac OS X Server allows groups to contain *other groups*. Your Writers group may be broken down further into yet other groups based on the types of articles they write, such as features or columns.

If ACLs permit multiple groups assigned to a folder, you might wonder why nesting groups are required. For example, why assign the Writers to the Submissions folder instead of directly assigning access to the three groups (Feature Writers, Staff Writers, Ad Copy Writers)? The effect would be the same.

Breaking groups down into subgroups can make your access easier to understand as an administrator. If you need to come back to your server a month later and give all your writers access to a new folder, you would have to recall the organizational details of your groups. Are you going to remember that to grant all writers access, you need to assign the Feature Writers, Staff Writers, and Ad Copy Writers groups to the new folder? With an all-inclusive group such as Writers, your job is simpler.

You can use nested groups to reflect the structure of your organization. We used a publishing example, but another example is a school: a grade level could be a group, which contains the individual classes of students.

While nested groups are powerful, they should be used with care. If you build a deep, complex hierarchy, you may find that access is harder—rather than easier—to understand. Mirroring your organizational structure is usually safe and useful. However, be wary of ad hoc groups that don't relate to any external structure. It may be a quick way to give access to some users, but later on may make it more difficult to understand your access.

Inheritance

Another feature of ACLs is *inheritance*: items inside a folder acquiring the ACLs of the enclosing folder. Users will normally be dealing with inherited permissions for files. As users create files on the server, the tools they use, even the Finder, do not set any explicit ACLs on the item being copied. In this case, the permissions on the file are the permissions on the enclosing folder.

Inheritance is another tool you can use to enable your structure. The publishing workflow example using multiple groups is fairly simplistic in that a user either has full read-write access to a folder and its contents, or can't see anything inside that folder. With inheritance, your actual permissions can be more subtle. You may want the Editors group to have read-only access to the Submissions folder, but still allow only the Writers group to be able to make changes to files or add new files. Inheritance allows this. Give the Editors read access on the Submissions folder, and by inheritance they also have read-only access to all files in the Submissions folder.

POSIX Permissions Versus ACL Settings

ACLs provide you the ability to set a finer grain of control over access settings that are compatible with the Windows environment. Seventeen additional settings can be made on a folder (or share point) from inside Server Admin. This allows a richer set of capabilities to be defined for read and write access as well as for administrative control (such as who can change permissions on or ownership of a folder). In Server Admin, these settings are enabled on folders, not individual files, although files can obtain these permissions through inheritance. This folder-level control allows a finer level of management, without having to worry about administering permissions for thousands or millions of individual files.

The POSIX settings available in the Finder were limited to Read & Write, Read Only, Write Only, and None. The following dialog displays the ACL settings available from Server Admin.

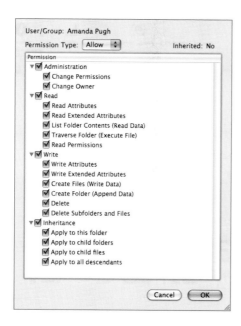

NOTE ▶ Access-control settings are made on a container basis for either folders or share points, not on individual files themselves. Individual files obtain their respective ACL settings from their containing folder.

The inheritance configuration determines where the ACL settings are propagated to, such as to the folder itself, any files or folders one level down, or to files or folders descendant from this folder. While the initial inheritance setting applies only for files and folders created afterward, you can propagate these settings manually to apply them to enclosed files or folders.

How File-System ACLs Work

When you use Server Admin to define ACLs, you are creating individual *access control list entries* (ACEs). These entries and lists are specific to a file-system location and are set on container objects—either share points or folders. Each ACE contains the following information:

- ▶ User or group associated with this entry
- ▶ Type of entry (Allow or Deny)
- ▶ Permissions (Full Control, Read & Write, Read, Write, or Custom, along with inheritance settings)

The order of entries is important, because lists are evaluated top to bottom by Mac OS X Server.

Allow and Deny matches work differently for ACLs. Allow matches are cumulative for all matches that apply to a user, whether from user or group matches. Deny matches apply on the first match.

ACLs on a file do not change when you move a file from one folder to another on the same volume. In this situation, the file is not copied and deleted. Instead, there is a change to the pointer to where the file is located. If you move between volumes, a copy and delete does occur and the file inherits the ACLs from the new enclosing folder.

Allow Access Is Cumulative

In the following diagram, assume that algebra tutors are algebra students, and that all algebra students are students. The folder has three entries in the ACL:

- ▶ All students can read the contents of the folder (inherited from the parent).

▶ Algebra students can write to the folder.

▶ Algebra tutors can administer the folder.

All students in the school can see the selected folder and files inside that folder. Algebra students have write access by virtue of their membership in the Algebra Students group, but they also have read access by virtue of their membership in the All Students group. Thus, Algebra Students have read-write access. Algebra tutors, who are algebra students, can read, write, and make administrative changes, such as change permissions or ownership.

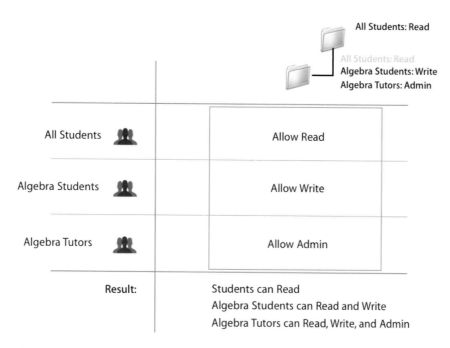

Notice that inherited permissions have to be considered for the cumulative Allow access. Algebra students and algebra tutors can read by virtue of being in the All Students group. If that is not what you intended, you could remove inherited privileges from the folder using Workgroup Manager.

Now suppose that inside the Math folder is a folder containing student evaluations. It is important that no student gain access to this folder or its contents. Notice that because of inheritance, students would normally have read access to the folder. In order to keep students out of this folder, you can place a Deny access control on the folder for the All Students group. This Deny access control should be placed above the Allow access controls, since access control entries are evaluated from top to bottom.

The Deny access at the top overrides all other access controls on the folder for the specified group. Even though algebra tutors have a read access ACE (from their membership in the Students group), a write access ACE (from their membership in the Algebra Student group), and an admin access ACE (from their membership in the Algebra Tutors group), the Deny access—which applies to all students—overrides all of these ACEs because it is placed at the top of the list, and no student can access this folder.

Group Membership and ACLs

Using ACLs to control access to server resources can be extremely valuable, as long as care is taken up front to organize your user and group accounts appropriately. The recommended way to approach this management is to take advantage of using smaller groups to correctly mimic the needs of your organization, including nesting groups within groups. Use these group accounts to manage access on a more granular basis.

You could address your classroom situation by creating a single group for all teachers, which is made up of two groups: Staff Teachers and Student Teachers. You could then manage staff and student teachers independently and assign access rights as needed. Over time, if a student teacher becomes a full-time teacher, you can simply move the student teacher's account into the Staff Teachers group. This enables you to continue managing access on a group/organizational basis, instead of dealing with access entries for individual teachers, which can get quite unwieldy.

Access Control Configuration

In this section, you will create a folder hierarchy and a means of controlling access to facilitate the workflow of the users and groups on your server. Using only file-system ACLs, you will follow the path of an example project from development. You will discover that the ability to manipulate a file can be determined by where the file is located in the system, rather than by who created or owns the specific file.

It is important to note that changes take effect only when you save. It is good practice to save your work frequently.

To properly configure your server, you will need to understand the intended workflow of your users. You have set up two groups, Engineering and Marketing, and each group needs different access to files at different times during a project. For this exercise, you will be adding new groups to this equation: a Projects group and a Contractors group.

Create the Folder Structure

In the example being used in this lesson, the folder structure is project-based, not department-based. As a document meets a particular milestone, it will be moved from one location to another. You will create project folders and assign ACLs for those folders to control workflow. This may be different from the way you managed documents with POSIX permissions.

The first step is to create a project folder hierarchy. You can create the folders in the Finder, but you can also use Server Admin, which enables you to create folders on your server remotely without having physical access to it.

1   On your client computer, open Server Admin and connect to your server.

2   Click the File Sharing button in Workgroup Manager's toolbar.

The main window displays the volumes or current share points, as either a list or in a column browse view, and the owner and groups assigned to them, as well as their access permissions.

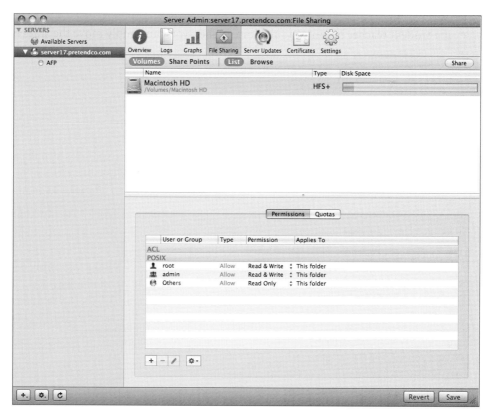

3   Click Volumes, followed by Browse.

This view enables you to navigate the local hard drive and set permissions on folders not contained within a share point.

4   In the left column, click the startup volume.

In this example, the name of the volume is Macintosh HD.

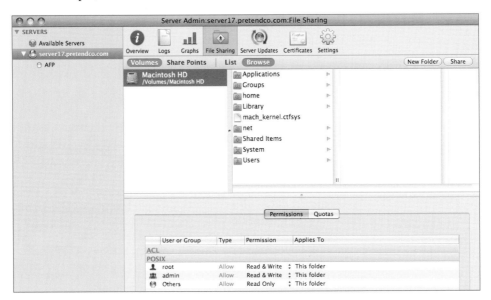

5   Click the Shared Items folder in the list of folders.

6   Click the New Folder button in the upper-right corner of the window.

This creates a new folder within the Shared Items folder.

7   In the Name field, enter *Project Phantom*.

This folder will be used for the development product.

8 Inside the new folder create three subfolders: Development, Pre_Release, and Release.

> **NOTE** ▸ If you don't deselect and reselect the parent folder, subsequent folder creations will nest within the newly created folder.

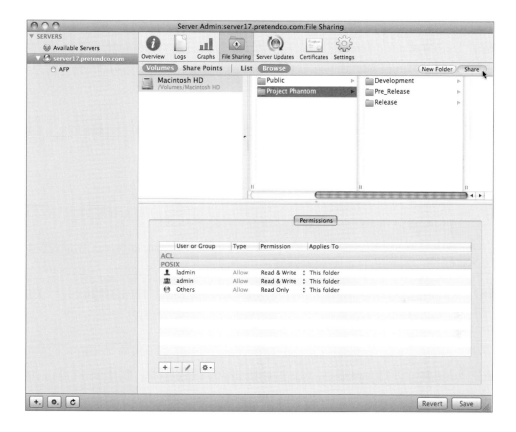

9 With the Project Phantom folder selected, click the Share button in the upper-right corner.

> **NOTE** ▸ Again, deselect, then reselect the Project Phantom folder before clicking the Share button to avoid just sharing one of the folder's newly created subfolders.

10 Click Save.

This turns the Project Phantom folder into a share point that will be mountable by your users.

Create Additional Groups and Remove a Member From a Group

As mentioned before, in addition to using the existing Marketing and Engineering groups, you need to create two additional groups for this exercise: Projects and Contractors. These will represent project management and temporary employees. Also, to demonstrate changing access, you must make sure that the user Warren is part of the Engineering group only, not part of the Marketing group.

1   Return to Workgroup Manager, and reconnect to your server if you are no longer connected to it.

2   Click the Accounts button in the toolbar, click the Groups icon on the left side, and create two new groups, Projects and Contractors. When creating these groups, just use their default settings.

These groups are empty now; you will add users later.

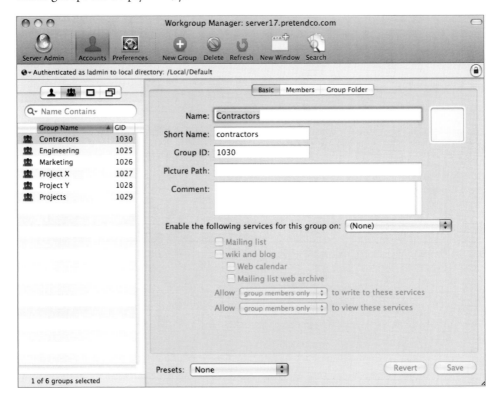

3   Select the Marketing group.

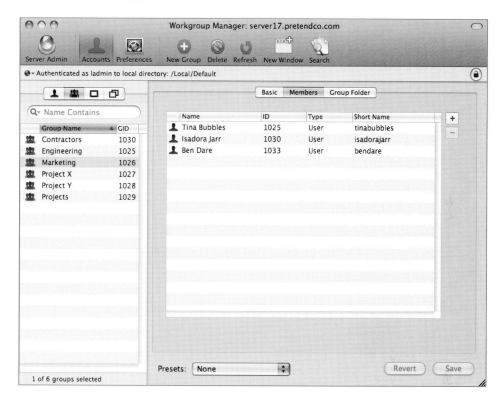

4   Remove Isadora Jarr from the Marketing group if she is a member by selecting her and clicking the Delete (−) button, and then click Save.

Set Ownership and Permissions for the Development Folders

Now that you have created the folder structure, you need to assign group ownership and permissions of each of the folders.

1   Return to the Server Admin application and reconnect to your server if you are no longer connected.

2   Click the File Sharing button in the toolbar and select the Development folder. You'll have to navigate to it inside the Project Phantom share if you closed your window earlier.

   The fields in the Permissions pane show that the Development folder is currently owned by the ladmin, and admin is the group assigned to this folder.

The admin group is a reserved group account that is created when Mac OS X Server is installed. The root account, also known as the System Administrator or superuser account, is also created when Mac OS X Server is installed. Because it is a system-level account, it is not listed in the Users Accounts list in the Accounts pane, but it is listed in the Users list in the Users and Groups drawer.

This window shows that the owner, ladmin, has read-write access to this folder, as do members of the admin group. The Others permissions are set to Read Only.

The Development folder will be left with POSIX permissions for the first phase of the exercise to illustrate the power of using ACLs. Remember, there will be a Contractors group and associated users.

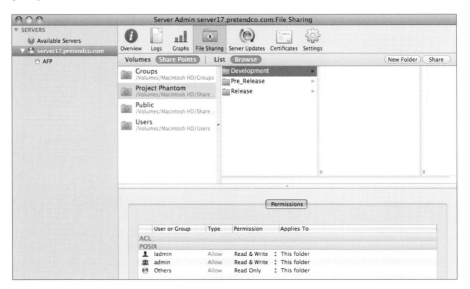

3   Click the Add (+) button to open the Users and Groups drawer.

Now drag users and groups to the POSIX list inside the Permissions pane to replace the existing permissions:

▶   Set the Owner permissions for the Development folder to warren by dragging warren over the single-person icon currently held by ladmin.

▶   Set the Group permissions for the Development folder to Engineering by dragging Engineering over the multi-person icon currently held by admin.

▶   Set the Others permissions for the Development folder to None by changing the pulldown menu in the Permissions column.

4   Click Save.

Will members of the Contractors group be able to access the Development folder that is owned by Warren Peece with a group of Engineering and Everyone No Access? No. They would need to be made part of the Engineering group or Everyone would have to have some type of access. What POSIX permissions would you need to set to allow them access? Everyone would need to have Read and Write access.

Set the Access Control for the Pre_Release Folder

You will use an ACL instead of POSIX permissions for the Pre_Release folder.

1   If not already selected, click the File Sharing button in the toolbar and select the Pre_Release folder inside the Project Phantom share.

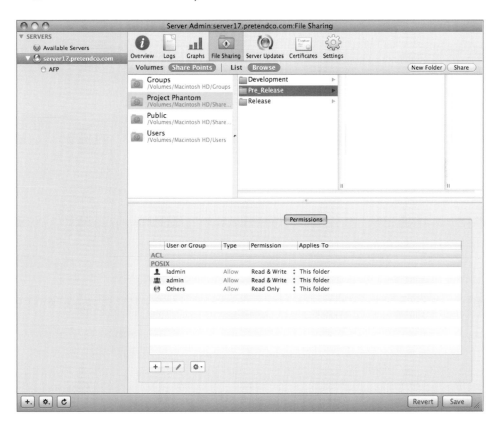

2   Click the Add (+) button to open the Users and Groups drawer, click Groups, and drag the Marketing group to the ACL list in the Permissions pane. Click Save.

3   Select the Marketing entry in the ACL list and, in the Permission column, give the Marketing group Full Control.

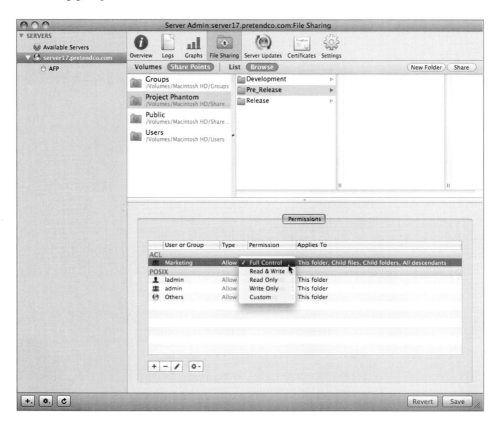

4   From the Groups list, drag the Engineering group into the ACL list. Click Save.

5   Select the Engineering group in the ACL list and give it Custom access that permits reading and writing but does not let them delete files or folders. Click OK.

Effectively, you have allowed the Engineering group full edit control, but group members cannot remove items.

6   Click OK, then click Save.

Set the Access and Permissions for the Release Folder

Just as you did for the Pre_Release folder, you must set the access controls for the Release folder. The group for the Release folder will be Projects. You do not need to assign members in that group to establish access; all access will be determined by the ACLs, as with the Pre_Release folder. If later you want to grant access to this folder, you can add users or groups to the folder ACLs.

1   If not already selected, click the File Sharing button in the toolbar and select the Release folder.

2   Click the Groups button in the Users and Groups drawer and drag the Projects group to the ACL list in the Permissions pane. Click Save.

3   Select the Projects entry in the Access Control List box and give the Projects group
Full Control.

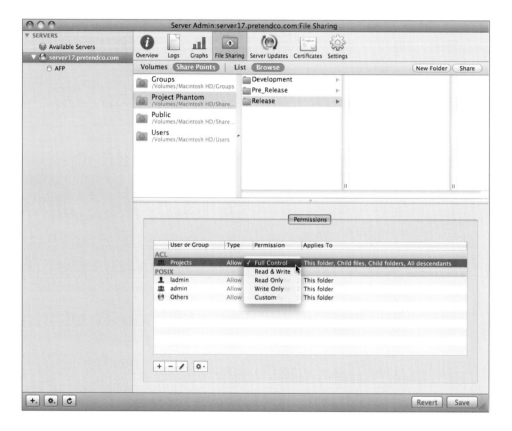

4   Drag the Marketing group to the ACL list.

5   Select the Marketing entry in the ACL list and give them custom access that permits
reading and writing but does not let them delete files or folders. Click OK.

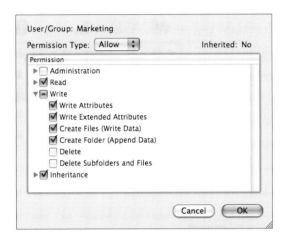

6 Drag the Engineering group to the ACL list.

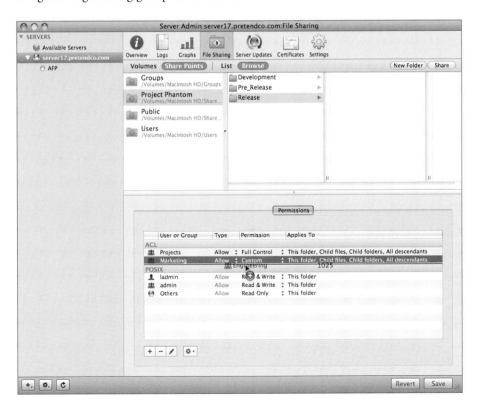

7   Double-click the Engineering entry in the ACL list and click OK to give the
Engineering group read-only access.

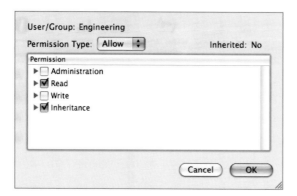

8   Click Save.

Add New Users

Now that you have created the folder structure, create two additional users and
assign them to groups, as you learned earlier in the section "Configuring Local User
Accounts":

▶   Project manager *Pamela Clarke*, short name *pclarke*, password *pclarke*, in the
Projects group

▶   Contractor *Mike Smith*, short name *msmith*, password *msmith*, in the
Contractors group

Turn on the File Server

Now that we've created a file share, we need to start the file server if it's not running already.

1   In Server Admin, select the AFP service in the left frame.

2   Click Start AFP at the bottom.

Watch the Workflow

You have now configured the server with the proper project folders and appropriate users
and groups. You will now create a document and watch the access during a normal workflow.

1   From the client machine, connect to the server machine as Warren.

2   Select the Project Phantom share point. Click OK.

3   Using TextEdit, create two text files, one named Engineering Spec and one named First Source, and place them in the Development folder.

Warren has full access to the Development folder.

4   Create a subfolder inside Development called Code and move the First Source file into that subfolder.

5   Option-drag the folder from Development to Pre_Release.

This copies the folder and its contents instead of moving it.

6   Disconnect as Warren and connect as Tina Bubbles.

7   View the permissions on the files in the Development folder.

As a member of the Marketing group, Tina does not currently have access to the Development folder. Because there are no ACLs on the Development folder and Tina isn't a member of the Engineering group, she cannot see the files in that folder.

8   View the files in the Pre_Release folder.

9   Edit the First Source file by adding some text to the file and save it in a new folder called Reviewed.

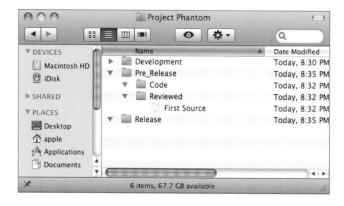

10 Move the Reviewed folder from Pre_Release to the Release folder.

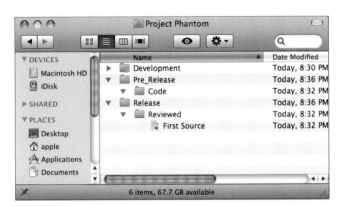

This indicates a project ready for production.

11 Disconnect as Tina and connect as Pamela Clark.

12 View the documents in the other folders.

13 Create a new folder inside Release named Ready and move the file First Source into it.

The other groups should still have read access to the Ready folder. View the file and folder info in the Finder using the Get Info command.

Add Groups to the Access Path

Now that you have configured a basic set of access to the program folders and viewed how the access changes when a document or folder is moved from one container to another, you will add groups to groups and see how that impacts the access.

1   Disconnect as Pamela and connect as the contractor Mike Smith.

2   Verify that you can access the data in the Pre_Release and Release folders.

3   Disconnect as Mike Smith.

4   Open Server Admin, click File Sharing, and navigate to the Development folder in the Share Points list.

5   Click the Add (+) button and click the Groups button in the Users and Groups drawer.

6   Drag the Engineering group to the ACL pane and give it Full Control. Click Save.

You've added ACLs to the Development folder. You will now give the Contractors group access to the Development folder.

7   Drag the Contractors group to the ACL pane and give them read and write access without allowing them to delete files or folders by using a Custom permissions setting.

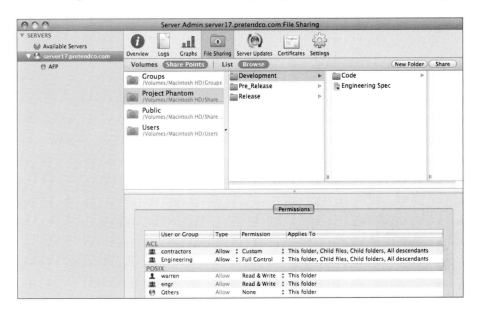

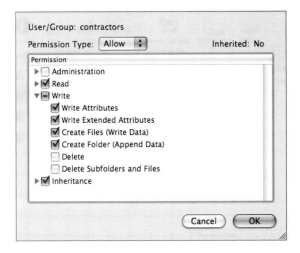

8   Click Save.

Add Deny Type Access

You just gave the Contractors group access to the Development folder. (The Marketing and Projects groups still do not have access.) An easy way to do that would have been to add the Contractors group to the Engineering group once you set the Development ACLs, but that would have given the contractors additional access that you don't want them to have. With Deny access, you can limit users and groups to better narrow down the permissions model you are seeking.

1   In Workgroup Manager, click Accounts and click the Groups button.

2   Add the Contractors group to the Engineering group by clicking the Add (+) button and dragging the Contractors group into the Members list of Engineering and click Save.

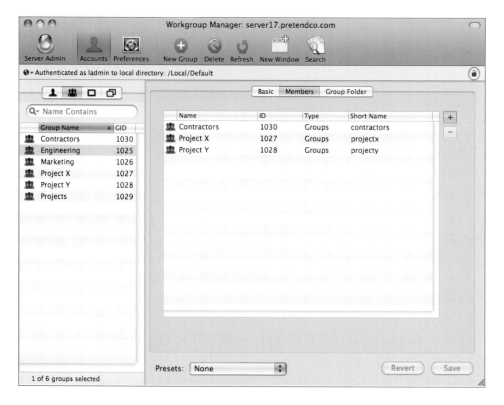

3   In Server Admin, click File Sharing and navigate to the Pre_Release folder.

4   Click the Add (+) button and click the Groups button in the Users and Groups drawer.

5   Drag the Contractors group to the top of the ACL list.

6   Double-click the Contractors group, choose Deny from the Permission Type pop-up menu, and click OK.

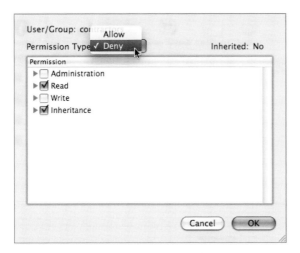

7   Click Save.

Even though the Contractors group would normally now have access as part of the Engineering group, it is explicitly denied access.

For this exercise, do not change the ACLs on the Release folder. Take some time to log in as various users and notice how your access changes. The Contractors group was denied access to the Pre_Release folder but picked up Engineering access to the documents in the Release folder.

Clean Up Folders on the Server
You have created the Phantom Project folder and viewed how the workflow can occur when documents are moved from folder to folder. You can now remove the folder from the server.

1   On your client computer, open Server Admin and connect to your server.

2   Click the File Sharing button in Workgroup Manager's toolbar, select the Phantom Project share point, click the Unshare button in the upper-right corner, and click Save.

3   Quit Server Admin.

4   In the Finder on the server, delete the folder Phantom Project.

Controlling Access to Your Server

In addition to file-system ACLs, Mac OS X Server also supports *service ACLs*, or SACLs, which are separate from file-system ACLs in implementation and purpose, despite the similar name. Service ACLs enable you to define who has access to specific services on Mac OS X Server. You could use SACLs to allow all users to log in via AFP connections, but restrict SSH (Secure Shell) connections to administrators.

SACLs are stored simply through membership in a specially named group. For example, the SSH SACL is controlled by membership in the group named com.apple.access_ssh. Once you configure SACLs, it's possible that you may see similarly named groups on your system. In most circumstances, you should leave those groups alone and instead use the Server Admin application to define SACLs as explained in the specific service lessons throughout this book. To modify SACLs, you need to have administrative rights on the server.

Promoting a User to an Administrator

As we mentioned before, you use the Workgroup Manager application to define a user as an administrator. Follow these steps to upgrade one of your existing user accounts to an administrator:

1 Open Workgroup Manager, if it's not already open.

2 Click the Accounts button on the toolbar.

3 Select the Tina Bubbles user.

4 In the Basic pane, check the box for "User can administer this server."

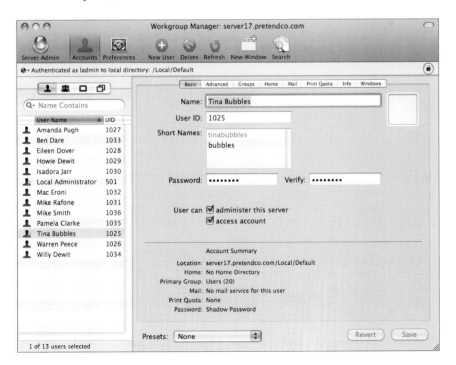

5   Click Save.

You'll notice that after an account is set as an administrator that the icon next to the user's name changes to a person with a pencil to indicate that the user can edit server settings.

6   Test the new administrator access by opening the Server Admin application and logging in using the tinabubbles user.

Configuring Service ACLs

As with files, you can configure SACLs for individual users, groups, or a mix of both. Similarly, you may find that long-term administration will be easier if you assign SACLs based on organizational roles assigned to groups rather than to individual people. This will make it much easier when there are changes within your company, because you will only need to change group membership rather than modifying individual file and service permissions for each person.

1   Open the Server Admin application and connect as tinabubbles.

2   Select the name of your server in the left column.

3   Click the Settings button in the toolbar.

4   Click Access.

5   Click "Allow only users and groups below."

6   Click the Add (+) button near the bottom to open the Users and Groups drawer.

7   Click Groups in the Users and Groups drawer.

8   Select the Marketing group, and drag it into the list of allowed users and groups.

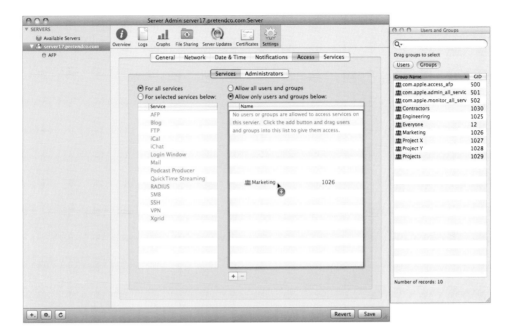

9 Click Save.

10 In the Finder, try making an AFP connection to your server as Mike Smith.

Because Mike Smith is not in the Marketing group, you should see a failure when trying to authenticate. This error will look like a normal password failure, even if you type the password correctly.

11 Back in Server Admin, add the Contractors group to the list of allowed users and groups.

12 Click Save.

13 Try connecting to your server as Mike Smith (msmith) again.

Because Mike Smith is in the Contractors group, the connection should work this time.

Granting Different Access for Different Services

In many cases, you may want to offer different groups different access to the server. For example, you may wish to give most of your groups access to the AFP service, while giving only the Engineering group access to the SSH (Remote Login) service.

1   In Server Admin, click "For selected services below."

2   Select the AFP service.

3   Click "Allow only users and groups below."

4   Drag the Contractors, Engineering, Marketing, and Projects groups into the list of allowed users and groups.

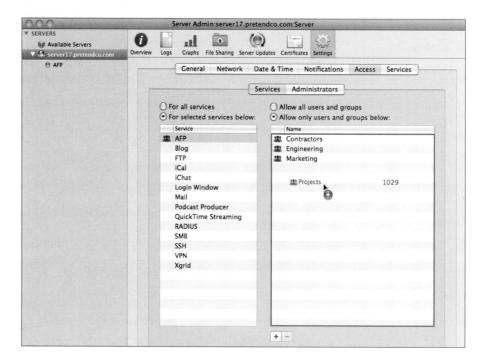

5   Click the SSH service.

6   Drag the Engineering group into the list of allowed users and groups.

7   Click Save.

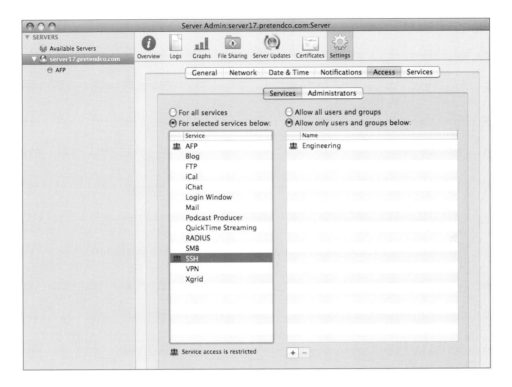

You'll notice that when you're specifying different access for specific services that services with controlled access will have an icon shown next to the name of the service, while the other services don't have an icon. If a service isn't listed as having access restricted to a list of users, that service is open to everyone. You may wish to restrict those others services to something as a security measure, unless you truly do want them open to everyone.

Limiting Administration Capabilities

There are often situations where you want to grant a group of users only partial administration abilities. These are cases where the roles of your organization might require a group of users to be able to do something that requires administrator privileges, but where you don't feel comfortable granting full rights to those users. An example of this situation may be in a school environment. You may have a group of students responsible for monitoring your services. Another group may be responsible for managing the access control of your Podcast Producer users and the list of allowed machines for your NetBoot service. Using the new limited administrator features of Mac OS X Server v10.5, you can configure access as described in the following steps while not granting access to the entire server.

1   Open the Server Admin application.

2   Click the name of your server in the left column.

3   Click the Settings button in the toolbar.

4   Click Access.

5   Click Administrators.

6   Click the Add (+) button to open the Users and Groups drawer.

7   Drag the Contractors group into the list of users allowed to administer or monitor.

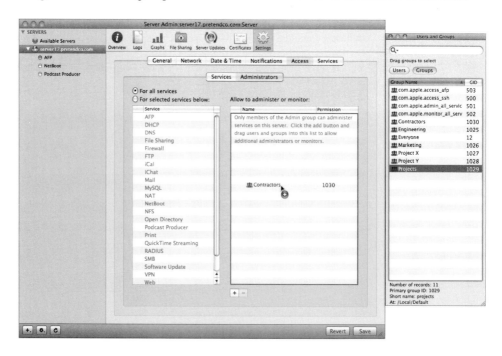

8   Click Save.

You'll notice that the permission defaults to Monitor. This means that, in addition to anyone defined as an Administrator in Workgroup Manager, anyone in the Contractors group can monitor, but not change, all of the services on your server.

You may also wish to add a different group of users to have administrative rights.

9 Drag the Engineering group into the list of users allowed to administer or monitor.

10 Change the pop-up menu option next to the Engineering group from Monitor to Administer.

11 Click Save.

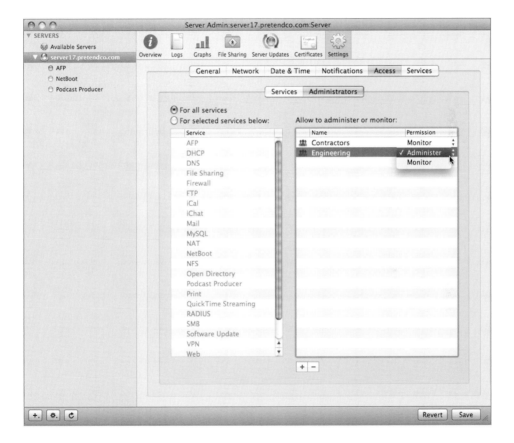

This will allow members of the Engineering group access to make changes to any of the services as well as keep the ability for any member of the Contractors group to monitor all of the services. In many cases, you may find that even that access is too broad, though, and you may wish to restrict access to only certain services for those groups.

12 Click "For selected services below."

13 Select Firewall.

14 Drag the Contractors group to the list of users allowed to administer or monitor.

15 Drag the Engineering group to the list of users allowed to administer or monitor.

16 In the Permission pop-up next to Engineering, change Permission to Administer.

17 Click Save.

This configuration will grant only contractors extra access to monitor the Firewall service (such as logs), and will grant members of the Engineering group access to make changes to the firewall configuration. Any other service will require the user to be a total server administrator.

Clean Up Authorization on Your Server

For the rest of this book, we'll want the server returned to a state where all the users can connect and only administrators have administrative access. Follow these steps to open your server access back up to everyone.

1   Open Server Admin.

2   Click Settings on the toolbar.

3   Click Access.

4   Click Services.

5   Click "For all services."

6   Click "Allow all users and groups."

7   Ensure that the list of allowed users and groups is empty. If there are any entries, select them and click the Remove (–) button.

8   Click Save.

9   Click Administrators.

10 Click "For all services."

11 Ensure that the list of users and groups is empty. If there are any entries, select them and click the Remove (–) button.

12 Click Save.

Troubleshooting

File-system ACLs can be very confusing and can grow out of hand very quickly. If someone doesn't have the access to a file or folder that you think they should have, be sure to use the Effective Permissions Inspector in Server Admin's File Sharing permission setting menu to evaluate the permissions that they have on an object.

For service ACLs, it can be somewhat confusing if someone is trying to connect to a service for which they don't have permission. Despite the fact that they are typing their password correctly, they may actually see an error message indicating that they haven't. It may be useful to have the user try to authenticate to a service that they do have access to so you can confirm that their password isn't the problem.

What You've Learned

▶ Authentication gets a user into the server. Authorization determines what the user can do after getting in.

▶ User accounts for Mac OS X Server are created in Workgroup Manager. You can configure two types of accounts with Workgroup Manager: user and administrator. An administrator account is the same as a user account except it has the authority to administer the server.

▶ Group accounts enable administrators to quickly assign a set of permissions to multiple users. You create and manage group accounts in Workgroup Manager. You can add users to groups and group membership to user accounts.

▶ You use Server Admin to create share points and to assign permissions to the share points.

▶ Mac OS X Server includes support for access control lists (ACLs), which provide a higher granularity for setting permissions. These ACLs are compatible with ACLs from the Windows world and work in addition to the standard POSIX (UNIX) permissions found on Mac OS X.

▶ Mac OS X Server includes support for Service ACLs (SACLs), which limit access for certain services to specified users or groups.

▶ Mac OS X Server v10.5 adds support for limited server administrators.

References

The following documents provide more information about users, groups, and ACLs with Mac OS X Server. (All of these and more are available at www.apple.com/server/documentation.)

Administration Guides

File Services Administration (http://images.apple.com/server/macosx/docs/File_Services_Admin_v10.5.pdf)

Server Administration (http://images.apple.com/server/macosx/docs/Server_Administration_v10.5.pdf)

User Management (http://images.apple.com/server/macosx/docs/User_Management_v10.5.mnl.pdf)

Upgrading and Migrating (http://images.apple.com/server/macosx/
docs/Upgrading_and_Migrating_v10.5.pdf)

Apple Knowledge Base Documents

You can check for new and updated Knowledge Base documents at www.apple.com/support.

Review Quiz

1. Describe the difference between authentication and authorization, and give an example of each.

2. What is the difference between user and administrator accounts on both Mac OS X and Mac OS X Server?

3. What tool is used to configure user, group, and share point settings on Mac OS X Server? What tool is used to change user and group permissions on Mac OS X?

4. Where do you set file or folder access ACLs?

5. What is the difference between Service ACLs and Limited Administrator settings?

Answers

1. Authentication is the process by which the system requires you to provide information before it allows you to access a specific account. An example is entering a name and password while connecting to an Apple file server. Authorization refers to the process by which permissions are used to regulate a user's access to specific resources, such as files and share points, once the user has been successfully authenticated.

2. User accounts provide basic access to a computer or server, while administrator accounts allow a person to administer the machine. On Mac OS X, the administrator account is typically used for changing settings or adding new software. On Mac OS X Server, the administrator account is typically used for changing settings on the server machine itself, usually through Server Admin or Workgroup Manager.

3. Workgroup Manager is used to configure users and groups, and Server Admin is used to manage share points on Mac OS X Server. Get Info is used to change permissions on Mac OS X.

4. Server Admin

5. Service ACLs determine which users are allowed to utilize a given service, while Limited Administrator settings control who can monitor or change a service.

4

Time   This lesson takes approximately 4 hours to complete.

Goals   Understand the four Open Directory service roles you can configure on Mac OS X Server

Configure Mac OS X Server as an Open Directory master

Locate and identify Open Directory–related log files

Use the Mac OS X Server DHCP service to provide Open Directory information to a Mac OS X computer

Examine the contents of an Open Directory archive and restore those contents

Describe authentication types

Understand basic Kerberos infrastructure

Using Open Directory

This lesson describes how using a directory service can help you manage users and resources on your network. You will learn about the features of Apple's Open Directory and how Open Directory can be integrated with other directory services in a mixed environment. You will also learn how to set up and manage directories and user accounts with Server Admin, Workgroup Manager, and Directory Access—the three main tools you'll use with Open Directory. Finally, you will become familiar with common Open Directory issues and learn how to correct them.

Open Directory is extremely versatile when dealing with a variety of other directory services, such as Active Directory, eDirectory, and Network Information Servers (NIS) directory servers. This lesson deals with a Mac OS X Server–to–Mac OS X directory service scenario.

Introducing Directory Services Concepts

Giving a user multiple user accounts on different computers can cause problems. For instance, if each computer in a network has its own authentication database, a user might have to remember a different password for each computer. Even if you assign the user the same password on every computer, the information can become inconsistent over time, because the user changes passwords in one location but forgets to do so in another. A single authentication database can solve this problem.

Directory services provide this central repository for information about the computers, applications, and users in an organization. With directory services, you can maintain consistent information about all the users—such as their names, passwords, and preferences—as well as about printers and other network resources. You can maintain this information in a single location, rather than on individual computers.

For example, users can freely log in to any Mac OS X computer that is bound to a Mac OS X Server providing a shared directory and have their session managed based on who they are or the group to which they belong. Using a shared directory service also permits the user's home folder to be located on another server and automatically mounted on whatever computer the user logs into, so long as that computer is bound to the share directory.

What Is Open Directory?

Apple's extensible directory-services architecture, called Open Directory, is built into Mac OS X Server. Many services on Mac OS X require information from Open Directory to function. Open Directory can securely store and validate the passwords of users who want to log in to client computers on your network or use other network resources that require authentication. You can also use Open Directory to enforce policies such as password expiration and minimum length and to manage user preferences.

Open Directory can also authenticate Windows users for directory login, file services, print service, and other Windows services that Mac OS X Server provides. Open Directory is integrated with Samba 3, which allows an Open Directory server to function as a Windows primary domain controller (PDC) or a backup domain controller (BDC).

Overview of Open Directory Components

Open Directory is based on OpenLDAP, an open-source implementation of the Lightweight Directory Access Protocol (LDAP), a standard protocol used for accessing directory-service data. In addition to LDAP, Open Directory includes plug-ins for several other directory types, including Active Directory, and NIS.

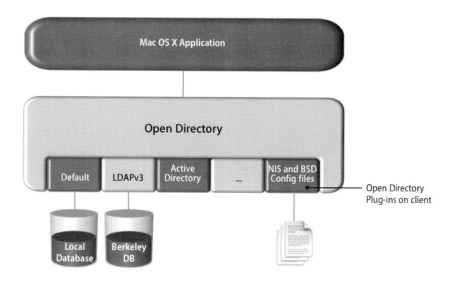

While LDAP was used in Mac OS X Server v10.3 and v10.4 for its shared database, earlier versions of Mac OS X and Mac OS X Server used the NetInfo directory service for local directory services. Starting with Mac OS X v10.5, NetInfo has been replaced with flat files. This structure, coupled with the Directory Utility application and the Kerberos utility, comprise the bulk of Open Directory on Mac OS X.

Open Directory acts as an intermediary between directories (which store information about users and resources) and the application and system software processes that want to use the information. Open Directory leverages other open-source technologies, such as Kerberos and LDAP, and combines them with powerful server administration tools to deliver robust directory and authentication services that are easy to set up and manage. Because there are no per-seat or per-user license fees, Open Directory can scale to the needs of an organization without adding high costs to an IT budget. Administrators can deploy Open Directory configuration information automatically using DHCP or manually using the Directory Access application at the computer.

By default, Mac OS X computers request network configuration information, including LDAP configuration, from a DHCP server. If the DHCP and LDAP servers are set up correctly, the client automatically gets access to network resources, including user authentication services, network home folders, share points, and preferences.

Configuring Open Directory

Using Server Admin, a computer running Mac OS X Server can be set up in four ways:

▶   As a standalone server, the server does not provide directory information to other computers or get directory information from an existing system. The local directory can't be shared.

▶   As a server connected to a directory system, you can set up the server to provide services that require user accounts and authentication, such as file and mail services, but use accounts that are set up on another server.

▶   As an Open Directory replica, a server hosts a replicated version of a directory. The replica is synchronized periodically with the master.

▶   As an Open Directory master, a server can provide directory information and authentication information to other systems as the host of a shared LDAP directory.

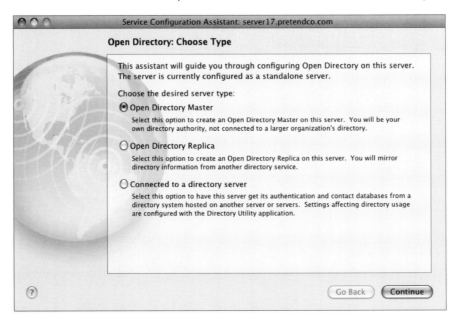

As you plan directory services for your network, consider the need to share user and resource information among multiple Mac OS X computers. If the need is low, then little directory planning is necessary; everything can be accessed from a local server directory. However, if you want to share information among computers, you need to set up at least one shared directory.

Connecting to an Existing Directory System

If you intend to set up multiple servers, it would be extremely inefficient to populate each server with the same user accounts. Instead, your Mac OS X Server computer can be a node connected to a directory system. In this role, the server gets authentication, user information, and other directory information from a directory system hosted on another server or servers. The Mac OS X server still gets some directory information locally from its own directory and provides authentication based on this information for local users. This puts one server at the pinnacle of your setup and other servers that obtain their directory information from this original server. This server does not have to be an Open Directory server; it could be another directory server such as Active Directory.

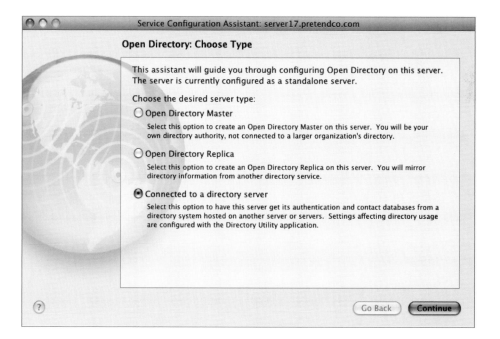

To configure your server to obtain directory services from an existing Open Directory master server:

1   Open Server Admin. Select Open Directory in the Available Servers list. Click the Settings button in the toolbar, then click the Change button near the top of the window. Select "Connected to a directory server" from the Server Configuration Assistant and follow the steps.

2   Open Directory Utility (located in /Applications/Utilities). If necessary, click the Lock icon and authenticate to make changes, and then click the Show Advanced Settings button.

3   Click the Add (+) button and type the fully qualified domain name of the Open Directory master.

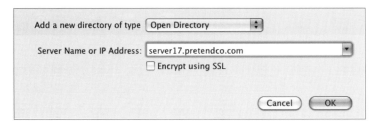

4 Enter the Computer ID (usually the Computer Name of the server that will connect to the Open Directory master).

5 Click OK.

You can then view your Open Directory master server in the Directory Servers list.

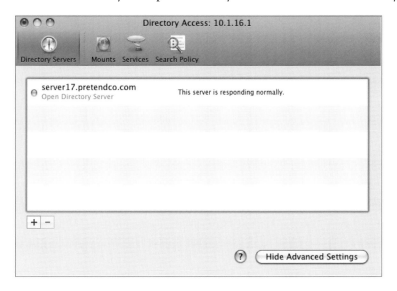

Your server is now bound to another Mac OS X Server Open Directory master.

Configuring an Open Directory Master

Instead of binding to another server for directory services, you can set up Mac OS X Server to host a shared LDAP directory, providing directory information and authentication to other systems. To do so:

1   Click the Change button in the Settings pane to open the Server Configuration Assistant.

2   Enter a Name, a Short Name, and a Password for a new account that will administer the shared LDAP directory. You can use the default user name and diradmin as the password as your initial LDAP account.

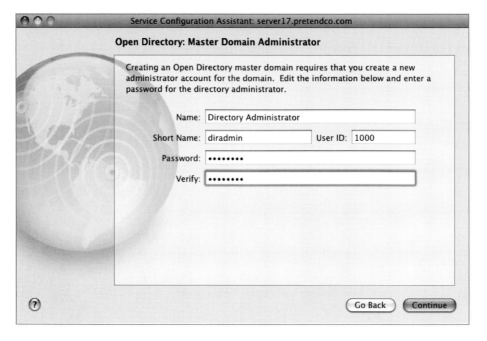

Once you have set up your server to be an Open Directory master, you can configure other computers on your network to access the server's shared LDAP directory.

> **NOTE ▶** Once you have added accounts to the Open Directory directory on your server, do not change the Open Directory role setting. If you do, you may lose all your account information and orphan your users' data.

NOTE ▶ Determine a standard for your UNIX user UIDs as you enter user records. Perhaps have your administrators in a separate range for easier searching. Workgroup Manager allows filtering, and UNIX user UID or UNIX group ID GID is a powerful way to search for users or groups.

To recap, you began with a local database for your local users. That database still exists. The administrator of that database is ladmin. You have now created a secondary, shared LDAP database. The administrator of that database is (by default) diradmin. Each database is separate and requires different authentication to manage either one. You have also created a Password Server database to store LDAP user passwords and a Kerberos Key Distribution Center (KDC). You will learn about those later in this book.

Managing Network User Accounts

Once you have created shared LDAP directories, you need to populate them with information. User account information is probably the most important type of information you can store in a directory. User accounts that are stored in a shared directory are accessible to all the computers that search that directory; those accounts are referred to as *network user accounts*.

To create user accounts, use Workgroup Manager. If you click the small Globe icon on the upper left of the Accounts pane below the Admin button in the toolbar, you can choose a directory from a pop-up menu. This enables you to create user accounts in different directories. Use the Basic pane to create an account, and then use the other panes to set the account's attributes, such as login shell.

NOTE ▶ If you are creating user accounts that other computers will use, make sure you have chosen a shared directory from the directory pop-up menu before you create the account. Workgroup Manager will display a warning whenever you start to add accounts to the local directory; this will help prevent you from accidentally creating an account in the local directory instead of a shared one.

> **NOTE ▶** You can also add users and/or groups from one directory to groups from another directory. This increases the flexibility of your system and servers, but it can be very easy to create an overly complex model across directory servers. Always make sure you know which directory you are editing before making changes.

You can use Workgroup Manager to configure both local and network user accounts. Workgroup Manager is essentially a directory-services editing tool.

Use the following steps to verify the configuration and verify that Workgroup Manager can see both databases.

1   Open Workgroup Manager on your Mac OS X computer and connect to your server computer using the following settings:

   ▶   Address: *server17.pretendco.com*

   ▶   User Name: *ladmin*

   ▶   Password: the password you chose when setting up your server

   You should see the LDAP directory, but it won't be authenticated.

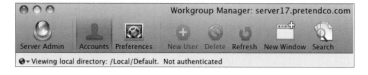

2   If you don't see the LDAP directory, click the small Globe icon at the left, beneath the toolbar, to display the Directory Node pop-up menu, and choose Other.

3   In the "Select a directory" sheet that opens, select LDAPv3, select 127.0.0.1, and click OK.

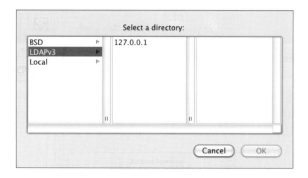

NOTE ▶ Authentication lasts for a set period of time—usually five minutes. You may see a locked option if the authentication has timed out.

4 Click the Lock icon on the right under the toolbar and authenticate as diradmin.

5 In the left pane of the Workgroup Manager window, click the Users button, then click the New User button in the toolbar.

6 Enter the following values:

▶ Name: *John Soward*

▶ Short Names: *john*

▶ Password: *johnsoward*

7 Click Save.

You have just created a user account in your shared directory domain. John Soward is now listed in the left pane. The only other user currently in the shared LDAP directory is Directory Administrator.

8 Create five more users and give them long names, short names, and passwords.

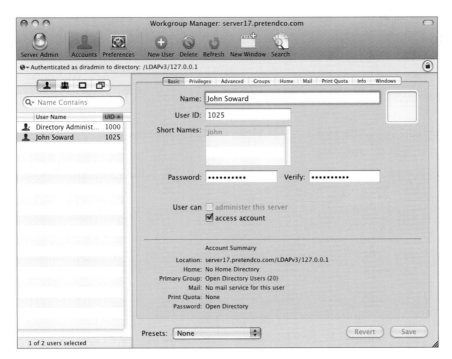

Connecting to the Shared LDAP Directory

Once you have an Open Directory master set up, you must configure the client computers to connect, or *bind*, to the server. Using Directory Utility on each client computer, you create an LDAP configuration that has the address and search path for your Open Directory master. This method forces you to visit every computer running Mac OS X, which can be quite time-consuming if you have a few hundred Mac OS X computers that need to be bound to your server.

You will now configure your Mac OS X computer to use authentication services from your Mac OS X Server. You just configured a shared directory, so your Mac OS X computers must be able to see the shared directory in order to authenticate against it. There are two main ways to do this, manually define the Open Directory master on your Mac OS X computer or receive the information via DHCP. Using Mac OS X Server's DHCP service is an excellent way to permit Mac OS X computers to obtain the shared directory information.

You will configure your Mac OS X computer to use authentication services on your Mac OS X Server. Once you have configured a shared directory on Mac OS X Server, you need to set the client machines to look for it. You can configure DHCP to provide the information required to locate the shared directory or you can set it up manually. Any client bound to the server can authenticate users using the data in the shared directory. Your Mac OS X computer must be using the static IP address (10.1.17.2) manually assigned in Lesson 3, "Authenticating and Authorizing Accounts," for this next set of steps.

Set Static LDAP Binding to Your Server

The Mac OS X computers need to bind to your Open Directory master server to connect. In the following steps, you will set the binding manually, and then set the client to use the server for authentication information.

1   On the Mac OS X computer, open Directory Utility (located in /Applications/Utilities). If necessary, click the Lock icon and authenticate to make changes, and then click the Show Advanced Settings button.

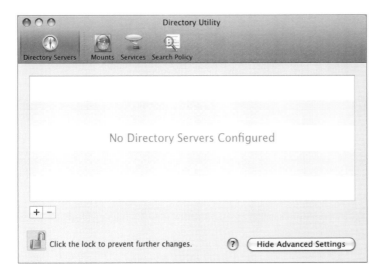

2   Click the Add (+) button and type the fully qualified domain name of the Open
    Directory master.

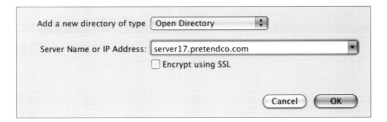

3   The Computer ID field will be automatically populated with the predefined name of
    the computer. Click OK.

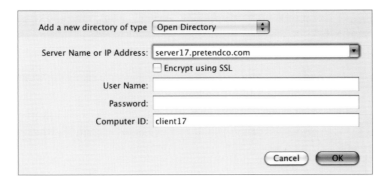

4 Click OK, and the Mac OS X computer is now bound to the Open Directory master.

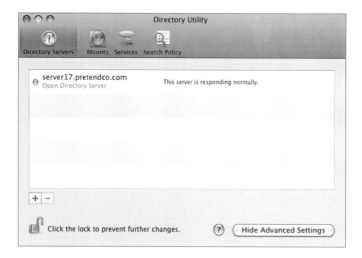

Verify Authentication

Now that binding is complete, you must verify that you are using the server for authentication information.

1 Click the Search Policy button in Directory Utility and verify that /LDAPv3/ server17.pretendco.com is in the list.

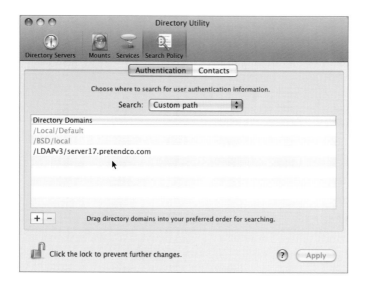

2   If the server path is not in the list, you will need to add it (you will not need to complete the following steps if the authentication is set for you):

▶   Choose Custom path from the Search menu.

▶   Click the Add (+) button.

▶   Select server17.pretendco.com.

▶   Click Add.

▶   Click Apply.

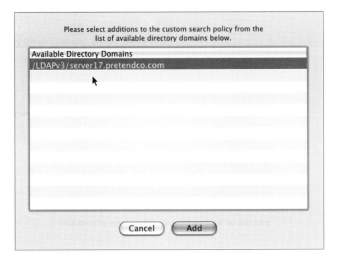

3   Quit Directory Utility.

4   Quit any applications and log out of your Mac OS X computer.

You have now bound your Mac OS X computer to your Mac OS X Server. Your login
window now has the option for Other, and you could use that to log in as a network user,
something you will do in a later lesson.

> **NOTE** ▶ You should delete this configuration from your Authentication Search path
> and remove the configuration from the LDAP list (essentially backing out of the pre-
> vious steps) if you are going to attempt the following exercises. Please remember to
> click the Apply button when fully backed out of the previous exercise.

Using DHCP to Obtain LDAP Directory Information

An alternative to manually setting the address on each computer is to provide the LDAP binding information through the DHCP service. You can configure the Mac OS X Server DHCP service to provide connection information for an LDAP server. After the DHCP service has been configured, the client computer receives the address of an LDAP directory server from the DHCP service that also supplies the computer's IP address, router address, and DNS server addresses. If the Directory Utility is set to use that LDAP information, the LDAP server's address automatically becomes part of your Mac OS X computer's search path.

1   Using Server Admin, enable the DHCP service by clicking the checkbox next to that service in the Services list.

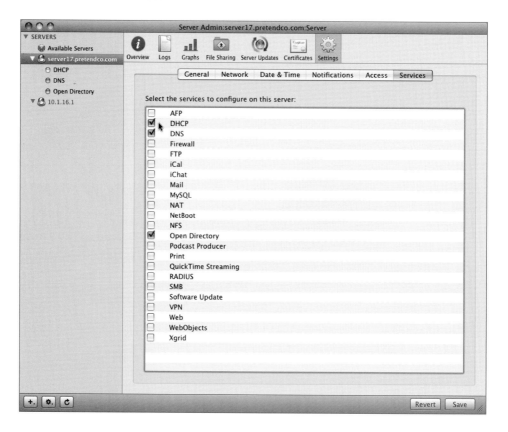

2   Select the DHCP service from the server list on the left, select the Subnets button
in the toolbar, enable the subnet, click the General tab below the list of subnets, and
configure it with the following parameters:

▶   Subnet Name: *Mac OS X Server Essentials Book Subnet*

▶   Starting IP Address: *10.1.17.10*

▶   Ending IP Address: *10.1.17.11*

▶   Subnet Mask: *255.255.0.0*

▶   Network Interface: *en0*

▶   Router: *10.1.17.1*

▶   Lease Time: *2 hours*

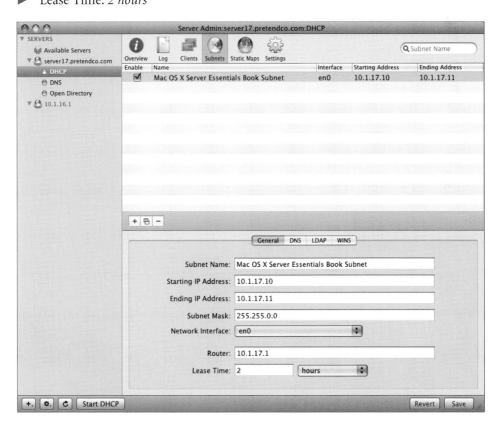

3 Select the DNS tab below the list of subnets, and configure it with the following parameters:

▶ DNS Servers: *10.1.17.1*

▶ Default Search Domain: *server17.pretendco.com*

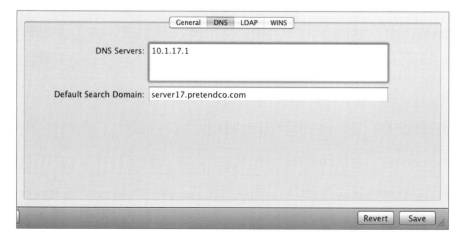

4 Select the LDAP tab below the list of subnets, and configure it with the following parameters:

▶ Server Name: *server17.pretendco.com*

▶ Search Base: *dc=server17,dc=pretendco,dc=com*

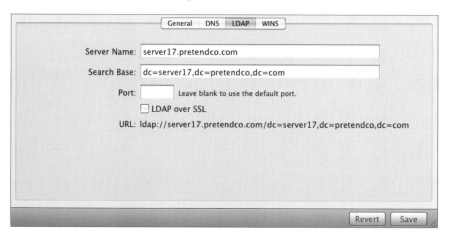

5 Leave the Port field blank, save the changes, click the Start DHCP button in the bottom of the Server Admin window, and quit Server Admin.

6 On your Mac OS X computer, create a new network location, call it *Using DHCP*, and ensure that your built-in Ethernet is using DHCP. You should obtain an IP address from your server after a few moments.

Now that you have obtained an IP address, you have also obtained your shared LDAP directory information. You must now tell the Directory Utility to look for that information.

7 On the Mac OS X computer, open Directory Utility (located in /Applications/ Utilities). If necessary, click the Lock icon and authenticate to make changes, and then click the Show Advanced Settings button.

8 Select the Services button in the toolbar, then select the LDAP service.

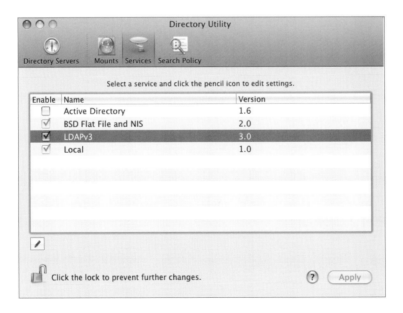

9 Click the Pencil icon (or double-click the LDAP service) to edit the service.

10 Select the "Add DHCP-supplied LDAP servers to automatic search policies" checkbox and click OK, then click the Apply button if necessary.

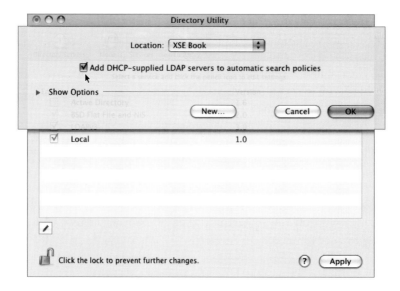

11 Confirm the LDAP information is supplied by clicking the Search Policy button in the toolbar and ensuring Automatic is selected in the pop-up menu. You should see your server's fully qualified domain name in the list.

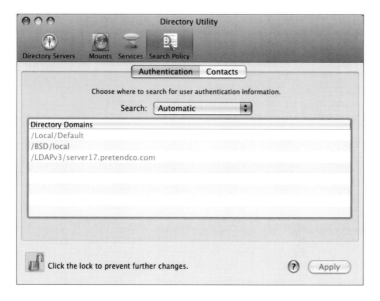

Your Mac OS X computer is now bound to the Mac OS X Server's LDAP server simply by using the information provided by the DHCP server.

Configuring an Open Directory Replica

Open Directory enables you to replicate servers, that is, to create and maintain one or more exact copies of your server's LDAP, password, and Kerberos databases. Open Directory also provides automatic load balancing between replicated servers. As a result, you can scale your directory infrastructure and improve search-and-retrieval time on distributed networks. Replication also protects against network outages because client systems can use any replica in your organization.

In Mac OS X Server v10.5, you can create nested replicas, that is, replicas of replicas. One master can have up to 32 replicas, and those replicas can have 32 replicas each; this totals 1056 replicas and one master, totaling 1057 authentication servers for a single Open Directory domain. Nesting replicas is accomplished by joining one replica to your Open Directory master, and then joining other replicas to the first replica.

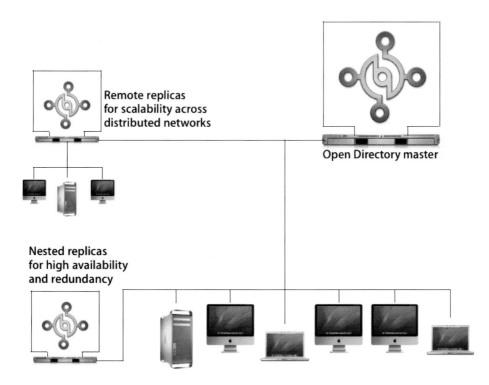

If you already have an open directory master server set up, you can configure a second Mac OS X server as a directory replica to provide the same directory information and authentication information as the master. The replica server hosts a copy of the master's LDAP directory and its Kerberos KDC. The Password Server authentication database is copied and is also writable on the master and any replicas. When data is transferred from the master to any replica, that data is encrypted as it is copied over. Replicas need a serial number that is different from that of the master, unless a site license is purchased from Apple.

Configure Your Server to Host a Replica of an Open Directory Master

You will be stepping through the process of hosting a Replica of your Mac OS X Server Open Directory master. If you have only one Mac OS X Server and one Mac OS X computer, you can read through this exercise but not complete it.

1   Launch Server Admin and select Open Directory in the services list on the left and add Open Directory, as shown in the following figure.

   Alternatively, you can follow the instructions on adding a service in Lesson 2, "Providing Basic DNS Service" (when the DNS service was added).

   Whatever the current role of the server, the goal is to make the server an Open Directory replica.

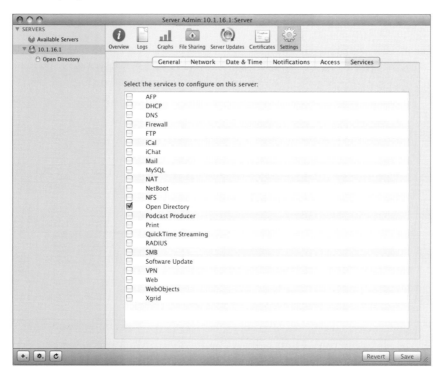

2 Select the Settings button in the toolbar, click the General tab, and click the Change button to launch the Service Configuration Assistant, just as you did when you created an Open Directory master from a standalone server earlier in this lesson.

NOTE ▶ You can't create a replica if you do not have an Open Directory master on your network.

3 Once the Service Configuration Assistant opens, select Open Directory Replica in the list and click Continue.

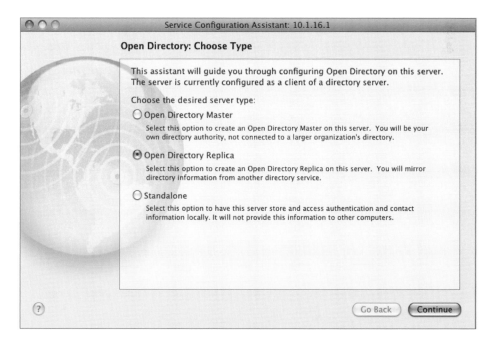

4 Configure the replica with the following parameters:

▶ IP address or FQDN of the Open Directory master

▶ Root password on Open Directory master

▶ Domain administrator's short name

▶ Domain administrator's password

NOTE ▶ It is important that the replica know the root password of the Open Directory master because initial information is passed using this account.

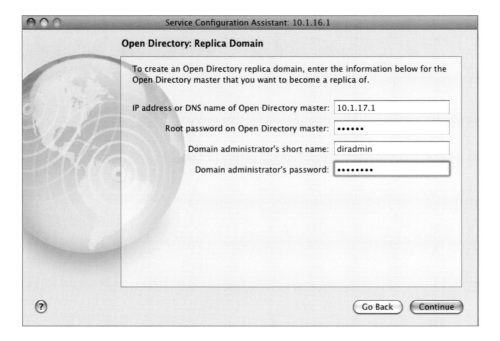

5 Click Continue.

At this point, the server is becoming a replica of an Open Directory master.

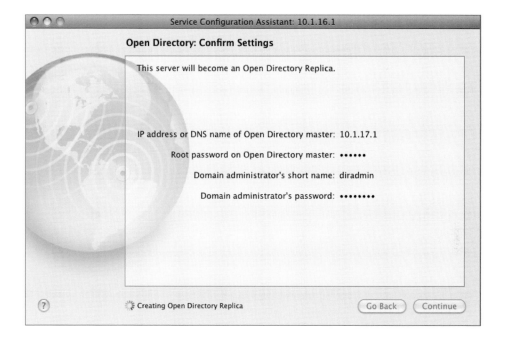

NOTE ▶ If this server is already an Open Directory master, the current LDAP database will be emptied of all its contents.

Once the replica has been established, viewing the Open Directory general settings of either the Open Directory master server or the Open Directory replica server will display the IP address of the Open Directory master and the IP address(es) of any Open Directory replicas.

NOTE ▶ Once you have set up your server to be an Open Directory replica, other computers can connect to it as needed automatically. The Open Directory master will also update the replica automatically or at specific intervals.

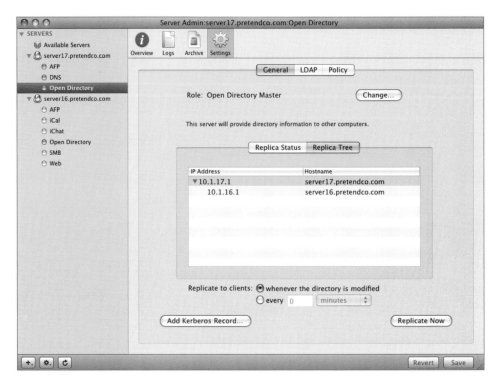

Once a single replica has been established, other Mac OS X Servers can be set up as replicas of replicas. This increases the redundancy and potentially improves performance of the entire Open Directory structure.

> **TIP** Because replication uses timestamps, it is best to use NTP to synchronize the clocks on all Open Directory masters, replicas, and servers using existing masters. You enable NTP services in Mac OS X Server in Server Admin. You configure a server to use NTP services in the Date & Time pane of System Preferences.

Using Authentication Methods on Mac OS X Server

Open Directory offers a variety of options for authenticating users whose accounts are stored in directories on Mac OS X Server, including Kerberos and the many authentication methods that network services require. Open Directory can authenticate users by using:

▶ Single sign-on with the Kerberos KDC built in to Mac OS X Server

- A password stored securely in the Open Directory Password Server database

- A password stored as several hashes including LAN Manager, NTLMv1 and NTLMv2 (NT LAN Manager), and Microsoft Challenge Handshake Authentication Protocol (MS-CHAPv2), used for VPN—in a file that only the root user can access

- An older crypt password stored directly in the user's account, for backward compatibility with legacy systems

- Local-only accounts, in which a shadow password is used, stored in a location accessible only by root

In addition, Open Directory lets you set up a password policy that affects all users (except administrators) as well as specific password policies for each user, such as automatic password expiration and minimum password length. (Password policies do not apply to crypt passwords.) Even though Mac OS X Server supports all of these different authentication methods, you should not use all methods. Crypt password support, for example, is provided for backward compatibility with older computers, but using crypt passwords is not as secure as using the Open Directory Password Server.

Configuring User Authentication

To authenticate a user, Open Directory first must determine which authentication option to use: Kerberos, Open Directory Password Server, shadow password, or crypt password. The user's account contains information that specifies which authentication option to use. This information is called the *authentication authority attribute*. The attribute is not limited to specifying a single authentication option. For example, an authentication authority attribute could specify that a user can be authenticated by Kerberos and Open Directory Password Server.

You can change a user's authentication authority attribute by changing the password type in the Advanced pane of Workgroup Manager. By default, the password type is Open Directory, which means that Mac OS X Server uses either Kerberos or Open Directory Password Server. Open Directory passwords are stored securely in a separate database, not in the user account.

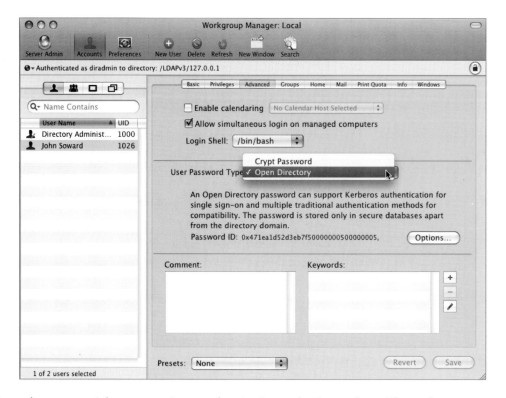

A user's account might not contain an authentication authority attribute. If a user's account contains no authentication authority attribute, Mac OS X Server assumes a crypt password is stored in the user's account. For example, user accounts created using Mac OS X v10.1 and earlier contain a crypt password but not an authentication authority attribute.

> **NOTE** ▶ Crypt passwords are inherently less secure, because they are stored in the directory database and are subject to dictionary attacks. Configure a user account to use a crypt password only if you need to provide compatibility with a computer running Mac OS X v10.1 or earlier.

> **TIP** ▶ If you are using a server that was upgraded from an earlier version of Mac OS X Server, you should examine the password type for all the user records stored on the server. If any records are still using a crypt password, you should upgrade the password type for the account to Open Directory.

Disabling a User Account

If you want to disable a user from logging in, you can temporarily disable that user by using Workgroup Manager to remove access to his or her account. Doing so does not delete the user, nor does it change his or her UNIX user ID or any other information. Nor does it delete any of the user's settings, preferences, or files created by that user. It simply prevents that user from authenticating and gaining access to the server via any method.

1 Open Workgroup Manager and select the directory where the account resides that you want to disable. Generally, you will disable the OpenLDAP accounts, but you can also disable local accounts.

2 Click the Accounts button, select the account, click the Basic tab, and deselect the "access account" checkbox.

3 Save the changes.

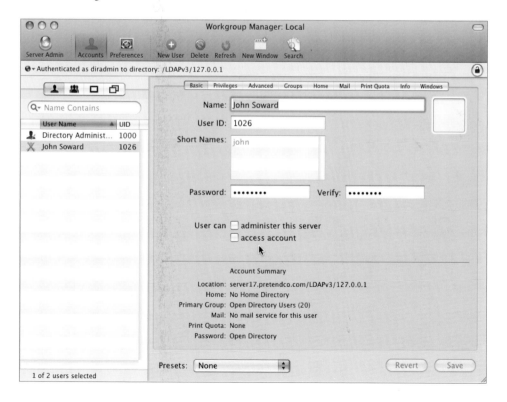

NOTE ▶ When a user account is disabled, you will see a red X through the user's icon in the list of users.

Setting Account Password Policies

Once you create new users, it is useful to establish password policies for their network accounts. (There is more on setting these policies later in this lesson.) Should the users change their passwords next time they log in? Should there be a minimum password length? You can use Workgroup Manager to establish these and other policies for your users. These password policies can apply to just one user or to all users. Password policies applied with Workgroup Manager are called user account settings and are set for each user by clicking the Advanced button, then clicking the Options button.

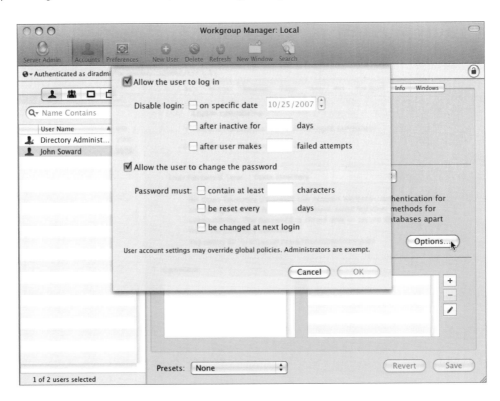

TIP ▶ Per-user policies can be set for more than one user by selecting more users prior to clicking the Advanced tab and subsequent Options button.

Password policies applied with Server Admin are called global policies. In Mac OS X Server, user account settings may override global policies. Administrators are exempt from both types of policies. You will learn how to set global policies later in this lesson.

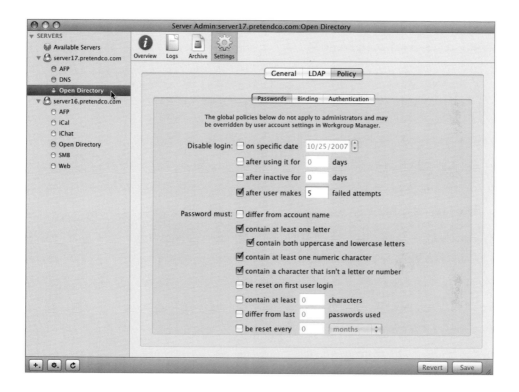

Set User Account Settings (Per-user password policies)
You will now set policies on a per-user basis as opposed to a global basis.

1   Open Workgroup Manager and insure you are in the LDAP directory (LDAPv3/ 127.0.0.1). Select the user accounts you created earlier in this lesson and click the Advanced tab.

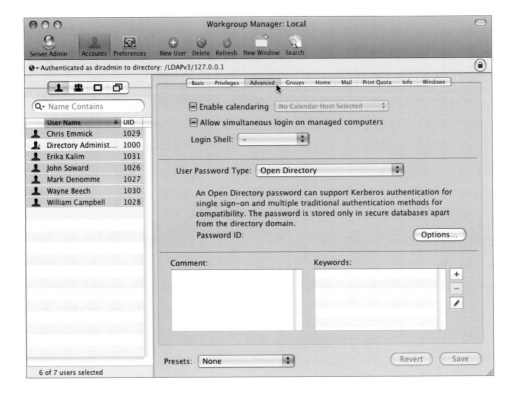

2   Click the Options button.

3   Select the following checkboxes:

   ▶   Disable login on specific date

   ▶   Disable login after user makes *N* failed attempts

   ▶   Allow the user to change the password

   ▶   Password must contain at least *N* characters

   ▶   Password must be changed at next login

   "Allow the user to log in" will already be selected.

4   In the "Password must contain at least *N* characters" field, enter 8.

   The next time any one of the highlighted users logs in, they will need to change
   their passwords; the password will need to be at least eight characters long, and their
   account will be disabled on the date you chose.

NOTE ▶ You will notice when you choose more than one user that dashes appear in all checkboxes. Clicking a dash changes it to a checkbox, indicating that the selection is now set for all highlighted users.

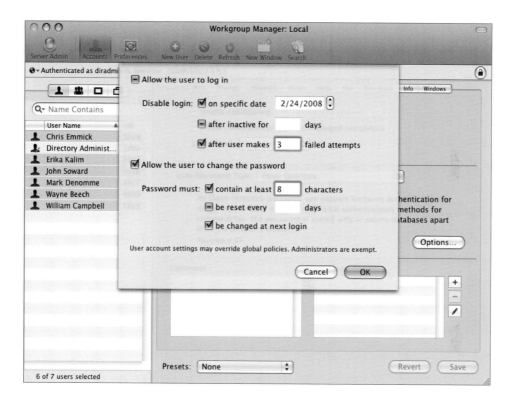

5 Click OK, then click Save.

Set Single User Account Settings

Now, perhaps you want to have only one of those users not be able to change their passwords, as in the case with a novice user.

1 Select one of your users, click the Advanced tab if not already selected, and click the Options button.

2 Edit the checkboxes to disallow all options under the criteria for password and disable the checkbox allowing the user to change his or her password.

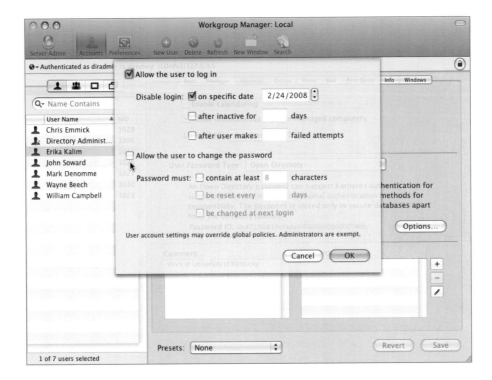

3   Click OK, then click Save.

Now, this user can't change his or her password, and it is still set to expire on a given date.

> **TIP** ▶ There are two places to deny access to a specific user account: the Basic pane and the Advanced pane. Changing the settings in the Basic pane will automatically affect the Advanced settings, but changing the data in the Advanced pane does not affect the Basic settings. If you want to deny access to a specific user account, make sure that settings in both the Basic and Advanced panes are configured appropriately. Make sure to save changes so that the new settings will be written to the directory.

Test User Account Policies

You will now move from your Mac OS X Server to your Mac OS X computer to test these policies.

1   On the client computer at the login window, click Other, then attempt to log in as John Soward using the initial password set for john.

Because you previously bound to the Open Directory master and there is no account record for John Soward on the Mac OS X client computer, the client searches the shared directory on the server to find a user account that matches.

2 You are prompted to enter a new password, because you configured directory services to require the password to be changed at the next login.

3   Enter *johnj* in the New Password and Verify Password fields, and then click Log In.

This login fails because earlier you set the password policy to require at least eight characters.

4   Enter *johnjohnjohn* into the New Password and Verify Password fields, and then click Log In.

Because of the way Mac OS X Server functions, you still won't be able to log in as john from your Mac OS X computer. This is because you haven't set a home folder for the user john. However, the login fails and the login window shakes, even though the password has been changed. This can be confirmed by watching the Password Service Server log file in Server Admin. (Directory-related log files will be covered at the end of this lesson.)

Setting Global Password Policies

Open Directory enforces per-user and global password policies. For example, a user's password policy can specify a password expiration interval. If the user is logging in and Open Directory discovers that the user's password has expired, the user must replace the expired password. Open Directory can then authenticate the user.

Password policies can disable a user account on a certain date, after a number of days, after a period of inactivity, or after a number of failed login attempts. Password policies can also require passwords to be a minimum length, contain at least one letter, contain at least one numeral, be mixed case, contain a character that is neither a number or a letter, differ from the account name, differ from recent passwords, or be changed periodically.

Open Directory applies the same password policy rules to the Password Server and Kerberos. Password policies do not affect administrator accounts. Administrators are exempt from password policies because they can change the policies at will. In addition, enforcing password policies on administrators would subject them to denial-of-service attacks.

Kerberos and Open Directory Password Server maintain password policies separately. Mac OS X Server synchronizes the Kerberos password policy rules with Open Directory Password Server password policy rules.

After global password policies are put into effect, they are enforced for all users created or imported. For example, an existing user with the password wayne will not be required to change his or her password, even though you may have required more than eight characters and required the password to be different from the short name. This is because wayne's account and password existed prior to the global policy being in place. In this case, it is best to require the user to change his or her password at the next login, thus forcing the user to conform his or her password to the recently set global password policies.

1 Open Server Admin, if not already open, and select Open Directory from the list of services on the left.

2 Click the Settings icon in the toolbar, then the Policy and Password tabs, in that order.

3 Choose your own criteria to disable the login, choose what parameters the user's password must meet, and click Save.

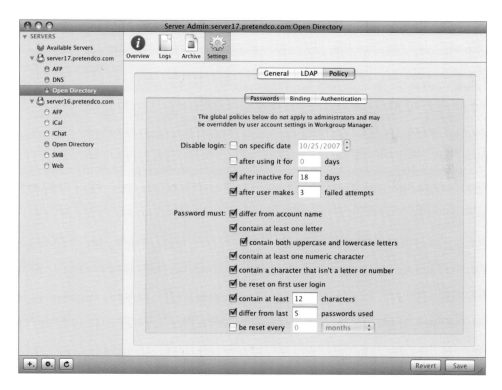

TIP ▶ It is important to obtain your organization's password policies if known prior to setting these options. If you miss certain criteria that are required by your organization and all users have been imported and have passwords set, changing these parameters may require users to change their passwords again to conform to the newer standards.

NOTE ▶ Because we don't have home directories set at this point, you will be unable to test these policies at the login window.

Using Single Sign-On and Kerberos

Frequently, a user who is logged in on one computer needs to use resources located on another computer on the network. Users typically browse the network in the Finder and click to connect to the other computer. It would be a nuisance for users to have to enter a password for each connection. If you've deployed Open Directory, you've saved them that trouble. Open Directory provides a feature known as *single sign-on*, which relies on Kerberos. Single sign-on essentially means that when users log in, they automatically have access to other services they may need that day, such as email, file servers, chat servers, VPN connectivity, and others without entering another password.

Defining Kerberos Terms

There are three main players in a complete Kerberos transaction:

▶ The user

▶ The service that the user is interested in accessing

▶ The KDC, which is responsible for mediating between the user and the service, creating and routing secure tickets, and generally supplying the authentication mechanism

Within Kerberos there are different *realms,* specific databases or authentication domains. Each realm contains the authentication information for users and services, called Kerberos *principals.* For example, if you have a user with a long name of John Significant and a short name of johnsig on a KDC with the realm of SERVER17.PRETENDCO.COM, the user principal would be johnsig@SERVER17.PRETENDCO.COM.

For a service to take advantage of Kerberos, it must be *Kerberized* (modified to work with Kerberos), which means that it can defer authentication of its users to a KDC. Not only can Mac OS X Server provide a KDC when configured to host a shared LDAP directory, but it can also provide several Kerberized services. An example of a service principal would be afpserver/server17.pretendco.com@SERVER17.PRETENDCO.COM.

Finally, Kerberos enables you to keep a list of users in a single database, called the KDC, which is configured on Mac OS X Server once an Open Directory master has been created. When a network user logs in on a Mac OS X v10.2 or later client computer, that computer negotiates with the KDC. If the user provides the correct user name and password, the KDC provides an initial ticket, called a Ticket Granting Ticket (TGT) that enables the user to sub-sequently ask for service tickets so they may connect to other servers and services on the network for the duration of the login session. During that time, the user can access any net-work service that has been Kerberized without seeing a password dialog.

Kerberos is one of the components of Open Directory. The reason a user's password is stored in both the Password Server database and the Kerberos principal database is to allow users to authenticate to services that are not Kerberized. However, users must enter a password every time they access those services. Open Directory uses Password Server to provide support for those authentication protocols.

Because Kerberos is an open standard, Open Directory on Mac OS X Server can be easily integrated into an existing Kerberos network. You can set up your Mac OS X computers to use an existing KDC for authentication.

One security aspect to using Kerberos is that the tickets are time sensitive. Kerberos requires that the computers on your network be synchronized to within 5 minutes by default. Configure your Mac OS X computers and your servers to use the NTP, and syn-chronize to the same time server so this doesn't become an issue in preventing you from getting Kerberos tickets.

Examining Kerberos Tickets

Even though you do not have a home folder at this point, you can examine your Kerberos Ticket Granting Ticket.

1   Log in to your Mac OS X computer as cadmin.

2   Navigate to /System/Library/CoreServices/ and open the Kerberos application.

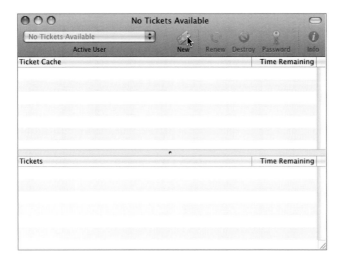

3   Click the New button in the toolbar to obtain a new Kerberos ticket.

Notice that because you are bound to the Mac OS X Server, you have SERVER17.PRETENDO.COM listed in your Realm field.

4   Enter the short name and password that you entered earlier in Workgroup Manager and click OK.

5   Because you set parameters on changing the password at next login, you are presented with a dialog asking you to change your password if you wish to obtain a ticket. Click Yes.

6   Enter the old password you chose for the user, then enter and reenter a new password that conforms to the criteria you set earlier on password restrictions and click OK.

You should now be able to view your Kerberos Ticket Granting Ticket. In later exercises, you will have a home folder and be able to view service tickets along with your TGT.

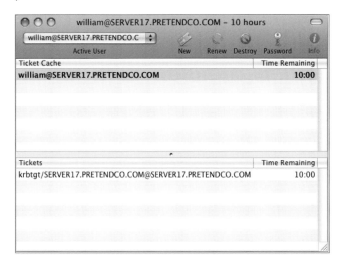

Notice that even though you logged in at the login window as cadmin, you were able to get a Kerberos TGT as another user. This is because you authenticated locally to your Mac OS X computer as cadmin, while your authentication mechanism for your other account originated on your Mac OS X Server, to which you have been bound during this lesson.

Archiving and Restoring Open Directory Data

Once your Open Directory master (and any replicas) has been established, it is advisable to archive all of your Open Directory data. This enables you to quickly recover all LDAP user information, passwords, and machine configuration information quickly. It also permits the transferring of Open Directory from one computer to another by restoring the Open Directory information, provided the IP address of the new machine is the same as the old one.

Understanding the Archival Structure

When you archive the Open Directory data, Server Admin creates an encrypted sparse disk image and stores it wherever you choose. The items archived include all three major components of Open Directory masters, which are the LDAP database, Password Server database, and Kerberos Key Distribution Center, along with the local database and passwords, the local KDC, and the host name and directory service files.

> **NOTE ▶** It is wise to store or copy this critical information to another device for safekeeping, should the server disks suffer catastrophic failure.

Archiving the Open Directory Master

You will now archive all your critical information related the your Open Directory master.

1   Open the Server Admin tool if it is not already open and select Open Directory in the service list on the left.

2   Select the Archive icon from the toolbar, click the Choose button next to the "Archive in" field, and navigate to the location you want to archive the information.

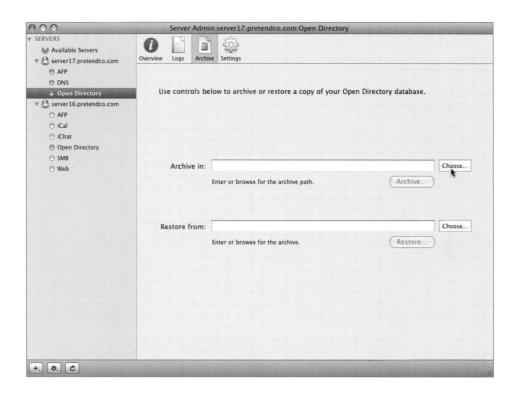

3   Once the location is selected, you are asked to name the disk image and supply a password.

NOTE ▶ It is crucial that you name the archive something useful, such as putting the date of archival in the name. Also, there is no password verification field, so type your password carefully and check to ensure the Caps lock key is either intentionally enabled or disabled.

You can now view the progress bar during the archival process.

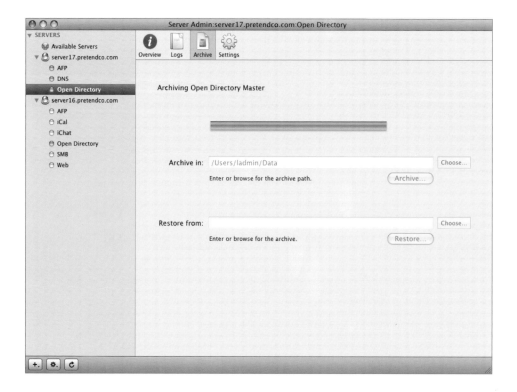

4   Navigate to and locate your sparse disk image to ensure the archival creation actually took place, then copy the image off the server for safekeeping.

NOTE ▸ You may also want to open and mount the disk image to peruse the contents of the archive.

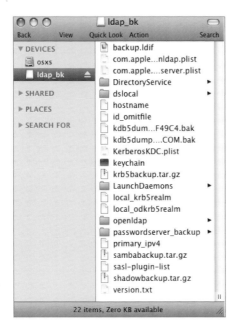

Restoring Directory Data to the Open Directory Master

Once Open Directory data has been archived, it can be restored just as easily.

1   Quit Workgroup Manager if it is open and open Server Admin.

2   Select Open Directory in the services list, select Settings from the toolbar, and click the General tab.

3   Change the role of the server from an Open Directory master to a standalone server using the Change button, which launches the Service Configuration Assistant.

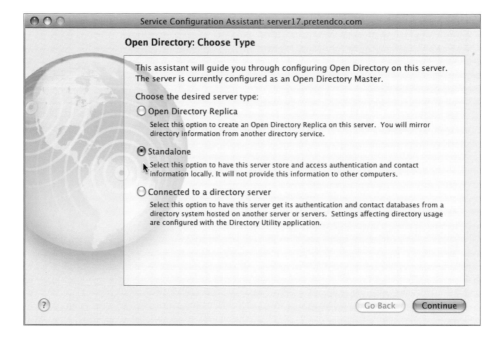

4   Select Standalone and click Continue two times to remove the LDAP database, Password Server database, and Kerberos KDC—all of which comprise the Open Directory master. Click Close to close the Service Configuration Assistant.

You now have no LDAP database and, consequently, no users in that database.

5   Click the Change button to launch the Service Configuration Assistant again, select Open Directory master in the list, and click Continue.

6   Select the defaults for UNIX user ID and short name, enter the same password you used when you first set up the Open Directory master (the password was the same as the short name, diradmin), and click Continue.

7   Accept the defaults for the Kerberos KDC and LDAP information and click Continue two more times.

8   Click Close to close the Service Configuration Assistant, then verify in Server Admin that the Role is an Open Directory master.

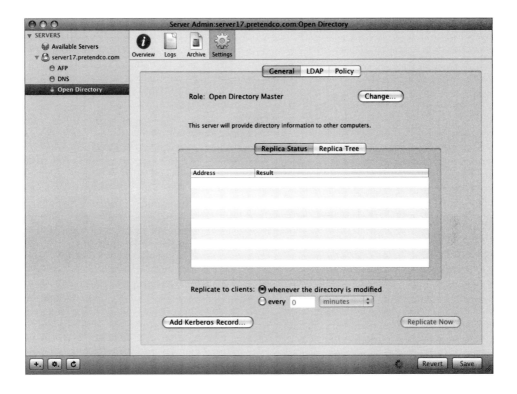

9   Click the Archive button in the toolbar, click the Choose button next to the "Restore from" field, and navigate to the location of your archived sparse disk image. Click Choose to select that image for restore.

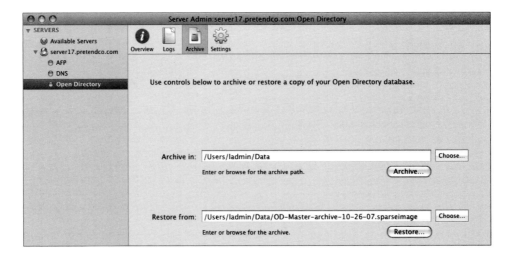

10 Click the Restore button, then enter the password for the encrypted sparse disk image.

Other than a progress bar, there is no indication that you successfully completed a restore of your Open Directory data.

11 Open Workgroup Manager and view the LDAP database to ensure all users are restored.

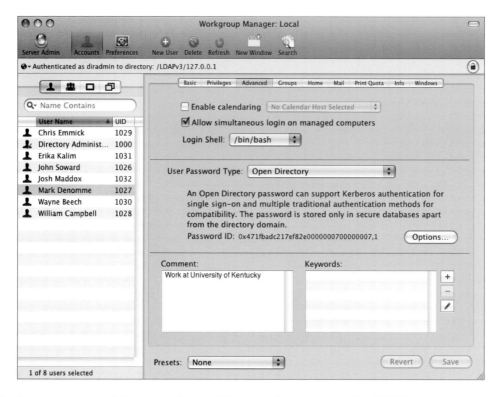

You have now successfully restored Open Directory data to your Mac OS X Server.

> **NOTE ▶** Although you can back up an Open Directory replica, there is no real need to do so. In fact, restoring a replica can be dangerous, because it puts an outdated copy of the account information on the network. Because a replica is a copy of the master, the master effectively backs up the replica. If a replica develops a problem, you can just change its role to standalone server. Then you can set up that server as though it were a brand-new server, with a new host name, and set it up as a replica of the same master as before.

Troubleshooting

Because Open Directory includes several services, there are several log files used for tracking status and errors. You can use Server Admin to view status information and logs for Open Directory services. For example, you can use the password-service logs to monitor failed login attempts for suspicious activity, or use the Open Directory logs for all failed authentication attempts, including IP addresses that generate them. Periodically review the logs to determine whether there are numerous failed trials for the same password ID, indicating that somebody might be generating login guesses. It is therefore imperative that you understand where to look first when troubleshooting Open Directory issues.

Accessing Open Directory Log Files

Generally, the first place to look when Open Directory issues arise is log files. Recall that Open Directory comprises three main components: the OpenLDAP database, the Password Server database, and the Kerberos Key Distribution Center. Mac OS X Server's Server Admin tool allows for easy viewing of all server-related Open Directory log files with respect to these three components.

The main log files are:

▶ Directory Service Server Log

▶ Directory Service Error Log

▶ Configuration Log

▶ Kerberos Administration Log

▶ Kerberos Server Log

▶ LDAP Log

▶ Password Service Server Log

▶ Password Service Error Log

▶ Password Service Replication Log

To access these log files:

1 Open the Server Admin tool and select Open Directory in the service list on the left.

2 Select the Logs icon from the toolbar, then choose the Password Service Server Log in the pop-up menu at the bottom of the window.

3 Type the word *john* in the search box at the upper right of the window to confirm that john's password was changed in the earlier exercise.

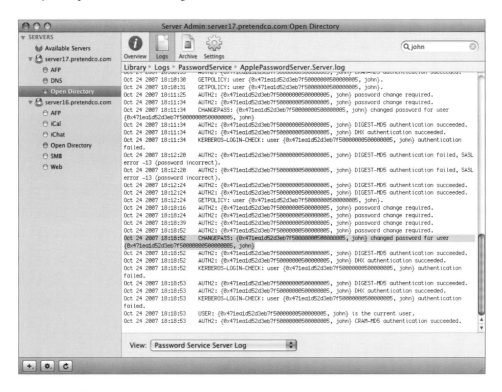

Interpreting log files can be a difficult task, and you may need the help of a more experienced system administrator. You can email the appropriate log file to the administrator. To find out where in the system the log file is stored, choose the log file from the View pop-up menu in Server Admin. The path to the log file will be displayed below the toobar.

Troubleshooting Directory Services

If Mac OS X or Mac OS X Server experiences a startup delay and a message about LDAP or directory services appears above the progress bar, the computer could be trying to access an LDAP directory that is not available on your network.

There are several ways to begin troubleshooting when you are unable to connect to a directory service. These include the following:

▶ Use Directory Utility to make sure the LDAP and other configurations are correct.

▶ Use the Network pane of System Preferences to make sure the computer's network location and other network settings are correct.

▶ Inspect the physical network connection for faults.

If you can't modify the password of a user whose password is authenticated by Open Directory, or if you can't modify a user account to use Open Directory authentication, one of two things might be wrong:

▶ Check to make sure you are authenticated as that particular directory administrator.

▶ Your administrator user account might not be configured for Open Directory authentication. If you have upgraded from an earlier version of Mac OS X Server, the account might have a crypt or shadow password rather than an Open Directory password.

Troubleshooting Kerberos

When a user or service that uses Kerberos experiences authentication failures, try these techniques:

▶ Ensure that DNS is resolving addresses correctly. This is especially important at the time you are promoting a server to Open Directory master. If the DNS doesn't resolve addresses correctly, the incorrect address will be written to the Kerberos configuration files. Kerberos tickets won't be usable.

▶ Kerberos authentication is based on encrypted timestamps. If there's more than a five-minute difference between the KDC, client, and service computers, authentication may fail. Make sure that the clocks for all computers are synchronized using the NTP service of Mac OS X Server or another network time server.

▶ Make sure that Kerberos authentication is enabled for the service in question.

▶ Refer to the password service and password error logs for information that can help you solve problems. You can sometimes detect incorrect setup information, such as wrong configuration filenames, using the logs.

▶ View the user's Kerberos ticket. The Kerberos tickets are visible in the Kerberos application, which is found in /System/Library/CoreServices.

What You've Learned

▶ Directory services centralize system and network administration, and simplify a user's experience on the network.

▶ Open Directory is Apple's extensible directory-services architecture.

▶ Directories store information in a specialized database that is optimized to handle a great many requests for information and to find and retrieve information quickly. Information may be stored in one directory or in several related directories.

▶ Open Directory uses the LDAP standard to provide a common language for directory access, enabling you to maintain information in a single location on the network rather than on each computer.

▶ The Open Directory service window of Server Admin lets you configure how a Mac OS X server works with directory information.

▶ Workgroup Manager enables you to create both local and network user accounts.

▶ Directory Utility is the primary application for setting up a Mac OS X computer's connections with directories, and it exists on both Mac OS X and Mac OS X Server.

References

The following documents provide more information about installing Mac OS X Server. (All of these and more are available at http://www.apple.com/server/macosx/resources/.)

Administration Guides

Open Directory Administration (http://images.apple.com/server/macosx/docs/Open_Directory_Admin_v10.5.pdf)

Upgrading and Migrating (http://images.apple.com/server/macosx/docs/Upgrading_and_Migrating_v10.5.pdf)

User Management (http://images.apple.com/server/macosx/docs/User_Management_v10.5.mnl.pdf)

Open Directory (http://images.apple.com/server/macosx/docs/L355770A_OpenD_TB.pdf)

Apple Knowledge Base Documents

You can check for new and updated Knowledge Base documents at www.apple.com/support.

Books

Carter, Gerald. *LDAP System Administration* (O'Reilly, 2003).

Bartosh, Michael, and Faas, Ryan. *Essential Mac OS X Panther Server Administration* (O'Reilly, 2005).

Garman, Jason. *Kerberos: The Definitive Guide* (O'Reilly, 2003).

URLs

Massachusetts Institute of Technology Kerberos release: http://web.mit.edu/kerberos/www/

Designing an Authentication System: A Dialogue in Four Scenes: http://web.mit.edu/kerberos/www/dialogue.html

Review Quiz

1. What is the main function of directory services?

2. What standard is used for data access with Open Directory? What version and level of support is provided for this standard?

3. How can network administrators automatically configure clients with Open Directory configurations?

4. What four roles can be used by Mac OS X Server when speaking about Open Directory?

5. What are the two methods of applying password policies and where are they located?

Answers

1. Directory services provide a central repository for information about the systems, applications, and users in an organization.

2. Open Directory uses the Lightweight Directory Access Protocol (LDAP) standard to provide a common language for directory access. Full read-and-write support for LDAP is provided with Mac OS X Server.

3. System administrators can use DHCP to dynamically assign IP addresses as well as provide computers with the settings on where to find DNS and LDAP servers on the local network. Armed with these settings, clients can then place requests for directory services to the correct authority.

4. Open directory master, standalone server, connected to a directory system, open directory replica.

5. Per-user policies are defined in Workgroup Manager, and global policies are defined in Server Admin.

5

Time   This lesson takes approximately 3 hours to complete.

Goals   Configure Mac OS X Server to control access to files and
                provide services based on user and group accounts

                Configure Mac OS X Server file services for Macintosh and
                Windows clients

                Configure Mac OS X Server to share files with Macintosh,
                Windows, and UNIX clients

                Configure Mac OS X Server to provide file services to
                FTP clients

                Troubleshoot file services on Mac OS X Server

                Configure Mac OS X Server to provide dynamic automounts

Lesson 5
Using File Services

This lesson addresses the topic of using Mac OS X Server to share files across a network. It begins by exploring the challenges associated with file sharing and the issues to consider when setting up file sharing. The main focus of the lesson covers setting up share points with appropriate access settings, and configuring the specific sharing protocols that Mac OS X Server will use. This lesson also addresses network mounts and general file-sharing troubleshooting issues to consider when enabling file services on Mac OS X Server.

Mac OS X Server has many different ways to manage share points and permissions. This lesson takes you through using Server Admin and Workgroup Manager to set up and maintain file sharing.

Challenges of File Sharing

When setting up file services, there are a number of issues to consider. The obvious ones are what types of clients will be accessing your file server, what protocols they will be using, and what access levels they will need.

At first glance, these questions might seem relatively easy to answer, but the true requirements can get very complex. For example, a network share point might require access by Windows and Mac users, using their native protocols, where both platforms might be reading and writing to the same files at the same time. In other cases, you might need a complex workflow to be supported, such as in a print production environment, where the traditional UNIX permissions model is not sufficient to support the workflow. In other cases, you might have a large number of users and the challenge is managing their appropriate access over a period of time, as user and departmental needs change.

Historically, Mac OS X Server supported multiple platforms, but the experience may not have been optimal. Whereas Mac OS X Server implemented the UNIX permissions model, Windows NT servers and later implemented a much different permissions model based on ACLs. Accessing a server from a nonnative client, such as a Windows XP client accessing a Mac OS X v10.3 server, might have led to a confusing interpretation of the permissions available to that user, because the Windows client would have expected the more granular permissions model. Mac OS X Server v10.4 addressed this issue and others by supporting new features, such as ACLs, at both the file-system and service levels.

The challenge also lies in the setup of the share points themselves. Careless layout of share points results in a more complex permissions matrix than necessary.

Different Protocols for Different Clients

Mac OS X Server includes a number of ways to share files. The method you select depends largely on the clients you expect to serve (although security is another factor to consider). Mac OS X Server provides the following file-sharing services:

▶   Apple Filing Protocol (AFP): This protocol is useful mainly for sharing files with Macintosh clients, both older Mac OS 9 clients and the latest Mac OS X clients.

▶   File Transfer Protocol (FTP): This file-sharing protocol is lightweight in the sense that it is simple and does not have all the features available in the other file-sharing services in Mac OS X. FTP allows you to transfer files back and forth between client and server, but you cannot, for example, open a document over an FTP connection. The primary benefit of FTP is that it is ubiquitous: It is hard to find a Transfer Control Protocol (TCP)–capable computer that does not support FTP.

▶ Network File System (NFS): NFS is the traditional method of file sharing for UNIX-based computers. NFS has its heritage in research facilities and academia in the 1980s. While it can be very convenient and flexible, it can suffer from some security holes that do not affect the other protocols. The primary use for NFS is to provide files to UNIX or Linux computers. Although Mac OS X has a core based on UNIX, you should normally use AFP for Macintosh clients.

▶ Windows file service: This service uses the Server Message Block (SMB) protocol, also sometimes called the Common Internet File System (CIFS). SMB is the native file-sharing protocol for Windows but is also used widely in UNIX environments. Mac OS X Server can appear to be a Windows server, even showing up in the Windows Network Neighborhood just as a Windows server would.

You can also share a folder over several different protocols simultaneously.

Planning File Services

When setting up file services on Mac OS X Server, proper initial planning can save you time in the long run.

Setting Up File Services

Follow these guidelines when you first start planning to implement file services.

Plan Your File-Server Requirements

Determine your organizational requirements:

▶ How are your users organized?

▶ Is there a logical structure to follow for assigning users to groups that best address workflow needs?

▶ What types of computers will be used to access your file server?

▶ What share points and folder structures will be needed?

▶ How will users interact with one another when accessing these share points?

These answers will dictate the file services you configure, as well as how you might organize groups and share points.

> **NOTE ▶** One of your early considerations is whether to use the access-control features available in Mac OS X Server. This decision will dictate how you proceed with setting user and group access rights to share points and folders, as well as how files and folders created over time on your server will be shared.

Use Workgroup Manager to Configure Users and Groups

The main goal is to end up with a group structure that best matches your organizational needs and allows easy maintenance over time. Setting up users and groups at the beginning is trivial. Setting up users and groups that continue to work as the organization goes through natural changes over time is not as simple as it first appears. Nevertheless, having a logical group structure that can be used to allow and deny access to your server file system will save you from continually adjusting file-service access later on. Mac OS X Server supports groups within groups, using groups as owners of a folder, and setting access-control lists on folders. Additionally, since Mac OS X Server v10.4, users can be members of more than 16 groups.

> **TIP ▶** For testing of groups, share points, and ACLs, you do not need to have all users entered. You may decide to test with a skeletal set of users and groups that meet the business requirements of your organization. After verifying the groups and share points, you can then enter or import the full set of users.

Use Server Admin to Configure Share Points, Permissions, File Services and Access to File Services, and to Start the Services

Server Admin is the main application you use to configure share points, file permissions, and specific file services—AFP, FTP, NFS, Windows (SMB/CIFS). You first configure the settings for each service, addressing such options as maximum number of clients, guest access, logging levels, and other service-specific settings. Once the services are configured, set and test appropriate access for users to the specific services. For example, you may have one group of users that needs access from both Windows and Mac clients, while another group is using only Linux clients. For security reasons, you might limit the first group's access to the AFP and Windows services, while limiting the Linux users to NFS or FTP services. Next, you define which folders should be shared by your file-sharing services, and what permissions each folder should have. Once everything has been properly secured, then you can use Server Admin to start each of the services you will be using and let users start accessing their appropriate file service.

NOTE ▶ Service ACLs should not be confused with file-system ACLs, which were covered in Lesson 3, "Authenticating and Authorizing Accounts." Service ACLs will be covered in-depth later in this lesson.

Adjust Settings over Time and Continually Monitor Your File Server for Signs of Problems

There are several ways to monitor your server services and manually adjust user and group settings:

▶ Use Server Admin to monitor logs and queues for specific services, to fine-tune any service-configuration settings, and to modify folder permissions and any file-service ACLs as required.

▶ Use Workgroup Manager to adjust users and groups.

▶ Use other appropriate applications for either monitoring or securing the server.

Once a server is deployed, you'll need to perform regular maintenance. This includes monitoring service usage to determine if it is addressing the needs of the organization, as well as looking for any security issues or unexpected activity. You might use additional software, such as Console, Terminal, or even third-party security software. As organizations change, use Workgroup Manager and Server Admin to adjust groups, users, and access to file systems and services.

Creating Share Points and Setting Access Permissions

After determining server and user requirements and entering at least a sample set of users and groups that represents the organizational structure, the next step in sharing files is to create your share points. A *share point* can be any folder, drive, or partition that is mounted on the server. When you create a share point, you make that item and its contents available to network clients via the specified protocols. This includes deciding what items you want to give access to and organizing the items logically. It requires using your initial planning and knowledge of your users and their needs. You might decide that everything belongs in a single share point and use permissions to control access within that share point, or you might set up a more complex workflow. For example, you could have one share point for your copywriters and a separate share point for the copy editors. Perhaps you would have a third share point where they could both access common items or share files among themselves. Setting up effective share points requires as much knowledge of your users and how they work together as it does the technology of share points.

Remember that Mac OS X Server supports different file-sharing protocols for different clients. When you create a share point in Server Admin, you have the option of sharing it via any combination of AFP, FTP, SMB, or NFS. By default, any new share point is shared via AFP, FTP, and SMB. If you want to share it over NFS, you must explicitly enable that service for that share point. For each protocol, you should review the Server Admin settings for items such as allowing guest access, creating a custom share-point name, Spotlight searching, and deciding whether service-specific inheritance is to be configured for that service. It is also important to keep in mind that different protocols will handle issues like filename case-sensitivity and extended file permissions differently. For this reason, it is usually best to limit your file-sharing protocols to those needed by the clients that are connecting to your server. For example, if you have only Mac OS X clients connecting to your server, it will simplify things to only use the AFP service and disable the SMB and FTP service for that share point.

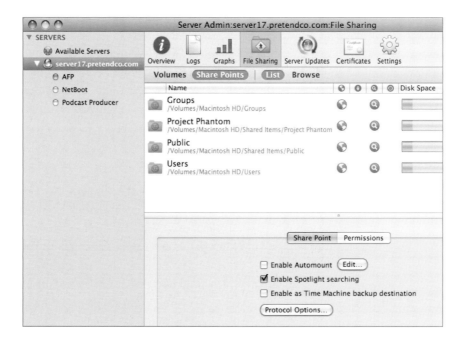

NOTE ▶ If inheritance is applied via file-system ACLs, then the separate inheritance settings, available from Server Admin's Protocol Options pane for Apple File Service and Windows file service, will be ignored.

Ultimately, how a share point is configured for access, combined with the access settings for each file-sharing service, determines whether users are able to log in via a file-sharing protocol, and if so, what share points they are able to see upon login.

Using Apple Filing Protocol

Apple Filing Protocol (AFP), has been the default sharing protocol for Mac OS X and its predecessors for quite some time. As Apple moves forward with an ever-widening set of options when dealing with permissions, it is important to understand the basics of POSIX permissions and their role in Mac OS X and Mac OS X Server.

Understanding AFP Share Points—POSIX Permissions vs. Inheritance

When determining how to set inheritance with a share point, you should first consider whether you will be using ACLs to set access permissions. If so, you should use the inheritance that is associated with ACLs. If you will be using traditional POSIX file permissions rather than ACLs to determine access to your share point, you should consider the specific options available for either the AFP or SMB sharing protocol.

For example, when configuring a share point with Server Admin, if AFP is chosen in the Protocol Options pane, you have the ability to use standard POSIX behavior or to inherit permissions from the parent folder for your AFP server. Historically, the inherited model was the only model available in AFP 2.1 and 3.0 (used in AppleShare IP 5.0 through Mac OS X v10.1). In this model, whenever you create a folder on a share point, the new folder inherits the owner, group, and permissions of the parent folder. This is also true if you are copying folders to a mounted server volume or duplicating files on a mounted server volume. However, when you create or copy files on a mounted volume set to use inherited permissions, the group and permissions are inherited from the parent folder, but the owner of the file is the user who created or copied the file.

> **TIP** ▶ The inherited permissions model applies only to items when they are created on the mounted volume. If you move an item from one folder to another folder on the same mounted volume, the item's permissions and ownership do not automatically change.

The other permissions model for new files and folders is the standard POSIX (UNIX) model. This model is available in AFP 3.1, which first appeared in Mac OS X v10.2. In the POSIX model, permissions depend on whether an item is new or a copy of an existing item. When you create a new item on a mounted volume or copy an item to a mounted volume, the new file or folder inherits its group from the enclosing folder, but the owner is always the user who created the file or folder. The difference is that copied files and folders maintain the permissions of the original item. New files and folders have the following predefined permissions:

▶   Owner: read/write

▶   Group: read only

▶   Others: read only

This is also known as a umask of 0022. You cannot change these predefined values. Under this model, if you create an item in a folder in which the group has read/write permission, the item will not inherit that permission. If you want to let other group members edit the new item, you must change its permissions manually, using the Finder's Get Info command. Server Admin gives you the option to choose between the POSIX permissions model and the inherited model for each share point shared via AFP.

In the following figure, we are looking at a file with read/write permissions set for the user (owner), group, and others (the first dash indicates a file and then rw- for user, rw- for group, and rw- for others). When this file is placed in an inherited permissions folder with the permissions set as rwx for user, rwx for group, and r-x for others, the file's write access for others is removed because it inherits the permissions of the folder. If that same file is dropped into a folder with POSIX permissions (rwx for user, rwx for group, and r-x for others), that file's final permissions are rw for only the owner, and group and others have read-only access. This is attributed to something called the *umask* in Mac OS X and Mac OS X Server and has its roots within UNIX. The default umask is to remove write access to group and others by default, hence the reason that the file shown in the figure had its write permissions removed regardless of what the folder permissions were.

NOTE ▶ Setting umask from a Terminal prompt affects only the shell that is currently running. It doesn't have a permanent effect on future shells (unless you change the shell initialization scripts), and it doesn't have any effect on the Finder.

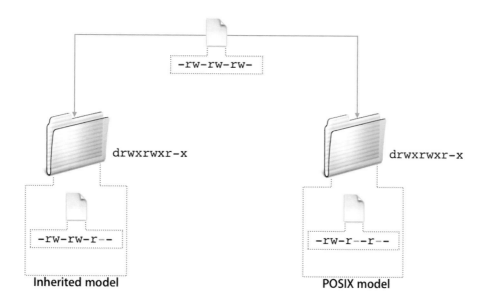

Setting Access to Share Points and Folders

Once you've created a share point and determined the protocols you will use, you can begin to address levels of access within that share point. You need to consider POSIX privileges (ownership and permissions) as well as file-system access permissions (set via ACLs), both of which were discussed in Lesson 3. Versions of Mac OS X Server prior to v10.4 supported only POSIX privileges with only a single user and group to define ownership. Mac OS X Server now also has the ability to have control settings available via ACLs. Using this very flexible system, you can apply access settings to any folder within your share points through inheritance or explicit support.

TIP ► You do not need to make a folder a share point to set its access level, because Server Admin allows you to browse the file system on your server. Also, you cannot set complex ACLs via the Finder using the Get Info command; you must use Server Admin for settings beyond the standard read/write, read-only, and none permission settings.

To configure access settings for share points or folders, use the Permissions pane when viewing that share point or folder in Server Admin. The standard POSIX settings are listed as Owner, Group, and Others in the bottom half of the pane; access settings using ACLs are set in the top half. POSIX privileges are always set for any file or folder in Mac OS X, while access-control settings (via ACLs) can only be set on folders and not on individual files. To see the result of access-control settings, you can use the Effective Permission Inspector, available from the Action pop-up menu in the lower-left corner of the Permissions pane.

TIP ► The best way to validate permissions is by logging in from client computers and testing access from valid user accounts.

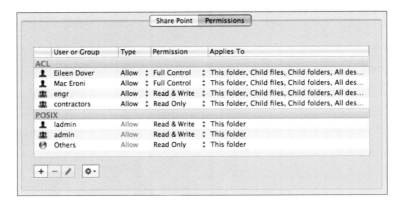

Creating and Enabling Service Access

The General and Access settings you configure for each service in Server Admin are part of the basic configuration steps you need to take regardless of which sharing protocols you decide to use. However, a few additional configuration settings are available for each share point from the pop-up menu in the Protocol Options pane in Server Admin.

When configuring Apple File Service for Macintosh clients, you must decide how you want clients to find this server. Do you want to require users to type an address when they need to connect, or should they be able to browse and pick the server from a list of servers? Either option may be appropriate, depending on how available you want the server to be.

AFP has only one option that enables your clients to browse your server. You can let users browse over IP by selecting "Enable Bonjour registration."

The Login Greeting field lets you specify a message to be displayed when a user connects. The message does not appear when users connect to their home folders.

Controlling Access

AFP gives you the option to use either Kerberos or standard authentication as a method of authenticating users. If you choose Any Method in the Authentication pop-up menu, AFP will first try to authenticate using Kerberos; if the connection cannot be established using Kerberos, it will use standard authentication.

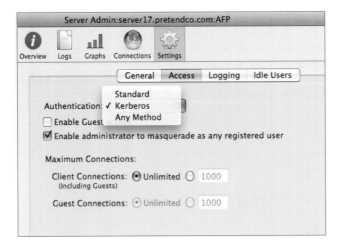

Once the user is authenticated, file permissions control access to the files and folders on your server. One setting should be called out with respect to permissions: the Others permissions. When you set Others permissions, those permissions apply to everyone who can see the item (either a file or folder) who is neither the owner nor part of the default group. You need to understand how Others permissions combine with another feature, guest access. As the name implies, guest access lets anyone who can connect to your server use its share points. A user who connects as Guest is given Others permissions for file and folder access. If you give read-only access to Others on a share point that allows guest access, everyone on your network (and possibly the entire Internet) can see and mount that share point.

If a folder is buried deep within a file hierarchy where guests can't go (because the enclosing folders don't grant access to Others), then guests can't use the Finder to browse to that folder. The Others permissions apply only to users who have been granted permission to see the enclosing folders but have not been granted permission to see that folder via their user and group settings. If a user knows the full pathname to the enclosed folder, he or she can navigate directly to that folder and view its contents if it has read access, even if the folders enclosing it do not support read access for that user.

Guest access can be very useful, but before you enable it, be sure you understand its implications in your permissions scheme.

Enabling Access

File ACLs control file-system access. Service ACLs control which service a user can access and provide an extra level of control when configuring your server. You can set service ACLs per service or globally for the entire server. It is important to understand the ramifications when enabling ACLs across all services. Therefore, as a cautionary measure, it is best to enable ACLs per service to reduce the amount of confusion for your users.

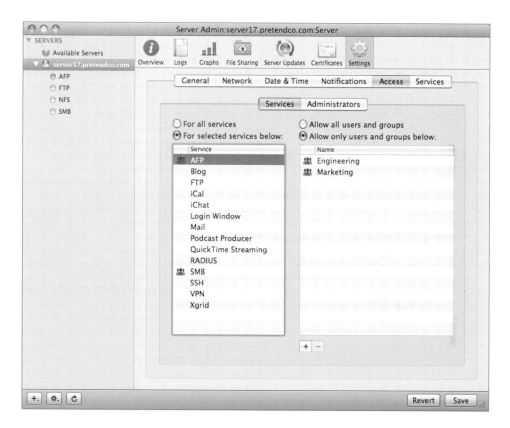

Logging Activity

Are you concerned that a user is accessing items that he or she should not have access to? Are you getting complaints from your users that their documents are disappearing or that they can't access things they should have access to? For troubleshooting these issues and more, logging is an invaluable resource.

AFP can keep two types of logs: the error log, which is always open by default, and the access log, which you must enable on the server using Server Admin (also used to view the logs). Enable the access log only when needed. Every action taken by a user is logged to this file, so it can become very large, very quickly and fill the available space in the file system. Logging all of these events for a busy server with a couple of hundred users can quickly result in a large log file that will be difficult to read through when attempting to diagnose the source of the issue. Alternately, you can configure the logging settings to save only certain events to the log, including Login, Logout, Open File, Create File, Create Folder, and Delete File/Folder. Another disk space–saving feature that is available to you is log archival. This will save (and compress) each log file after the specified period of time.

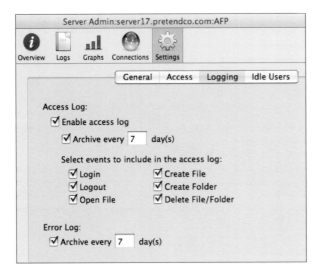

Troubleshooting and Monitoring Usage

In addition to the logs, Server Admin gives you graphical information about the current state of your server. You can view the number of connections, which users are currently connected, what protocol they used to connect, and how long they have been connected. In addition, the Graphs pane gives you a historical view of the amount of overall activity that the server has seen recently.

Monitoring server usage is a valuable tool to keep track of workflow. You can view graphs and watch for usual traffic patterns, usage spikes, and low usage periods that you could use to plan backups or perform server maintenance.

Configuring Apple File Service

You use Server Admin to make a folder on your server computer and share it via AFP.

Set Up a Folder for Sharing

Before a folder can be shared via any protocol, you must set it up for sharing.

1   If it has not already been done, log in to the server and use the Finder to create a new
folder: /Shared Items/*Apple File Services* (where *Apple File Services* is the name of the
new folder in the /Shared Items folder).

You do not have to be physically located near your server to create share points, as
you will see later.

2   If Server Admin is not open on your Mac OS X computer, open it and connect to
your server as ladmin.

3   Select your server from the Servers list if it is not already selected.

4   Click the File Sharing button in the toolbar, and then click the Refresh button in the
lower-left corner to have Server Admin refresh its view of the server.

5   Click the Browse button to navigate the entire contents of the hard drive. Go to
the Apple File Services folder you created in step 1, and then select the Apple File
Services folder.

6   Click the Share button in the upper-right corner, then click Save.

This item is now shared. By default, Mac OS X Server items over AFP, SMB, and FTP. Because you want this item to be viewable only by your Macintosh clients, you'll modify the default setting so that the item is shared only via AFP.

7   Click the Protocol Options button in the Share Point pane at the bottom of the window, and under AFP make sure that "Share this item using AFP" is enabled (it should be enabled by default).

8   Make sure the "Allow AFP guest access" checkbox is selected.

This allows users to connect anonymously, provided the AFP service is configured to allow guest users.

9   Change the AFP name to *Corporate AFP Server*.

This is the name that will be given to the volume when client computers connect to it, while preserving the original folder name when viewed from the server. On your server, you'll want to be sure to choose names for the shares that correlate to their use. You may also want to just retain the original folder name as the AFP name to avoid confusion between the name of the folder when viewed from the server versus when remotely connected from a client computer.

10 Select the option to "Inherit permissions from parent."

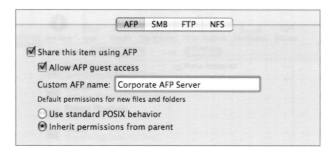

11 Click the SMB tab next, and deselect the "Share this item using SMB" checkbox.

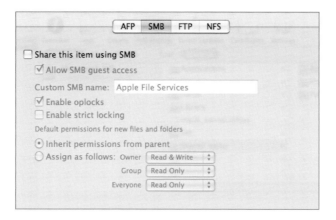

12 Click the FTP tab next, and deselect the "Share this item using FTP" checkbox. Click OK to dismiss the pop-up window, then click Save in the main Server Admin window.

Now your shared folder named Apple File Services is visible only to Mac clients using AFP. No action needed to be taken in the NFS pane because share points are not exported as NFS shares by default.

Configure and Start AFP Service

Because you want to share this folder using AFP, you must configure AFP service with Server Admin, and then start the AFP service.

1   In Server Admin on your Mac OS X computer, select the AFP service from the Computers & Services list on the left side of the window, and then click the Settings button in the toolbar.

   If the AFP service isn't listed, you must first add it by choosing Add Service from the + menu in the bottom-left corner of Server Admin.

2   In the General pane, make sure that "Enable Bonjour registration" is selected.

   This option lets clients browse for the share point using the Mac OS X "Connect to Server" command.

3   Click the Access tab, choose Standard from the Authentication pop-up menu, and select the "Enable Guest access" option. Click Save.

4   AFP should already be running from previous lessons. If it isn't, start it by clicking the Start AFP button.

5   On your Mac OS X computer, use Connect to Server to connect to your server at server17.pretendco.com.

6   Connect as a guest user.

7   Select the Corporate AFP Server share point and click OK.

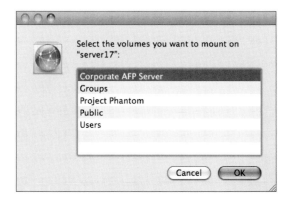

8   Verify that the network share appears on your Mac OS X desktop or in a Finder window's sidebar.

9   Unmount the Corporate AFP Server share point.

Restrict Access to Files

Now that you have shared the Apple File Services folder, modify the permissions to restrict access to the files.

1   On your Mac OS X computer in Server Admin, click the File Sharing button in the toolbar, and then click the Share Points button, followed by the Browse button. Select the Apple File Services share point.

2   Click the New Folder button in the upper-right corner of Server Admin to create a folder inside Apple File Services: *Press Releases*. Click Save.

You can create folders and share points using Server Admin without actually going to your server computer.

3   Deselect and reselect the Apple File Services folder, and create a second new folder inside Apple File Services: *Tiger Development*. Click Save.

NOTE ▶ If you don't deselect and reselect the parent folder, subsequent folder creations will be nested within the newly created folder.

4   Click the Refresh button at the bottom to have Server Admin refresh its view of the server.

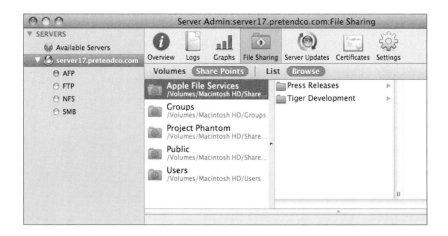

5   Click the Tiger Development folder in Server Admin.

6   In the Permissions pane, change the POSIX permissions as follows:

▶   Owner: bendare, Read & Write

▶   Group: admin, Read & Write

▶   Others: None

7   Click Save.

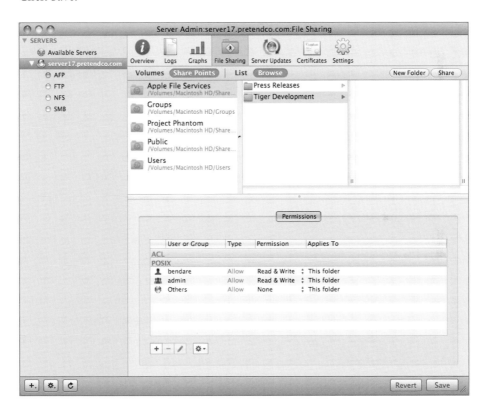

Set Other AFP Options

You now have a basic AFP share ready for use. However, it's possible you may need to set some additional settings. Next, we're going to look at the various other options you can configure for an AFP share.

1   In Server Admin, select the AFP service and click the Settings button in the toolbar.

2 In the General pane, type some text in the Login Greeting box.

This message will be displayed to each user who connects to the Apple File Service on your server. If users don't have to see the message every time they connect, you can configure the Apple File Service to display it just once for each user.

3 Click the checkbox for "Do not send same greeting twice to the same user."

Users will now only see the message the first time they connect. They won't see a message again until you change the greeting.

4 Click Save.

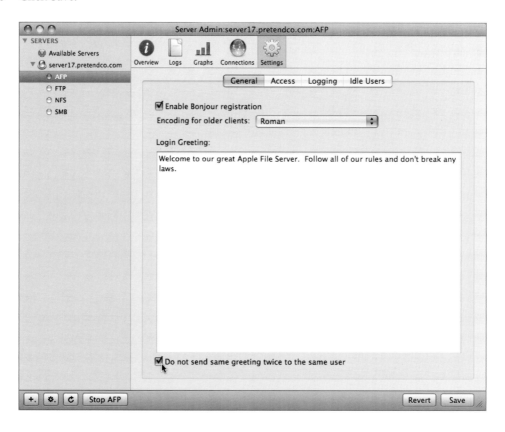

5 Click the Access tab.

6 Select "Enable administrator to masquerade as any registered user" if it isn't already selected.

This option allows any admin on the machine to connect with AFP as another user, but using his or her administrator password. This can be a useful troubleshooting step, particularly for permissions issues, by simulating the access of that user, without needing to know his or her password.

Limit Concurrent Users

In some cases, it may be useful to put limits on the number of users who can be connected to your server at any one time. This can be particularly useful if your server isn't very powerful, or if you have a very slow network connection. In most cases, you'll always want to set the number of maximum connections to a number higher than the number of guest connections to leave room for real users to connect to your server.

1 Under Maximum Connections, change the setting for Client Connections to *10*.

This limits the number of users who can be connected to the Apple File Service simultaneously to 10.

2 Change the setting for Guest Connections to *3*.

Of the 10 possible users who can be connected at one time, only three of them can be connected anonymously.

3 Click Save.

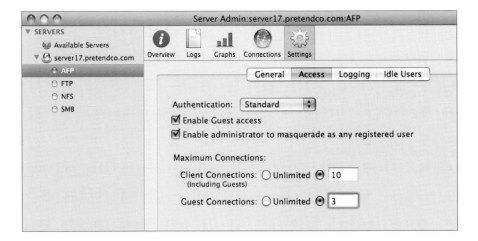

Set Idle User Options

If you've set low limits on the maximum number of connected users, as we've done here, you'll want to avoid the problem where someone forgets to disconnect and monopolizes one of those connections unnecessarily. This can be done with the Idle Users options.

1   Click the Idle Users tab.

2   To enable client computers to reconnect after sleeping less than an hour, select "Allow clients to sleep ___ hour(s)," and enter *1* in the field.

3   To disconnect users who have not accessed the file server in more than 30 minutes, select the option to disconnect idle users, and enter *30* in its field.

4   If they aren't already selected, select the options to exempt Guests, Administrators, Registered users, and Idle users who have open files.

5   Set the Disconnect Message text to: *Due to limited resources on this server, we had to terminate your idle connection. Feel free to reconnect when you return if needed.*

6   Click Save.

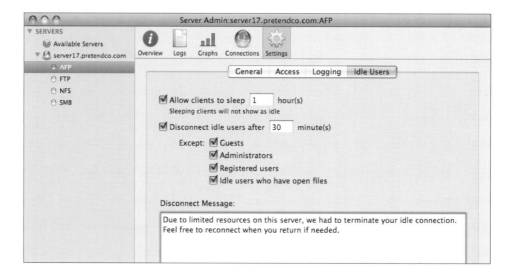

Keep Error and Access Logs

Logs are critical assets for diagnosing any problem, including AFP issues. Certain laws or company policies may also require you to keep logs of activity on your server. Configuring your server to create error and access logs is done through Server Admin as well.

1 Click the Logging tab.

2 Select every checkbox.

3 Click Save.

    This will enable all the possible logs, including both access and error logs. This will save information about such actions as when a user connects to your AFP server (Login), disconnects (Logout), reads or copies a file (Open File), creates a new file or folder, or when they delete a file or folder. Additionally, there is a setting to archive the logs after a specified number of days. This is useful on a high-traffic server where the logs would otherwise grow too large and possibly fill your disk.

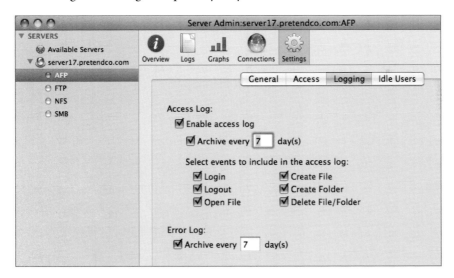

Enable Spotlight Searches

New functionality in Mac OS X v10.5 and Mac OS X Server v10.5 allows you to perform Spotlight searches of network file shares using AFP. This functionality is not enabled by default, however, and must be enabled for each share point. To turn on Spotlight indexing for a file share, follow these steps:

1 Open Server Admin and connect to your server. If Server Admin was still open, select your server from the Servers list.

2 Click the File Sharing button in the toolbar.

3 Select the share point for which you wish to enable Spotlight indexing.

4 Click the Share Point button in the middle of the window.

5 Select the "Enable Spotlight searching" option.

6 Click Save.

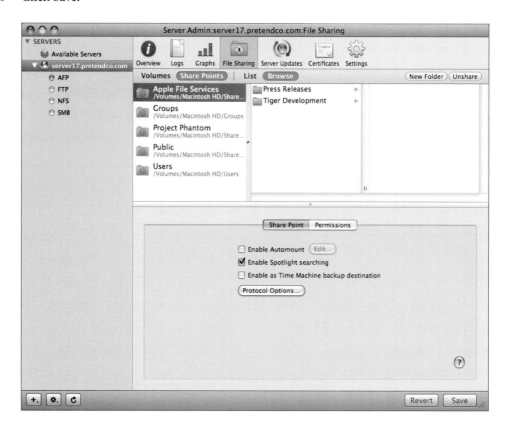

Use Your Server for Time Machine Backups

This pane contains two other important options. New in Mac OS X v10.5 is an automatic backup feature called Time Machine. Normally, Time Machine backups are saved to a second hard drive directly connected to a given machine. However, you can use a remote AFP share for this purpose as well by selecting the "Enable as Time Machine backup destination" option.

Monitoring AFP Activity

Earlier in this lesson, you configured the AFP service to log everything. Your settings indicated that the logs would contain user connects to your AFP server (Login), disconnects (Logout), reads or copies a file (Open File), creates a new file or folder, or when they delete a file or folder. Additionally, the logs will show more general information such as when the AFP server was stopped or started.

View Access and Error Logs

You can view both the Access and Error logs using Server Admin.

1 Open Server Admin and connect to your server.

2 Select the AFP service in the left pane.

3 Click the Logs button in the toolbar.

4 Select the Access or Error log using the View menu at the bottom of the window.

   The log will auto refresh while it is being displayed on your screen.

View Activity Graphs

Additionally, it may be wise to proactively monitor the amount of activity and usage your AFP server is getting. Server Admin presents this information in easy-to-view graphs. This will help you to identify anomalies such as abnormal spikes in traffic or number of connections that could lead to service degradation.

1 Open Server Admin and connect to your server.

2 Select the AFP service in the left pane.

3   Click the Graphs button in the toolbar.

4   Select whether you want to view the network throughput (bytes per second) at a given time, or the total number of connected users at a given time by using the menu at the bottom of the window.

5   Change the time period you wish to monitor using the other menu at the bottom of the window.

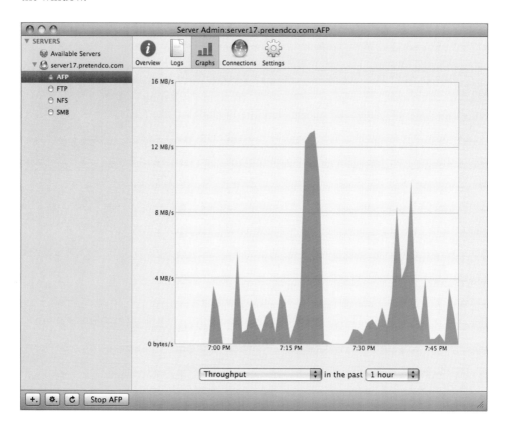

Using Windows File Service

Mac OS X Server permits you to share files over the SMB protocol. Sometimes referred to as CIFS, this is the primary protocol used by Windows clients to access files on a remote file server. It has some differences from AFP that you must explore. Understanding the fine differences between the two will lead to a better integration when sharing folders.

Windows Share Points

As shown in the following figure, when you use Server Admin to configure a share point for use with Windows service (SMB), you have a different set of options as to how new files or folders should behave (these options are ignored if ACLs are configured for the share point):

▶ *Oplocks* are opportunistic locks, a client-side performance enhancement that requires cooperation between the client and server. If a server supports oplocks, the client can cache changes to a file locally, and then tell the server that it has written its changes. The server does not let another client write to the file until the first client has finished writing. Do not enable oplocks on share points that also allow AFP access, otherwise data could become corrupted.

▶ "Enable strict locking" forces the server to treat files with byte-range locks as if the entire file were locked. Since Windows clients can lock a range of bytes within a file rather than locking the entire file, you should choose this option if the volume is being shared over other protocols, such as AFP, so that locked files are not overwritten.

▶ Inherit permissions from parent: This option means that the new item will have the same permissions as the folder that contains that item.

▶ Assign as follows: The owner receives read and write access, and Group and Everyone receive read-only access. The potential issue with this setting is that users often put a document on the server expecting their coworkers to edit it. With the default settings, this is not possible unless the original author specifically enables read and write access for his or her coworkers. Giving the group read and write access allows this automatically on all new files.

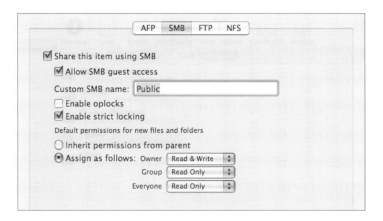

Server Name and Workgroup

The Windows service has a number of configuration options available in Server Admin. Just as Macintosh computers can browse for servers using Bonjour, Windows clients have their own way to find servers on the network, based on a protocol called Network Basic Input/Output System (NetBIOS). The Computer Name field in the General pane of the Settings pane defines the server's NetBIOS name. It is set automatically, but it is always best to make sure your server's Windows NetBIOS name matches the host name and the DNS name for your computers. That way, there is no chance for a client computer to get conflicting information if it tries to get the server name using different protocols.

Workgroups are another feature of NetBIOS. The workgroup name is an arbitrary text string used to group servers together. You often see descriptive workgroups, such as MAR-KETING, RESEARCH, and so on. Your server's Windows service will join whatever workgroup you specify. If you type the name of a workgroup that doesn't exist on your network, your server creates its own workgroup, and Windows computers will see that group.

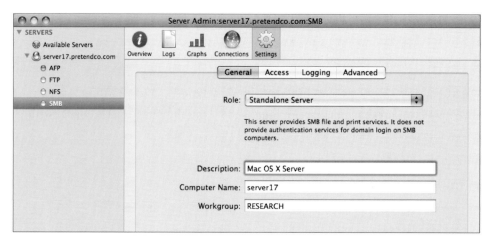

This is also the location where you choose the role of your Windows service on the server. A standalone server provides file service, but does not provide any Windows authentication services. Configuring the server as a domain member will provide file service by authenticating the user against an external domain controller. Since v10.3, it's been possible to configure your server as a primary domain controller (PDC), and since v10.4 as a backup domain controller (BDC). If your server is a domain controller, not only can you provide file service, but Windows clients can authenticate directly against your server.

Advanced Windows Services

The Advanced pane of the Settings pane lets you set other Windows configuration options:

▶ The Code Page pop-up menu refers to the character set supported by Windows service on this server. The default setting (Latin US) is correct for U.S. English. Other language settings can be chosen from the list.

▶ The Workgroup Master Browser option means your server can become a local master browser. It doesn't mean the server necessarily will be the local master browser, just that it will participate in the election process to determine who will serve as the local master browser.

▶ The Domain Master Browser option is similar to the Workgroup Master Browser option, but selecting its checkbox will now result in a possible election between your domain master browser and the Windows domain master browser.

  Browsing is a key element of a Windows network. Users can find shared resources on the network by using Network Neighborhood, a Windows utility. A Windows network maintains a list of all the computers connected to it by using central repositories known as workgroup master browsers (or simply master browsers) and domain master browsers.

  How do you know whether to select the browser options? You should consult with your Windows administrator. Generally speaking, if you are in a workgroup with a Windows server acting as a domain controller, you should not make Mac OS X Server the domain master browser. In that case, the Windows server is the domain master browser, and adding another domain master browser will result in an election process that the Windows administrator may not want to happen. When computers capable of acting as master browsers come online, they automatically elect a computer to be the master browser for a given network. Some Windows administrators may not feel comfortable with a non-Windows machine acting in such a role.

▶ Windows Internet Name Service (WINS) is Microsoft's implementation of NetBIOS Name Service (NBNS). WINS resolves NetBIOS names to IP addresses. You can distribute this information using the DHCP service in Mac OS X Server.

  How do you know if WINS needs to be configured? Again, you should consult the administrator who is responsible for your Windows computers. Selecting "Enable WINS server" makes your Mac OS X Server a WINS server. Selecting "Register with WINS server" allows you to become the client of an existing WINS server by specifying its IP address or name.

▶ Finally, if you want to host home folders for Windows users on your Mac OS X Server, make sure that the "Enable virtual share points" option is selected.

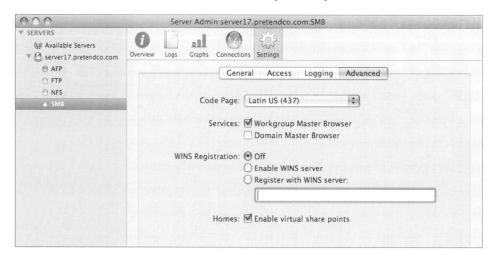

Browsing from a Windows Client

Once you configure your name, your workgroup, and—if necessary—the Advanced settings, Mac OS X Server can be browsed just like any other Windows server on the network. The following figure depicts Mac OS X Server showing up on a small network with no WINS service. A Windows server is creating the Example workgroup, and Mac OS X Server is creating the workgroup named Workgroup.

From a Windows computer, once you have chosen the Mac OS X Server as a share point, the Windows service in Mac OS X Server provides support for authentication via the protocols local area manager (LAN) Manager, NT LAN Manager (NTLM), and NTLMv2 and Kerberos (the last two being one option simultaneously).

SMB Activity Monitoring

Windows service logs are configurable in Server Admin; however, configuration is not quite as flexible as with AFP. Server Admin lets you configure three levels of detail—low, medium, or high—but you can choose a much more verbose level of logging by editing the SMB configuration file directly. Unless you are debugging a particular problem with Windows file sharing, you'll probably want to choose Medium from the Log Detail pop-up menu in the Logging pane. The lower the Log Detail setting, the better you preserve the server's resources.

As with the AFP service, Server Admin contains a simple-to-use graph feature that will show how many users are connected for any period of time. To access the SMB graphs:

1   Open Server Admin and connect to your server.

2   Select the SMB service on the left side of the window.

3   Click the Graphs button in the toolbar.

4   Change the time period, if desired, using the menu at the bottom of the window.

This exercise demonstrates some of the more useful features of Windows file service on Mac OS X Server. After creating a Windows share point, you will explore the Windows browsing features and browse to your Windows services using the Connect to Server command in Mac OS X.

Configuring Windows File Service

You use Server Admin to share a folder over SMB. This process is very similar to how you created an AFP share point, but it will be using the SMB (also known as CIFS) protocol to make the share point available to Windows clients.

1   On your Mac OS X computer in Server Admin, click the File Sharing button in the toolbar, and then click the Volumes button, followed by the Browse button. Navigate to and select the Shared Items folder.

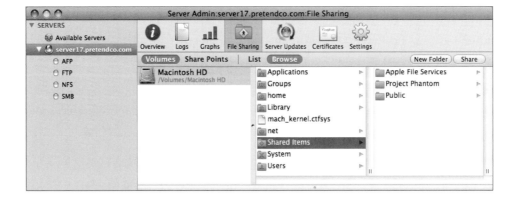

2   Click the New Folder button in the upper-right corner of Server Admin to create a
    folder inside Shared Items called *Windows Services*. Click Save.

    You can create share points using Server Admin without actually going to your server
    computer.

3   Click the Refresh button if necessary, and then select the Windows Services folder
    from the list. Click the Share button, and then click Save.

4   In the Share Point pane at the bottom of the window, click the Protocol Options
    button, and disable AFP and FTP services for this folder.

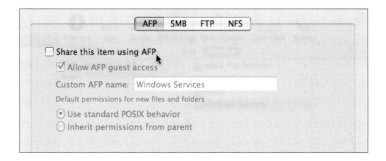

5   In the Protocol Options dialog, choose SMB, and be sure the "Share this item using SMB" option is selected.

6   Select "Allow SMB guest access."

This allows SMB connections to be made to this share point without providing a user name if the SMB service has been configured to allow guest access.

7   In the "Custom SMB name" field, type *Windows*.

This is the name that clients see when they browse for and connect to the share point using SMB.

8   Select "Enable oplocks" and "Enable strict locking."

9   Change the permissions model to "Assign as follows:"

▶   Owner: Read & Write

▶   Group: Read & Write

▶   Everyone: Read Only

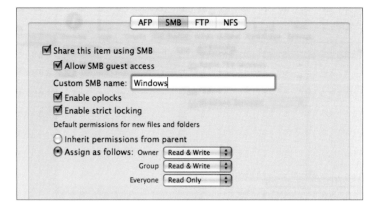

10 Click OK to close the Protocol Options dialog.

11 Click Save.

Configure Access and Start Windows File Service

Now it's time to configure access and start the Windows file service.

1 Select the SMB service on the left side of Server Admin, and then click the Settings button in the toolbar.

If the SMB service isn't listed, you must first add it by choosing Add Service from the + menu in the bottom-left corner of Server Admin.

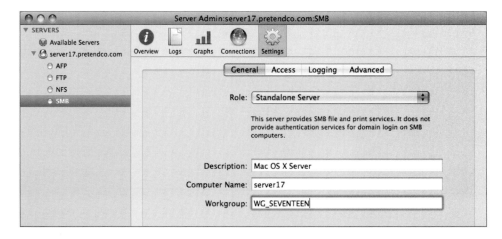

2   In the General pane, enter *server17* in the Computer Name field and *WG_SEVENTEEN* in the Workgroup field.

3   Click the Access tab, and select the "Allow Guest access" checkbox.

4   Set the maximum number of client connections to *15*.

Leave all the authentication models (LAN Manager, NTLM, and NTLMv2 & Kerberos) selected.

5   Click the Logging tab, and select a Log Level of High.

6   Click the Advanced tab. Select "Register with WINS server" from the WINS Registration options, and enter *10.1.17.1* in the "Register with WINS server" field.

Leave the default option of Workgroup Master Browser selected.

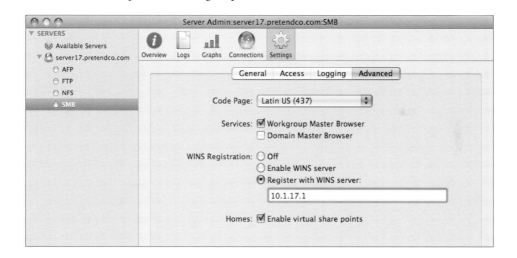

7   Click Save.

8   Start the SMB service by clicking the Start SMB button in the bottom-left corner.

Using NFS Share Point Access

Network File System (NFS) is one of the oldest shared file systems. Because of its deep roots among UNIX platforms, it is still used in a number of situations today. It is considerably different from either AFP or SMB service. The most outstanding difference is that NFS does not support user logins. When you try to connect to Windows or Apple services, the first thing you do is identify yourself with a user name and password. NFS does not give access to users; it gives access to computers. More accurately, it gives access to particular IP addresses. If your computer has one of these IP addresses, NFS lets you connect. It won't prompt you for a name or password.

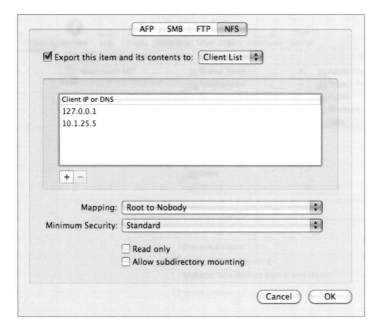

Starting with Mac OS X Server v10.3, NFS file and file-range locks (standard POSIX advisory locks) are enabled by default. This means that two users can safely edit the same file concurrently, as long as they are not editing the same section of the file. If two users attempt to modify the same section of a file, one is locked out in read-only mode until the other is done saving changes.

Mac OS X Server v10.5 added the ability to use Kerberos authentication for NFS. This increased security allows you to use NFS for home folders if desired, but requires updated NFS client software on your client computers to take advantage of Kerberos. AFP continues to be the preferred protocol since it is more compatible with prior versions of Mac OS X.

NFS Trusts the Client for User Authentication

If NFS doesn't prompt you for a name and password, how can it deal with permissions? If you sit down at a client computer and start using an NFS volume, how does it know if you're a member of the group that has access? Who does it assign as the owner of a file you create?

The server simply believes what the client tells it, based upon the user ID provided by the client. The client tells the server that user Jim is creating a folder or deleting a file, and the server believes it. If Jim has access to that file or folder, the operation is allowed. In Mac OS X, the user that the client reports to the server is normally the user who logged in at the login window. Two issues arise with this method of user identification:

▶   User mismatch: Maybe the user really is Jim, and your client is correctly reporting his identity to the server. What if the server doesn't know who Jim is? Or what if there are different Jims—one on the server and one on the client? Remember that each Mac OS X client has a list of users (configured in Accounts preferences), and Mac OS X Server has its own list of users (configured in Workgroup Manager). The two lists may not have any common users, or they may have users who appear to be the same but only coincidentally have the same information. NFS can't keep this straight on its own.

▶   Identity theft: Imagine you are a standard user on the server, but you are the administrator of your own PowerBook running Mac OS X. Because you control that PowerBook, you can create any user you want locally and thus pretend to be anyone you want to be. You can now see why NFS is a security concern.

User Mapping Can Increase Security

One response to the problem of identity theft is to map NFS users. Rather than accept what the client reports, the server can simply pretend that the user is "nobody," and hence the user gets the permissions that are assigned to everyone. You'll almost certainly want to select this mapping for the root user—the all-powerful superuser who can delete any item on a volume. It is just as easy to steal the root user's identity as it is any other user's. Beyond this, you can map all users to nobody and just ignore altogether what the client is reporting for a user. Checking both these options is similar to giving guest access under AFP.

Configuring NFS

Setting up NFS share points is similar to setting up AFP and SMB share points.

1 On your Mac OS X computer in Server Admin, click the File Sharing button in the toolbar, and then click the Volumes button, followed by the Browse button. Navigate to and select the Shared Items folder.

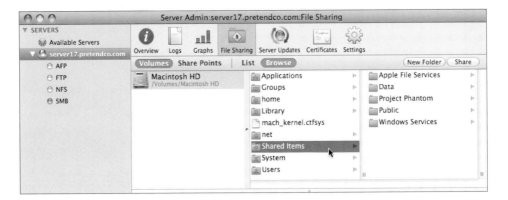

2 Click the New Folder button in the upper-right corner of Server Admin to create a folder inside Shared Items called *NFS Services*. Click Save.

You can create share points using Server Admin without actually going to your server computer.

3 Click the Refresh button if necessary, and then select the NFS Services folder from the list. Click the Share button, and then click Save.

4 In the Share Point pane at the bottom of the window, click the Protocol Options button, and disable AFP, SMB, and FTP services for this folder.

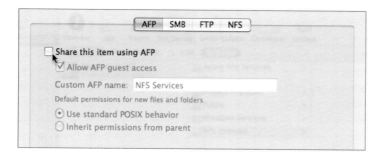

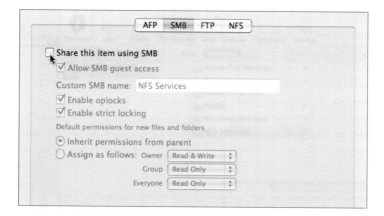

5 In the Protocol Options dialog, click NFS.

6 Select "Export this item and its contents to" and leave World chosen from the pop-up menu.

This setting allows any computer (unless blocked by a firewall) access to this NFS share, regardless of its IP address.

7   Set the Mapping pop-up menu to "Root to Nobody."

This setting blocks users from using the root user account (UID=0) to get unlimited access to the file on the share point. Anyone using a root user account will be treated the same as the nobody, or guest, user on the server.

8   Select the "Read only" option.

Because of the security deficiencies with NFS, many people choose to only offer file services via NFS in a read-only manner.

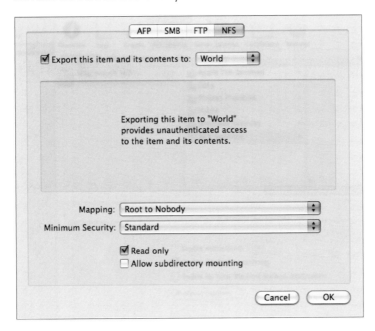

9   Click OK to dismiss the Protocol Options dialog.

10 Click Save.

Starting the NFS Service

In Mac OS X Server v10.4 and earlier, the NFS service would start automatically, but only after share points were configured to use NFS. Starting in Mac OS X Server v10.5, you start the NFS service in the same manner as other services.

1   In Server Admin, select the NFS service in the left column.

2   Click the Start NFS button at the bottom.

The NFS service Settings pane contains only a few options, which can safely be left at their defaults for basic NFS file servers.

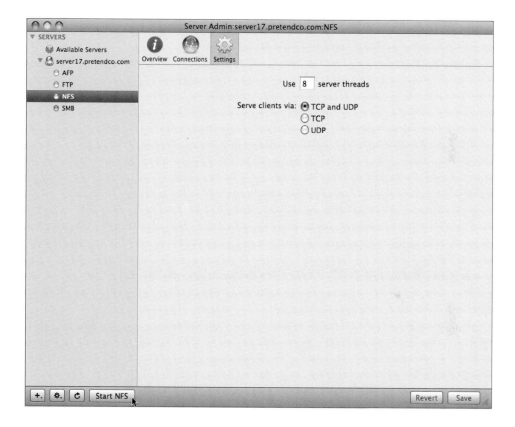

Connecting to an NFS Share

NFS has one major difference over other file-sharing protocols that comes up when you mount an NFS share from your client computer. With most sharing protocols, you connect to the share point without knowing where it is on the file server's file system. With NFS, you must specify the full path of the share point as it exists on the server. Also unlike other protocols, you won't be given a list of share points to choose from. If you need to know what shares exist on a server, you can type *showmount -e nfs.server.name* in a Terminal window.

1   In the Finder on your Mac OS X computer, choose Go > Connect to Server.

2   Type in this URL: *nfs://server17.pretendco.com:/Shared Items/NFS Services*.

3   Click Connect.

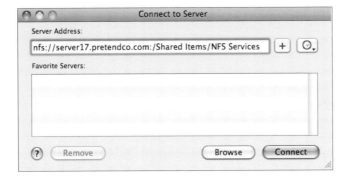

A new Finder window will appear. Note that you were not prompted for any user name or password. Also note the no-writing icon in the corner of the Finder window; it is shown because the volume is read-only, as you configured it to be earlier. Depending on your use of NFS, you may have a read-write NFS share, or you may limit NFS to read-only but also share the same folder using another protocol for any write actions.

Setting Other NFS Share Options

Usually for NFS you don't want to export (share) the folder to the entire world, but rather restrict it to a certain subnet or list of IP addresses.

1   In Server Admin, click the name of your server on the left, followed by the File Sharing button in the toolbar.

2   Click the Share Points button just below the toolbar.

3   Click the NFS Services share point.

4   Click the Protocol Options button.

5   Click the NFS tab.

6   Change the pop-up menu from World to Subnet.

7   Enter a Subnet address of *10.1.0.0*.

8   Enter a Subnet mask of *255.255.0.0*.

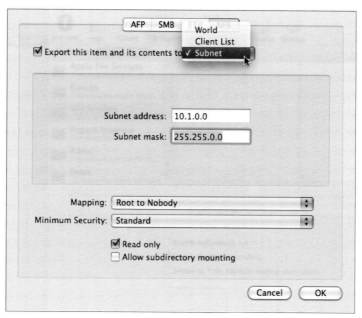

For even better security, if you have only a few machines that will be connecting to your NFS server, you would want to limit connections to just those IPs.

9   Change the pop-up menu at the top from Subnet to Client List.

10   Click the Add (+) button.

127.0.0.1 (localhost) appears in the list. You probably want to leave that IP there so the server can talk to itself.

11   Click the Add (+) button again.

12   Type an address of *10.1.17.17* (or use the IP address assigned to your Mac OS X client machine).

We'll also modify some additional NFS settings that might be appropriate for your use:

13   Change the Mapping to "All to Nobody."

This setting will completely ignore any user names on the client side, and treat any NFS client as if they were using the Nobody (guest) account on the server.

14 Change the Minimum Security setting to "Kerberos v5 with data integrity and privacy."

If you are in a fully Kerberos-aware environment, you may be able to take advantage of some of the new features of NFSv3 that now exist in Mac OS X Server v10.5. This setting indicates that clients must possess a Kerberos ticket, and it will authenticate both the client and server as well as encrypt all the NFS network traffic.

15 Click OK.

16 Click Save.

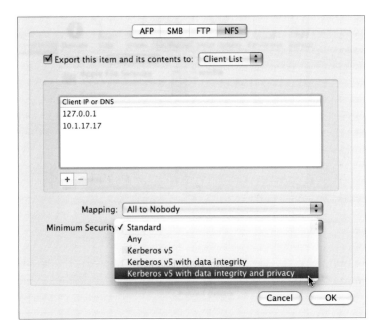

Using FTP File Service

FTP is a well-known, cross-platform way to transfer files. Mac OS X Server supports this method as a way to transfer files to and from your server. However, keep in mind that FTP is not known for its good security. Because of this, you should only use FTP in situations where it is needed. One such use might be to distribute your product documentation or drivers to everyone on the Internet. Such a situation would not fit well with other file-sharing mechanisms because you wouldn't know what platforms they are using and wouldn't want to create accounts for everyone.

Enabling FTP

You configure the FTP service in much the same way as you configure the AFP and SMB services—using Server Admin. The General pane of the Settings pane of Server Admin lets you control the number of users who can connect to the FTP service, the authentication protocol they use for connecting, and whether to let anonymous users connect. Anonymous FTP users are similar to guest-access users under AFP or SMB.

NOTE ▶ Although FTP service supports Kerberos authentication, neither the Finder nor the command-line FTP clients support Kerberos authentication.

By default, all share points you create in Server Admin are shared via AFP, SMB, and FTP. Simply turning on the FTP service gives access to these share points. The Advanced pane of the FTP service lets you modify this behavior. By enabling Home Directory with Share Points from the "Authorized users see" pop-up menu, you can force users to see only their home folders. FTP share points appear as a subfolder inside users' home folders. This is a good way to prevent users from having access to other users' home folders. The most restrictive option is "Home Directory Only." This selection gives users access only to their own home folders. If you have FTP share points set up, anonymous users have access to those share points.

When providing access via FTP, *passive FTP* can be a useful option. Passive FTP is commonly used to access an FTP server behind a firewall. If your network administrator doesn't allow any FTP access through your firewall, this option will not help you, but a common firewall configuration is to allow passive FTP but not active FTP. This is a client-side option. You do not need to configure anything on the server, but you may need to explain to your users that they must use passive FTP to connect to your server.

Understanding FTP File Conversions

One hidden, but useful, feature of the Mac OS X Server FTP service is its ability to perform automatic file conversions. The FTP server can automatically compress, archive, and encode files on the fly at the time they are requested. There are a few situations where this comes in particularly handy:

▶ MacBinary: Many files created with Classic applications, as well as many applications created for Mac OS 9, use a special type of file called a *forked* file. This type of file can cause difficulties with FTP, so the server encodes the file in MacBinary format before sending it. To request this type of encoding, simply add the extension .bin to the file you are requesting. For example, if the FTP server has a copy of SimpleText, you can ask for SimpleText.bin, and the server will encode and send the SimpleText file in MacBinary format. MacBinary can be combined with both .tar and .gz compressions.

▶ Automatic archiving: If you need an entire folder of documents, just ask for the folder with .tar added at the end before the transfer. The server creates a single archive file of the folder, and you can expand it after you have downloaded it. Be aware that this feature doesn't perform compression.

▶ Disk-image creation: When you include the .dmg extension in the URL, the FTP server converts the download into a disk-image file. This also works when downloading an application that has .app in the filename. In this case, the server automatically creates a .dmg file for the downloaded application.

▶ Automatic compression: If you are copying a large document, you can compress it by adding .gz to the end. This uses a UNIX-style gzip program. A useful shortcut is to chain archiving and compression. If you want a folder called bigfolder, you can ask for bigfolder.tar.gz, and the folder will be archived and compressed before it is sent.

Monitoring FTP Activity

The FTP server has a log that you configure in the Logging pane of the Settings pane. You can have the log keep track of uploads or downloads. You can view the activity in the FTP Log pane by clicking the Log button in Server Admin's toolbar.

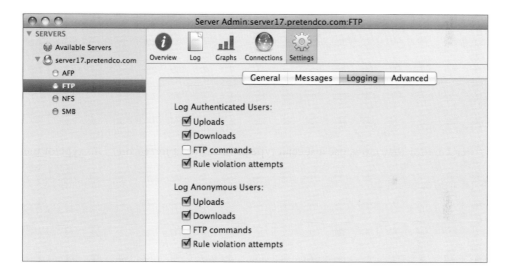

Configuring FTP Service

You use Server Admin to share a folder over FTP. As we've done previously with SMB and NFS shares, you'll create a folder and make it available to others using the FTP protocol.

1 On the server, use the Finder to create a new folder inside /Shared Items called *FTP Services*.

2 Use TextEdit to create a file, and save it as *ftp_file* in the FTP Services folder you just created.

3 On your Mac OS X client computer, open Server Admin and connect to your server.

4 Click the File Sharing button in the toolbar, then click the Volumes button, followed by the Browse button just below the toolbar. Navigate to and select the FTP Services folder you created in step 1 (click the Refresh button if necessary).

5 Click the Share button, and then click Save.

6 In the Share Point pane at the bottom, click the Protocol Options button and do the following:

▶ In the AFP pane, disable "Share this item using AFP."

▶ In the SMB pane, disable "Share this item using SMB."

▶ Click the FTP tab and select the "Share this item using FTP" checkbox.

7 Select "Allow FTP guest access" if it isn't already selected.

8 In the "Custom FTP name" field, type *FTP Services*.

9 Click OK.

10 Click Save.

Now your shared folder is visible only to FTP clients.

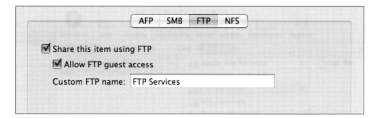

Modify Permissions

Now that you have shared the FTP folder, modify the permissions to control users' access to files.

1 On your server, use the Finder to create two new folders, *Public* and *Development*, in your FTP Services folder.

2 In Server Admin on your Mac OS X computer, click the Refresh button and select the Development folder.

3 Click the Development folder in the FTP Services share point, and in the Permissions pane, click the Add (+) button to open the Users and Groups drawer. By dragging the users and groups to the POSIX section of the Permissions pane, set the POSIX permissions as follows:

▶ Owner: bendare, Read & Write

▶ Group: admin, Read & Write

▶ Others: None

4   Click the Groups button in the drawer, and drag the Engineering group to the Access
Control List box. Click Save.

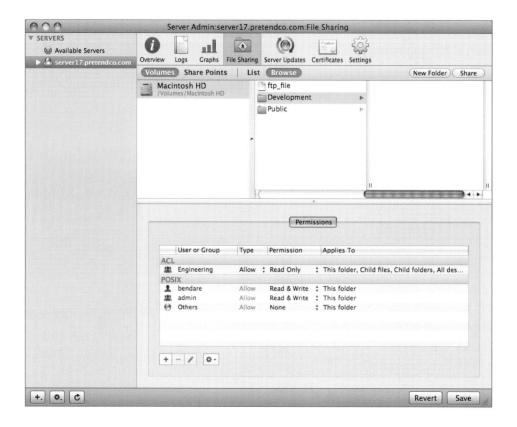

5   Select the Public folder and change the permissions as follows:

▶   Owner: ladmin, Read & Write

▶   Group: mktg, Read & Write

▶   Others: Read & Write

6   Click Save.

Allow Access for Selected Users and Groups

Next, you'll start the FTP service and allow access to FTP for certain users and groups.

1   On your Mac OS X computer, open Server Admin and authenticate if necessary.

2 Select the FTP service from the Computers & Services list, and then click the Settings button.

3 Choose Standard from the Authentication pop-up menu.

4 Disable the option to "Enable anonymous access."

5 Click Save.

6 Click the Start FTP button in the bottom-left corner.

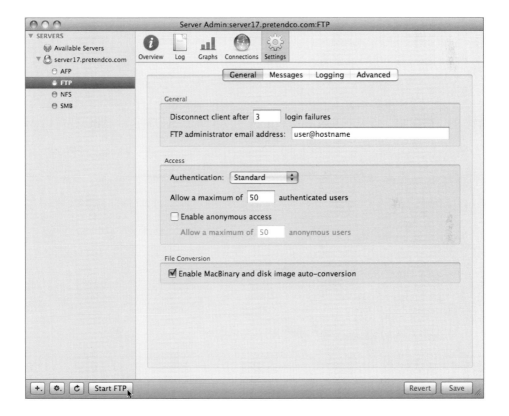

7 Select your server name (Server17) in the Computers & Services list.

Depending on how you connected to your server with Server Admin, you may see server17.pretendco.com, Server17.local, or 10.1.17.1. Any of these will work.

8 Click Settings, and then click the Access tab.

9   Select "For selected services below" and disable any older AFP Access settings.

10   Select FTP from the list.

11   Select "Allow only users and groups below" and click the Add Group Members (+) button.

12   Drag users Mike Rafone and Tina Bubbles from the Users and Groups drawer.

13   Click Save.

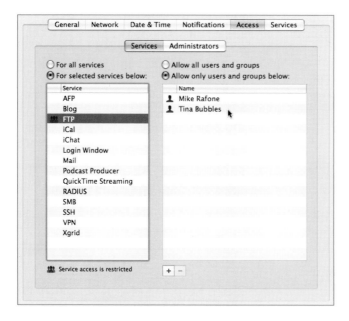

Connect to Server via FTP

Finally, you'll use the client computer to connect via FTP on the server.

1   Using your client computer from the Finder, choose Go > Connect to Server as warren, using ftp://server17.pretendco.com.

    You cannot connect as Warren because access has not been permitted; only Mike and Tina have access.

2   Using your client computer, connect as tinabubbles and note which folders you have access to in the mounted share point.

3   Unmount the FTP volume from your client computer.

4   Using your client computer, connect as Mike and note which folders you have access to in the mounted share point.

5   Unmount the FTP volume from your client computer.

Although it can be useful to restrict connections per service group user, it will interfere with future exercises.

6   On your Mac OS X computer, open Server Admin and authenticate if necessary.

7   Select your server (Server17) from the Computers & Services list.

    Depending on how you connected to your server with Server Admin, you may see server17.pretendco.com, Server17.local, or 10.1.17.1. Any of these will work.

8   Click Settings, then click the Access tab, and do the following:

    ▶   Select the "Allow all users and groups" option.

    ▶   Select the "For all services" option.

9 Click Save.

10 Choose FTP from the Computers & Services list, and stop and restart FTP service.

Network Mounted Share Points

You'll often need to make files and folders on a server available to users on client computers. One way to do that is to tell users to connect to the server from the Finder. Connecting
from the Finder is easy, but it requires users to remember which server to connect to and
where to find the files on that server.

For frequently accessed resources, such as applications, libraries, or fonts, you might want
to simplify your users' experience even more. If so, you can make a folder, disk, or partition
on a server mount automatically on some or all of the client computers in a domain. You
do this by configuring network mount share points.

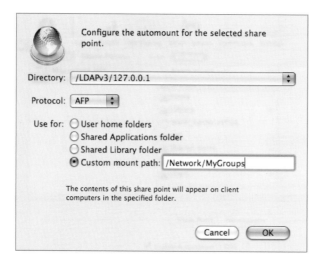

For example, suppose you want to have a specific set of applications available to every user
in a given LDAP directory. You could create a share point containing the desired applications
and then set the share point to automatically mount into a /Network/Applications folder on
client machines that can utilize either the AFP or the NFS protocol. To do this, you configure

the share points using Server Admin, and then select the Enable Automount checkbox and click the Edit button to configure those share points to automatically appear in a folder in the Finder windows of supported client computers. Information about these automatically mounted share points is stored in the LDAP directory.

Setting Up a Network Home Folder

You also can set up a network home folder for a network user. The user's home folder can reside in any AFP or NFS share point that the user's computer can access. The share point must be automountable—it must have a network mount record in the directory domain where the user account resides. An automountable share point ensures that the home folder is automatically visible in /Network/Servers when the user logs in to a Mac OS X computer configured to access the shared domain. Apple recommends storing home folders in AFP share points, because AFP provides authentication-level access security, which NFS does not provide. With AFP, a user must log in with a valid name and password to access files.

> **NOTE ▶** The home folder doesn't need to be stored on the same server as the directory domain containing the user's account. In fact, distributing directory domains and home folders among various servers can help you balance your workload.

When a network user logs in to a Mac OS X computer, the computer retrieves the account information from a shared directory domain on the accounts server. The computer uses the location of the user's home folder, stored in the account, to mount the home folder, which resides physically on a home folder server. Conversely, if you don't set up a home folder for a network user account, any changes the user makes to preferences are lost after logging out.

To set up a home folder for a network user in Workgroup Manager:

1   Click the Accounts button in the toolbar, then select the user in the user list.

2   Click Home to set up the selected user's home folder.

3   In the share points list, select the previously set automounted share point you want to use.

The list displays all the automountable network-visible share points in the search path of the server you are connected to. If the share point you want to select is not listed, try clicking Refresh. If the share point still does not appear, it might not be automountable. In this case, you need to set up the share point to have a network mount record configured for home folders. Note that automounts of user home directories will only work on users in the LDAP network domain, not the Local network domain.

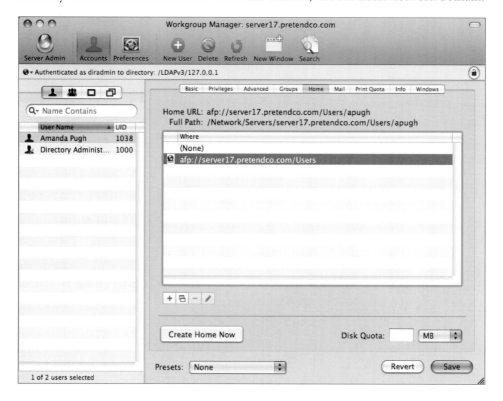

4   Click Create Home Now, and then click Save.

If you do not click Create Home Now before clicking Save, the home folder is created the next time the user restarts the client computer and logs in remotely. The home folder has the same name as the user's first short name. When having Windows users connect, the home folder should be created in advance of the Windows users' initial login.

Additionally, you can use the Disk Quota field in the Home pane to limit the disk space a user can consume to store files in the partition where the user's home folder resides.

For example, when user Sharon places files in user Rafael's folder, the size of the files affects either Sharon's or Rafael's disk quota, depending on the protocol Sharon uses to transfer the files:

▶ If Sharon uses AFP to drop files in Rafael's drop box, Rafael's quota is affected because the owner of the drop box (Rafael) becomes the owner of the files.

▶ If Sharon uses NFS to copy the files to Rafael's folder, Sharon is still the owner, and so copying affects Sharon's quota, not Rafael's.

Configuring Network Mounts

Next, you'll configure the /Users folder to be used for network home folders. This is required for your users to log in to local machines using network accounts maintained on the server.

1   If you have turned on Fast User Switching, you may encounter errors, which will prevent users from logging in to the Network account if they switch from a local account. Log off all users on your Mac OS X computer except your initial administrator account.

2   On your Mac OS X computer, open and authenticate as ladmin to Server Admin.

3   Click the File Sharing button in the toolbar, and then click the Share Points button. Select the Users folder.

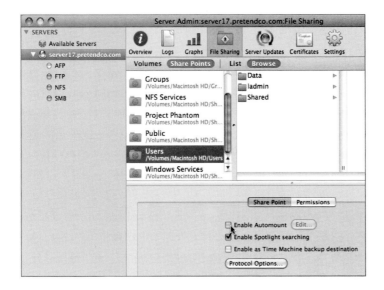

4   Click the Enable Automount checkbox.

5   Authenticate as your directory administrator if prompted.

6   Confirm that AFP is chosen in the Protocol pop-up menu.

7   Select "User home folders."

8   Click OK. Authenticate as your directory administrator if prompted.

9   Click Save.

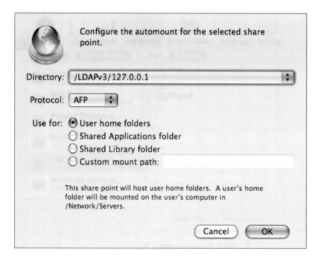

Configuring Users to Utilize Network Home Folders

You have configured the file server to share /Users for network home folders, but you must also point the user account record information to use these home folders. You must set each user account record to indicate the server and share that contains their home folder.

1   On your Mac OS X client computer, open Workgroup Manager and connect to your server.

2   Click the Accounts button in the toolbar, and make sure you are viewing the LDAP Directory, not the Local Directory. Authenticate if prompted.

This is the shared Open Directory domain you created in a previous lesson. User accounts defined in this domain are accessible from your Mac OS X computer via the network, as you have seen in a previous lesson. While you logged in successfully as another user, that user did not have a home folder.

3 Click the Users button in the toolbar, and select all the users except Directory Administrator. Click the Home tab and select the Users share point for your server.

4 Enter a Disk Quota of *50* MB for all of the selected users.

5 Click Save.

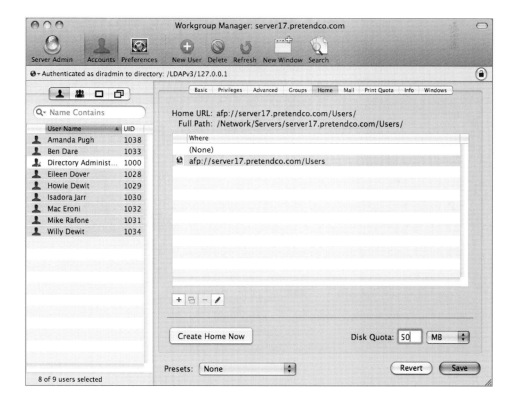

6 On your Mac OS X computer, open Directory Utility and verify that you are still bound to your server.

7 In Directory Utility, click the Search Policy button, and verify that your server is still listed in the Authentication path for your Mac OS X computer.

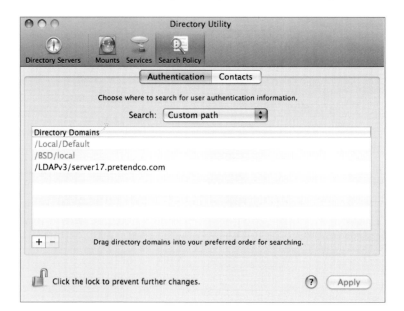

8 Restart your Mac OS X computer.

9 On the Mac OS X computer, log in as Warren Peece.

10 Verify that a new home folder is created in the /Users folder on your server computer.

The name of the new home folder matches the short name of the user (in this case, warren).

11 Log out as Warren Peece.

Using Automounts for Other Folders

Automounts can be used for more than just user home folders. Presets exist for creating shared Applications and Library folders, but any folder can be set to automount at any path. Next, you'll create a new folder, copy some applications into it, and share its contents as a network mount.

1   On the server, create two new folders in /Shared Items. Name the folders *Applications* and *Library*.

2   Copy Calculator and Stickies from /Applications to /Shared Items/Applications. You can make a copy, rather than moving the application, by holding down the Option key while dragging.

3   On your Mac OS X computer, log in using a local account, then open Server Admin. In the Computers & Services list, select AFP. Click the Settings button, and then click the Access tab to verify that "Enable Guest access" is selected; if it isn't, select it and click Save. Start the AFP service if it is not already running.

4   Click the name of your server in the Computers & Services list.

5   Click the File Sharing button in the toolbar, then click the Volumes button followed by the Browse button just below the toolbar. Navigate to /Shared Items/ Applications, click the Share button, and then click Save. Do the same for the /Shared Items/Library folder.

6   Reselect the Applications folder. In the Share Point pane at the bottom, select the Enable Automount checkbox.

7   Choose your LDAP directory in the pop-up menu, confirm that AFP is chosen in the Protocol pop-up menu, and select "Shared Applications folder." Click OK. Authenticate to your directory if prompted.

8   Click Save.

9   Select the /Shared Items/Library folder. In the Share Point pane at the bottom, select the Enable Automount checkbox.

10   Select your LDAP directory in the pop-up menu, confirm that AFP is chosen in the Protocol pop-up menu, and select "Shared Library folder." Click OK. Authenticate to your directory if prompted.

   The shared Library folder can be used for giving your client machines access to a shared set of fonts, preferences, or other objects that normally reside in your Library folder.

11   Click Save.

   If your server was bound to several other servers, you would see them in the Directory pop-up menu. In this case, all you see is the /LDAPv3/127.0.0.1 directory.

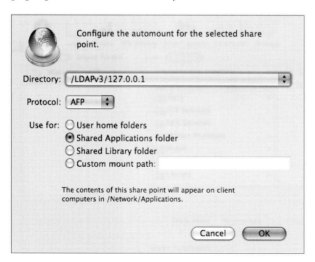

Testing Access to Shared Applications

Finally, test your new network mount point.

1   Restart the Mac OS X computer.

Shared volumes mount automatically only at startup. Simply logging in as a network user does not force the volume to mount.

2   Log in as Tina Bubbles.

3   Navigate to /Network/Applications and open Calculator.

When Calculator launches, your client computer has successfully accessed a shared application.

4   Log out from your Mac OS X computer as Tina Bubbles and log back in as your local administrator.

Controlling Access to Shared Folders

In many cases, you won't want everyone to have access to your file services. There are a few simple steps that can be followed to greatly increase the security of your file server.

Reduce the Number of File Sharing Services

First and foremost is reducing the number of services itself. Every service that's running on your server represents a potential point of entry for an unwanted visitor to your server. Reducing the number of services on your server will also reduce this risk. For example, if you have only Mac OS X machines connecting to your server, you probably don't need the SMB or FTP services running. Similarly, if you're only providing services to Windows computers, the AFP and FTP services likely won't be used and can be stopped. In most cases, the FTP service should only be used when you need to provide access to the broadest set of computers external to your organization.

Remove Guest Access for Every Share Point

The next thing to consider is guest access. If you are only sharing files with members of your organization who have accounts on your server, or if everyone is bound to the same directory server, you should consider removing guest access. Remember that there are a few places you can set this. First, remove guest access for every protocol on every share point.

1   Open Server Admin and connect to your server.

2   Click the File Sharing button in the toolbar.

3   Click the Share Points button just below the toolbar.

4   Select a share point.

5   Click the Share Points pane in the bottom half of the window.

6   Click the Protocol Options button.

    A dialog will appear with options for each of the protocol options that apply to that share.

7   For each protocol, deselect "Allow guest access."

8   Click OK.

9   Click Save.

10 Repeat for every share point on your server.

Remove Guest Access for Each Protocol

Next, remove guest access for each protocol itself. Though disabling guest access for each share point, or for the entire protocol itself, will accomplish what you're looking for, it's best to disable it in both places to minimize the risk of reactivation.

1   In Server Admin, click the AFP service in the left column.

2   Click the Settings button in the toolbar.

3   Click the Access tab.

4   Deselect "Enable Guest access."

5   Click Save.

6   Repeat the same steps for the FTP and SMB services.

Set Up Service ACLs

Next, review who has access to connect to each of your file-sharing services. This access is controlled through the use of Service ACLs, which was described in more detail in Lesson 3. Service ACLs will require explicit permission to connect to your file server. Each user, or a group the user belongs to, will need to be registered as being allowed to use a given service. You can set up Service ACLs using these steps:

1   In Server Admin, select your server name in the left column.

2   Click the Settings button in the toolbar.

3   Click the Access tab.

4   Select the services you wish to restrict.

5   Determine which users and/or groups should have access to that service.

6   Click Save.

Once complete, review the file system permissions on the folders that are your share points. The permissions of the folders that are your share points will control what share points are listed on the client when they connect to your server. In many cases, you should also review the permissions of the enclosed folders because a larger group will often have access to the share point than will have access to all of its subfolders.

Troubleshooting File Services

Whether AFP, SMB, NFS, or FTP, troubleshooting file services on Mac OS X Server typically involves the following considerations:

▶   User access: What users or groups should have access to the specific files and folders on the server, and are their appropriate permissions set correctly?

▶   Platform and protocol access: From what clients are users trying to access the server, such as Mac OS X, Mac OS 9, Windows, or Linux systems? What protocols are they using when accessing the server?

▶   Special needs: Are there any special circumstances, such as users' needing concurrent access to files or access to files in a nonnative format to the system they are using?

For troubleshooting access settings, you will want to test access by using the Effective Permissions Inspector and by logging in from remote clients. Here the biggest issue will be starting with an appropriate logical group structure and maintaining it over time.

While multiple platforms are supported through the different sharing protocols (AFP, SMB, FTP, NFS), this can become tricky either when trying to provide concurrent access to the same files or when platform-specific issues come into play. Concurrent access means that multiple users are trying to access or modify the same files at the same time. Many times this is dependent on the specific cross-platform applications knowing how to allow multiple users to access the same file. Because Mac OS X Server includes support for ACLs and these ACLs are compatible with ACLs from the Windows platform, permissions mapping between Windows clients will be in line with what Windows users expect to see. Previous to Mac OS X Server v10.4, this was not necessarily the case.

Another consideration is if the clients will be storing forked files on the share point. If you use Mac OS Extended for an SMB share point or an NFS export, files created or copied onto the server from the client side will have shadow files instead of resource forks. These files will not look right when viewed from the server. Conversely, files created from the server side will look wrong from the client, which cannot see the resource forks.

Case-Sensitivity Issues in File Sharing

Case sensitivity becomes an issue if you are copying files between two computers and only one of them has a case-sensitive file system. Beginning with Mac OS X Server v10.3, drives can be formatted as Hierarchical File System Plus (HFS+) case-sensitive volumes. Suppose you have two files, Makefile and makefile, in the same folder on a case-sensitive Mac OS X server. If you were to copy those files to a Mac OS X client computer, which is by default not case sensitive, you would run into problems. The operating system would attempt to overwrite one file with the other. When you copy files from a case-insensitive file system to a case-sensitive file system, you might have a problem with executable files. For example, suppose you had an executable script called Runscript on your case-insensitive file system. If you were to copy that file, without altering its name, to a case-sensitive file system, users would be able to run it from the command line only by typing *Runscript*. This could be problematic if the documentation called for typing *runscript* (all lowercase).

You need to be aware of the issues associated with case sensitivity now that Mac OS X Server can easily be configured to be case sensitive, while the Mac OS X client cannot. Not much can be done to synchronize case-sensitive and case-insensitive systems. You need to work around the incompatibility. Given that NFS, FTP, and AFP are case-sensitive protocols, mounting a share point using any of these protocols enables you to see the different case-sensitive files and download whichever one you'd like.

More specifically, SMB does not seem to be a case-sensitive protocol, but it has a distinct preference for uppercase filenames. For example, if your share point contains the files Runscript and runscript, and you use SMB to download either of these files to the client, only Runscript is downloaded, whether you asked for Runscript or runscript. Similarly, if you try to move runscript to a different folder in the share point, Runscript is moved, not runscript. Also, if you upload a local file named runscript to an SMB share point that already contains Runscript and runscript, you are prompted to replace the existing file, but then the operation fails and Runscript is deleted.

Here's what happens: When you attempt to copy runscript to the server, SMB detects the existence of a file with the same name and asks if you want to replace it. Once you click OK, SMB deletes the file Runscript and then attempts to copy runscript to the server. However, that operation fails because runscript still exists on the server. If you try the upload again, however, it succeeds, because now there is only one runscript on the server. When you tell the server to replace the file, it does so without confusion.

A Comparison of File-Sharing Protocols

This table gives a short comparison of the file-sharing protocols you have seen thus far. There really isn't one best protocol. Instead, think of the protocols as different tools at your disposal to give different types of access.

	AFP	SMB	NFS	FTP
Native platform	Mac OS	Windows	UNIX	Multi-platform
Security	Authentication is normally encrypted	Authentication is normally encrypted	Authentication only if using Kerberos	Uses cleartext passwords
Browsable	Bonjour	NetBIOS	Bonjour	Bonjour
Example URL	afp://server17.example.com/SharePoint	smb://server17.example.com/Share	nfs://server17.example.com/Volumes/Data/nfs_share	ftp://server17.example.com

AFP and SMB are both full-featured file-sharing protocols with reasonably good security.

NFS is not as secure as the other protocols, but it is very convenient for UNIX clients. Be careful before you "export" (share) a volume over NFS. With a Mac OS X server and a Mac OS X client, NFS volumes are browsable in Connect to Server; that is, a user can find them by browsing through a list of servers in the Connect to Server window.

FTP is useful because it offers maximum compatibility. However, FTP also offers a minimum feature set, and its passwords are sent over the network as cleartext unless you are using the Kerberos option and a supported Kerberos FTP client—something the Mac OS X Finder lacks.

Mac OS X supports secure File Transfer Protocol (SFTP), a secure alternative for FTP that uses SSH to encrypt the entire FTP connection. Of the four file-sharing protocols, only AFP has simple built-in support for encrypting connections. If you're in a fully Kerberized environment, you can also use NFS in an encrypted fashion, but you still must deal with its other shortcomings.

What You've Learned

▸ The first step when implementing file-sharing services is to plan out the shared services needed.

▸ A share point is any folder, drive, or partition that you make available to network clients. Share points are created and configured in Server Admin. A share point can be shared over AFP, SMB, NFS, or FTP. Access control lists can be used to set very flexible restrictions on share points and folders.

▸ Macintosh clients normally access share points over AFP, which is configured in Server Admin.

▸ Windows service allows share points to be accessed by Windows clients over SMB.

▸ NFS provides UNIX systems with access to share points. Unlike AFP and SMB, NFS relies upon the IP address of the computer for authentication (unless you're using Kerberos).

▶ Mac OS X Server provides FTP access for share points as well. Mac OS X Server's FTP service provides the additional feature of automatically encoding, archiving, or compressing a file on the fly, based upon the extension that the client adds to the filename.

▶ Automount share points and network home folders also can be configured on Mac OS X Server.

References

The following documents provide more information about installing Mac OS X Server. (All of these and more are available at www.apple.com/server/documentation.)

Administration Guides

Mac OS X Server Getting Started

Mac OS X Server Upgrading and Migrating for Version 10.5 or Later

Mac OS X Server File Services Administration for Version 10.5 or Later

Mac OS X Server Windows Services Administration for Version 10.5 or Later

Mac OS X Server User Management for Version 10.5 or Later

Mac OS X Server Command-Line Administration for Version 10.5 or Later

Apple Knowledge Base Documents

You can check for new and updated Knowledge Base documents at www.apple.com/support.

Document 301590, "Mac OS X Server: Admin Tools compatibility information"

Document 301272, "Mac OS X Server 10.4: Limit SMB connections to improve server reliability"

Document 107697, "Mac OS X Server 10.3 or later: SMB print queue names must not exceed 15 characters"

Document 107077, "Mac OS X Server: How to reshare NFS exports via AFP"

Document 152363, "Mac OS X 10.3 Help: Managing network and Internet services using Mac OS X Server"

Document 301183, "Mac OS X 10.4 Tiger: "Connection failed" error when connecting to an AFP server"

Document 301601, "Mac OS X Server 10.4: Inherit permissions does not work for AFP service"

Document 301310, "Mac OS X Server 10.4: Windows users cannot modify ACL permissions on the server"

Document 301069, "Mac OS X Server 10.3, 10.4: How to make a hidden directory a share point"

URLs

Mac OS X Server File-Sharing Issues: www.afp548.com

Review Quiz

1. Name four file-sharing protocols supported by Mac OS X Server and their principal target clients.

2. How does Mac OS X Server support browsing for Windows clients?

3. What is the primary security concern with NFS?

4. What does FTP file conversion do?

Answers

1. AFP for Macintosh clients; SMB for Windows clients; NFS for UNIX clients; and FTP for multiple, cross-platform client access are four file-sharing protocols supported by Mac OS X Server.

2. On smaller networks, Mac OS X Server uses NetBIOS to advertise its presence. On larger networks, Mac OS X can be a WINS server, or it can use an existing WINS server. If there are no other servers on the network, Mac OS X Server can be a workgroup master browser or a domain master browser.

3. Normally, NFS has no user-authentication process: NFS trusts that the client is who it claims to be. Beyond a security concern, this can also be a management issue if the client and server aren't working with a unified user list. If you're using Kerberos with NFS, you can authenticate the connection process, however.

4. FTP file conversion is a feature of the FTP server that automatically encodes a file or folder requested by an FTP client. The client appends .tar, .bin, or .gz to the end of the filename, and the server does the appropriate encoding.

6

Time   This lesson takes approximately 2 hours to complete.

Goals   Learn how Internet email travels from the sender's computer
            to the recipient's computer

            Configure the Mac OS X Server mail service

            Protect your mail service from spam and viruses

            Secure your mail service

            Restrict email abuse using quotas

            Create mailing lists for email distribution

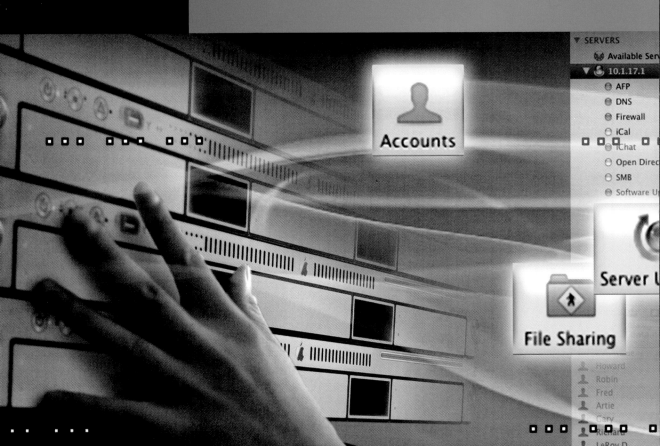

Lesson **6**

Hosting Mail Services

Electronic mail, or email as it is more commonly known, is one of the fundamental services on the Internet. Mac OS X Server includes a feature-rich email service that you can use to send, receive, and store email for your organization. Aside from the obvious reason of hosting an email server to gain an Internet identity, there are a number of other reasons that make hosting your own mail service advantageous. If you have a small office with a slow Internet connection, you may find that keeping all of your email within the building rather than using external email servers makes better use of your network bandwidth. This is especially true if typical messages within your organization include large attachments. Additionally, many organizations are required to keep the information held in their email messages secure for regulatory or competitive reasons. Hosting your own email server in-house can keep confidential data from falling into the wrong hands. You may also find that various third-party email services don't offer the exact services you want. By running your own mail servers, you can customize various options to meet the needs of your organization.

The mail service in Mac OS X Server is based on two open-source email packages:

▶ Postfix handles acceptance and delivery of individual messages.

▶ Cyrus accepts connections from individual users downloading their messages to their mail client.

In addition to those programs, the mail service in Mac OS X Server makes use of a number of other packages to provide features, such as web mail, spam and virus scanning, and mailing lists. Each of these will be discussed in-depth throughout this lesson, but first you must learn how Internet email works.

Understanding Internet Mail

Although email is one of the oldest and simplest systems on the Internet, it is composed of a number of different protocols. The primary protocol used by email is the Simple Mail Transfer Protocol (SMTP). SMTP is responsible for delivering a message from the sender to the recipient's email server and between email servers. When a message is sent, the outgoing mail server first looks up the address of the destination's Mail eXchange (MX) server using DNS. A given Internet domain can have multiple MX servers to help balance the load and provide redundant services. Each MX server is assigned a priority. The highest priority servers are assigned the lowest number and are tried first when delivering mail via SMTP.

To look up information about a domain's MX servers, you can use the Network Utility found in /Applications/Utilities on a Mac OS X computer.

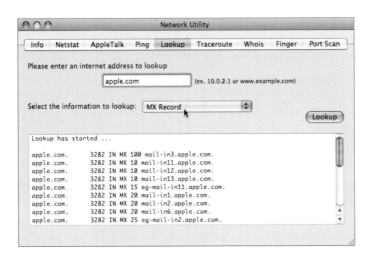

An individual email message may travel through many servers while en route to its final destination. Each server that a message passes through will tag a message with the name of the server and the time it was processed. This is done to provide a history of what servers handled a given message. To examine this trail using the Mail application, you can choose View > Message > Long Headers while viewing the message.

```
Received:  from cooper ([127.0.0.1]) by localhost (cooper.pretendco.com [127.0.0.1]) (amavisd-new, port
           10024) with ESMTP id 09379-03 for <david.pugh@pretendco.com>; Sat, 21 Sep 2002
           15:31:32 -0400 (EDT)
Received:  from mail-out4.apple.com (mail-out4.apple.com [17.254.13.23]) by cooper (Postfix) with
           ESMTP id 5D5B9B7C672 for <david.pugh@pretendco.com>; Sat, 21 Sep 2002 15:31:32
           -0400 (EDT)
Received:  from relay14.apple.com (relay14.apple.com [17.128.113.52]) by mail-out4.apple.com (Postfix)
           with ESMTP id 292BD251CA2; Sat, 21 Sep 2002 15:31:31 -0700 (PDT)
Received:  from relay14.apple.com (unknown [127.0.0.1]) by relay14.apple.com (Symantec Mail Security)
           with ESMTP id 0E96B20A4C; Sat, 21 Sep 2002 15:31:31 -0700 (PDT)
Received:  from [17.09.21.02] (sep21-2002.apple.com [17.09.21.02]) (using TLSv1 with cipher AES128-
           SHA (128/128 bits)) (No client certificate requested) by relay14.apple.com (Apple SCV relay)
           with ESMTP id E1B20A24685; Sat, 21 Sep 2002 15:31:30 -0700 (PDT)
```

Once the email message is delivered to recipient's mail server, it will be stored there until the recipient retrieves the message using either of two available protocols:

▶ Post Office Protocol (POP) is a common email retrieval protocol used on mail servers where disk space and network connections are at a premium. POP is preferred in these environments because a mail client will connect to the server, download the email, remove it from the server, and disconnect very quickly. Although good for the server, POP mail servers are typically less user-friendly because they don't support server-side folders and may cause difficulties for a user connecting from multiple computers.

▶ Internet Message Access Protocol (IMAP) is commonly used by mail services that want to provide more features to the user. IMAP allows the storage of all email and email folders on the server, where they are generally backed up. Additionally, a mail client will often remain connected to the mail server for the duration of the user session. This can result in quicker notification of new messages. The downside to using IMAP is that it puts a greater strain on the resources of the mail server.

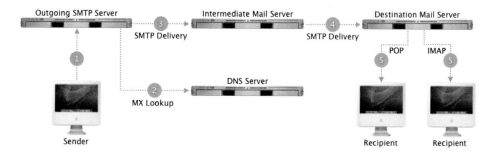

Setting Up the Mail Service

Setting up the Mac OS X Server mail service requires configuring a few different pieces that all work together. You need to have the MX records configured in DNS, your SMTP service configured to deliver outgoing mail and to accept incoming mail, and your IMAP or POP service configured to allow mail clients to retrieve their email. Additionally, you'll need to enable the mail service for each user. Later in the lesson, you'll take steps to refine your mail service by providing spam and antivirus filtering, along with setting other options.

Configuring DNS for Mail

When you send an email, you'll need to ensure that DNS is configured for your domain so that mail can be delivered to the proper address. Earlier in Lesson 2, "Providing Basic DNS Service," you configured the MX record for mail. We'll verify that now:

1   On your Mac OS X computer, open /Applications/Utilities/Network Utility.

2   Click the Lookup tab.

3   In the lookup field, type *pretendco.com*.

4   Choose MX Record from the "Select the information to lookup" pop-up menu.

5   Click the Lookup button.

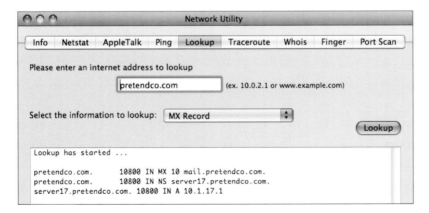

You should see MX 10 mail.pretendco.com listed, indicating that mail.pretendco.com is the mail exchanger, with a priority of 10. Next, we need to verify that mail.pretendco. com is a valid host name.

6 In the lookup field, type *mail.pretendco.com.*

7 Choose Default Information from the "Select the information to lookup" pop-up menu.

8 Click the Lookup button.

Did an address come back for mail.pretend.com? In the DNS lesson, you only configured the MX record for the domain as being mail.pretendco.com. You didn't actually create a DNS record for mail.pretendco.com itself.

9 On your Mac OS X computer, open Server Admin and connect to your server.

10 Select the DNS service in the left column.

11 Click the Zones button in the toolbar.

12 Select the pretendco.com entry in the list, and click the disclosure triangle to open the list of hosts.

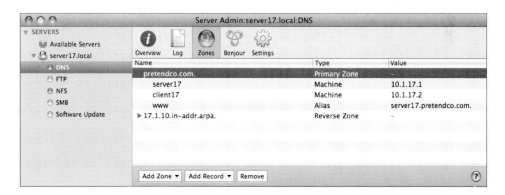

13 Click the Add Record button and choose Add Machine (A).

NOTE ▸ Internet standards dictate that you should use a Machine (A) record rather than an Alias (CNAME) record for the DNS records of mail servers, even if that server has other names.

14 Select the newMachine entry in the list at the top.

15 Change the Machine Name to *mail*.

16 Change the address to *10.1.17.1* in the IP Addresses list.

17 Click Save.

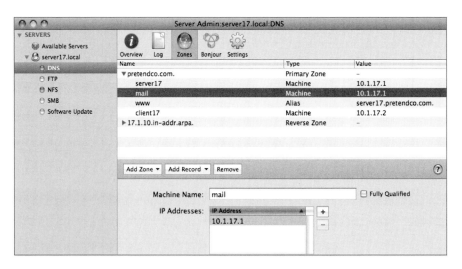

Now we'll repeat the host-name lookup in Network Utility.

18 If Network Utility is not running, open /Applications/Utilities/Network Utility.

19 On the Lookup tab, type *mail.pretendco.com* in the lookup field.

20 Choose Default Information from the "Select the information to lookup" pop-up menu.

21 Click Lookup.

You should now see that mail.pretendco.com has an address of 10.1.17.1.

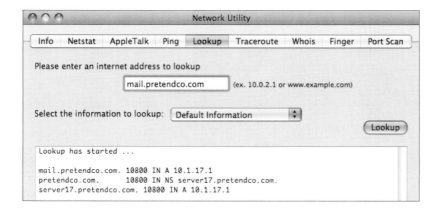

Enabling the Mail Service

Now that DNS is configured correctly for Mail delivery to your domain, we need to configure the Mac OS X Server mail service to process mail messages. This, like most other services, is done through Server Admin.

1 Open Server Admin and connect to your server.

2 Select the Mail service in the left column.

> **NOTE ▶** If the Mail service isn't listed, you can add it by selecting your server name in the left column, clicking the Settings button in the toolbar, clicking the Services tab, selecting the Mail service in the list, and clicking Save. After you've added the Mail service to your server, select it in the left column.

3 Click the Settings button in the toolbar.

4 Click the General tab if it's not already selected.

5 Configure the settings as follows:

▶ In the Domain name field, type *pretendco.com.*

▶ In the Host name field, type *server17.pretendco.com.*

▶ Select the option "Enable POP."

▶ Select the option "Enable IMAP."

▶ Select the option "Enable SMTP."

The option to "Allow incoming mail" should already be selected.

6 Click Save.

7 Click Start Mail in the lower-left corner of Server Admin.

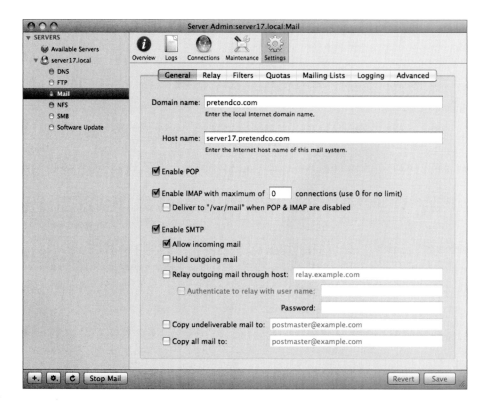

Configuring Users on Your Mail Server

Although you have a fully functional Internet email server running now, none of your users are configured to use it yet. There are two aspects to this. The first is to allow a user to receive email on your email server. The second option is to define your Mail application presets so when a client computer binds to your directory server, that user's Mail application will be automatically configured to use your mail server and the chosen protocol, IMAP or POP, for accessing his or her email.

1   Open Workgroup Manager and connect to your server.

2   Select all your users except any administrative accounts.

3   Click the Mail tab.

4   Click Enabled.

This option allows those users to receive email on your server.

5   Configure the settings as follows:

   ▶   Set the Mail Server to *server17.pretendco.com*.

   ▶   Set the Mail Quota to *500* MB.

   ▶   Set Mail Access to Both POP and IMAP.

6   Click Save.

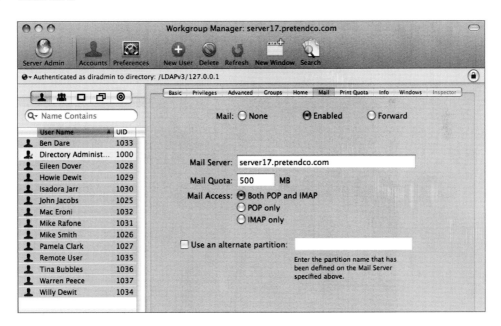

Enhancing Mail Service

Now that your users can use your mail server, there are a number of adjustments you can make to increase performance, add features, and secure your mail server.

Setting Server Connection Options

To conserve system resources, you can limit the number of concurrent IMAP connections that are allowed. It's best to base this number on actual usage to ensure that you have the proper balance between allowing all your users to be logged in at the same time and not overwhelming your server.

Some Internet service providers require that all outgoing email be routed through their SMTP server rather than being delivered directly to the destination. This could be for security, efficiency, or spam-prevention reasons. Additionally, some providers may require you to provide a user name and password to relay mail through their SMTP server. You can enter these here as well. These settings and requirements can be obtained from your ISP.

1   On the Server Admin Mail Settings General pane, change the maximum number of IMAP connections to *50*.

2   Select the option "Relay outgoing mail through host," and type *mail-relay.pretendco.com* as the host.

3   Click Save.

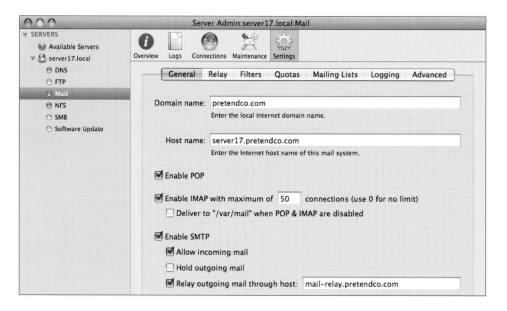

4   Click the Relay tab.

5   Under "Accept SMTP relay only from these hosts and networks," click the Add (+) button and add a network: *10.1.0.0/16*.

6   Click OK.

7   Click Save.

Server Admin automatically adds your subnet to the list, but your organization may be made up of other networks. To allow all of your computers to send outgoing email through your mail server, be sure that all of your organization's subnets are added here.

Clustering Mail Services

As of Mac OS X Server v10.5, you can create a mail cluster. A mail *cluster* is a group of servers that share a single mail store amongst all of the servers for the purposes of redundancy and load balancing. This requires each of the participating servers to share a common file system using Xsan 2.0. The messages will be kept in the shared file system and can be accessed from any of the servers once they've been configured to participate in the cluster.

1   In the Server Admin Mail Settings, click the Advanced tab.

2   Click the Clustering tab.

3   Click the Change button.

A setup assistant will appear and will walk you through configuring your clustered mail service.

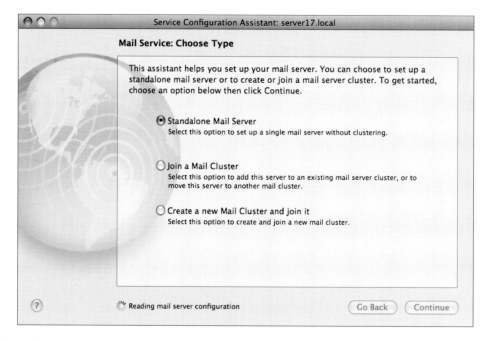

If you don't have an Xsan file system on your server, you can't cluster your mail servers, so the options to do so will be disabled. At this point just click the red button in the upper-left corner to close the setup assistant.

Accessing Mail on the Web

In addition to using an email client with POP or IMAP to access email, Mac OS X Server includes a web mail service that permits users to log in to a web page to access their email. Once you've configured your web server, you can enable this feature by selecting the Webmail option in the Web Services pane of a given web site. Web server configuration will be discussed in detail in the next lesson.

Securing Mail Service

Internet email is arguably one of the most used services available on the Internet. Along with significant use comes significant abuse. Mail, like any other Internet-enabled service, has numerous options that can increase the security of it and reduce or eliminate the risk for abuse. In this portion of the lesson, we'll focus on three primary areas of abuse and what can be done to reduce their impact on your users.

▶ Password security focuses on ensuring that your users' passwords are safe and that frequent checking of email does not expose their passwords.

▶ Spam prevention actually has two components. First, you want to keep other users from using your server for delivering their spam to others, and second, you want to reduce the amount of spam your users receive.

▶ Virus detection is used to protect the integrity of your users' computers by keeping known viruses out of their email.

Protecting User Passwords

Any time a user must authenticate to a service over the Internet, particularly over insecure wireless networks, his or her password is at risk. We can reduce this risk by taking advantage of higher levels of password hashing and by enabling encryption.

The mail service in Mac OS X Server offers a number of different authentication mechanisms. Each has varying levels of security, but more importantly, do not have support in every email client used. When selecting authentication methods, it's important to determine which email clients your users will be running and what authentication methods they support. Authentication methods range from Clear or PLAIN, which send passwords over the network completely unencrypted, all the way to Kerberos, which is considered one of the most secure because passwords are never sent over the network. If none of your users will be using a particular authentication method, you should disable that method. Additionally, if you want to force your users to only use more secure methods, you should disable the less-secure mechanisms such as Clear and PLAIN or require the connection to use SSL.

1   Open Server Admin and connect to your server.

2   Select the Mail service in the left column and click the Settings button in the toolbar.

3   Click the Advanced tab.

4   Click the Security tab.

5   In the SMTP column, select the CRAM-MD5 option.

6   In the IMAP column, leave CRAM-MD5 selected, and deselect Clear.

7   In the POP column, leave APOP selected, and deselect Clear.

NOTE ▶ APOP is a very weak form of password security, though still better than Clear which offers no encryption. For more protection, you should only use these when combined with SSL.

8   Click Save.

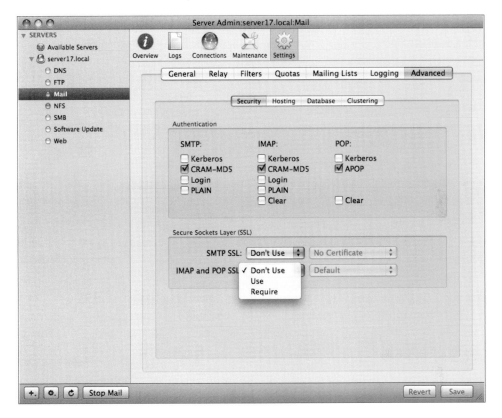

The authentication options protect only the user's password. To further protect the user's password and protect the message content from eavesdropping as well, you can also take advantage of SSL encryption. This provides the same level of protection used by secure websites, and can either be offered to compatible clients by choosing Use from the SSL menus, or can be required by selecting the Require option instead. Unless you have incompatible clients or don't want to manage SSL certificates for your server, you generally will want to set both of the SSL options to Require.

Preventing Spam

Spam, or unsolicited junk email, is a growing problem on the Internet. Although nearly impossible to eliminate altogether, there are steps you can take to reduce it. There are two main components to this. First, you want to keep your server from being misused, and second, you want to reduce the amount of spam your users receive.

Keeping Your Server from Being Misused

Now that you're running your own email server, you want to take steps to ensure that your server can't be misused by spammers to send their messages. Spammers make use of unprotected servers to send thousands of messages to lists of recipients. When this happens, users outside of your organization are using your server as their outgoing email server, thus providing an extra layer of anonymity to them. Servers that allow anyone to send messages through them are typically referred to as *open relays*. Fortunately, protecting your server from being used as an open relay is very simple. You can either require authentication for your SMTP server, or you can limit the networks that are allowed to relay through your server.

1   In Server Admin's Mail Settings, click the Relay tab.

2   Be sure "Accept SMTP relays only from these hosts and networks" is selected.

3   Click the Add (+) button to add any individual IP address or subnets that should be allowed to relay messages through your server.

    This list should always include the server itself by using the loopback address of 127.0.0.1 so the server can send error emails, and can also include any networks that are part of your organization.

4   Click Save.

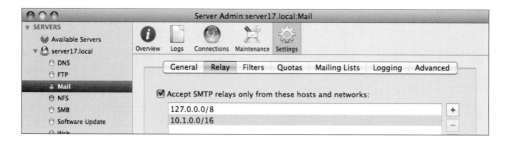

Once you've configured your server to prevent open relays, you'll want to confirm that it is, in fact, blocking open relaying. There are a number of websites that can verify this for you. A quick Internet search for "open-relay test" will bring up many third-party sites that can verify that your server is sufficiently protected.

Reducing Incoming Spam Using Known Sources

Now that your server can't be used to deliver junk mail to others, you should take steps to reduce the amount of junk mail your users receive. There are some key ways to accomplish this. One method blocks known sources of junk mail. Although this method is guaranteed to stop junk mail coming from known spam servers, you also run the risk of blocking legitimate messages delivered through a server that was misidentified as a spam server.

1 In Server Admin's Mail Settings, click the Relay tab.

2 Select the option to "Refuse all messages from these hosts and networks."

3 Click the Add (+) button.

4 In the dialog, type *10.54.199.3*.

   That address is a fictitious source of spam. In a real-world situation, you'd have to examine the headers of your spam messages to determine the origin of the spam.

5 Click OK.

6 Click Save.

Reducing Incoming Spam Using a Blacklist Service

Examining every spam message to try to determine its source would be a very tedious, and probably not very successful, method of spam prevention. An alternative would be to take advantage of one of the many blacklist services that exist. A *blacklist service* publishes and updates a list of known open relay servers.

You can configure your Mac OS X Server to reference such a service for determining whether you should accept mail from a given host. If, for example, there was a blacklist service offered by a server named blacklist.pretendco.com, you would follow these steps:

1   In Server Admin's Mail Settings, click the Relay tab.

2   Select the option to "Use these junk mail rejection servers (real-time blacklist)."

3   Click the Add (+) button.

4   In the dialog that appears, type *blacklist.pretendco.com*.

5   Click OK.

6   Click Save.

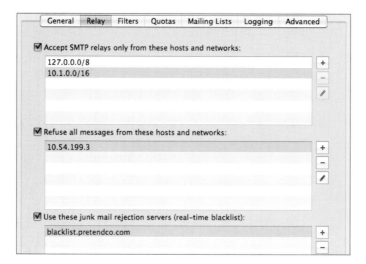

Reducing Incoming Spam Using Filters

Another type of spam reduction involves inspection of every incoming message. This method relies on recognizing patterns of text that are commonly seen in spam junk mail.

1   In Server Admin's Mail Settings, click the Filters tab.

2   Select the option to "Scan email for junk mail."

3   Adjust the Minimum junk mail score to 20 hits.

   This setting may need to be adjusted depending on the types of email your users are supposed to receive. If you set the number too high, your users will continue receiving spam. However, if you set the number too low, legitimate messages will be tagged as spam and may not be seen by their intended recipient. You may also find that you'll want to start with a high number, and once your server has received a sufficient amount of training, you can reduce the setting.

4   Set the option to indicate that "Junk mail messages should be Delivered."

   As with the previous option, this setting can either make life easier for your recipients by not delivering their spam messages or cause problems by not delivering messages misidentified as spam. Additional options include the ability to bounce messages identified as spam, which may tell the spam origin-ator that the email address they sent to was bad (even though it wasn't) and may result in a reduction of spam. You can also redirect all spam messages to another email address for collection. This may be handy for spam server training or a honeypot project.

5   Click Save.

Detecting Viruses

As with spam, no user wants to receive a virus in his or her email. Mac OS X Server includes virus scanning as well. This is enabled on the same settings pane as spam filtering.

1   In Server Admin's Mail Settings, click the Filters tab.

2   Select the option to "Scan email for viruses."

3   Select the option to indicate that "Infected messages should be Deleted."

4   Deselect the option to "Send notification to: virus-admin@example.com."

5   Select the option to "Notify recipients."

This option will send an email to the intended recipient telling them a message was detected as having a virus and was deleted. This option can be useful in cases where a legitimate attachment was misidentified as a virus so the user knows why they never received it.

6   Select the option to "Update the virus databases 4 times every day."

Updating more often will catch new viruses sooner, but also add extra load to your server and your network.

7   Click Save.

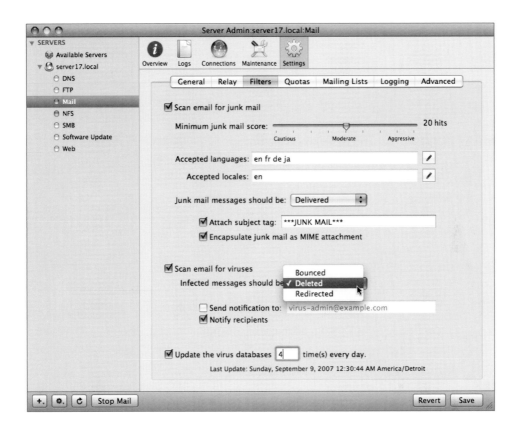

Maintaining the Mail Service

Now that you have your mail server configured with settings helpful to the users, you'll want to make some further adjustments that are helpful to you, the system administrator. These settings include options that will keep your server healthy, aid in diagnosing problems, distribute mail to multiple users, as well as options that may help you adhere to regulatory requirements.

Saving Disk Space

The most important settings to be aware of are those that affect disk consumption. Every message that arrives at your server will take up disk space. If your server runs out of free disk space, you won't be able to receive any more messages. There are two main methods to keep this from happening. The first method is by establishing mail quotas for your users. We set this number earlier in the lesson using Workgroup Manager when we enabled each of the users' mail access. This setting will control the total amount of disk space a given user can occupy with all his or her email that is stored on the server. The other item to keep in mind is the possibility of running out of disk space as a result of a few huge messages coming into your server. You can reduce this threat by limiting the maximum size of each individual message.

1   In Server Admin, select the Mail service, followed by clicking the Settings button in the toolbar.

2   Click the Quotas tab.

3   Refuse messages larger than 10 MB.

4   Select the option to "Enable quota warnings."

5   Click the Edit Quota Warning Message button and configure it as follows:

   ▶   From: *postmaster@pretendco.com*

   ▶   Subject: *Email Quota Warning*

   ▶   Body: *You are approaching your email storage quota. Please delete some messages soon to avoid blocked messages.*

6   Click OK.

7   Select the option to "Disable a user's incoming mail when they exceed 100% of quota."

8   Click the Edit Over Quota Error Message button and configure it as follows:

   ▶   From: *postmaster@pretendco.com*

   ▶   Subject: *Email Over Quota*

   ▶   Body: *You have exceeded your email storage quota. Until you delete some messages, you will no longer receive new email.*

9   Click OK.

10 Click Save.

Redirecting Messages

Because of company policy or in order to adhere to certain regulations, you may need to save copies of every message sent through your server, whether delivered or undelivered to a final recipient. Mac OS X Server offers easy configuration to meet these needs. You'll probably want to create a new user with no quota for these delivery email addresses and periodically archive the mail so it doesn't fill your mail server.

1   In Server Admin's Mail Settings, click the General tab.

2   Select the option to "Copy undeliverable mail to: *postmaster@server17.pretendco.com*."

3   Select the option to "Copy all mail to: *postmaster@pretendco.com*."

4   Click Save.

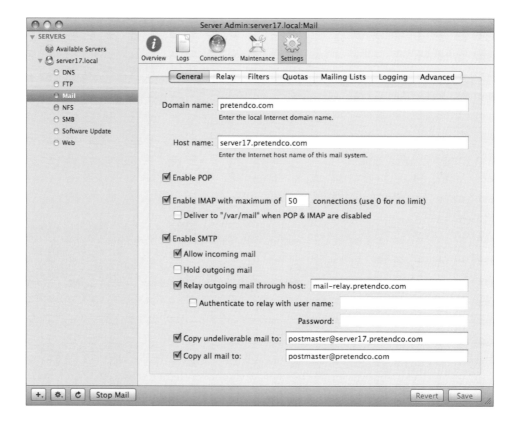

Creating Mailing Lists

You can also use Server Admin to set up mailing lists. This functionality is based on an open source project called mailman and allows you to create an email address on your server that will distribute a copy of every message it receives to all of the members of that list.

1   In Server Admin's Mail Settings, click the Mailing Lists tab.

2   Select the option to "Enable mailman mailing lists."

3   A dialog will appear. Configure it as follows:

   ▶   Master password: *Mail4Apple*

   ▶   Administrators: *warren@pretendco.com tinabubbles@pretendco.com*

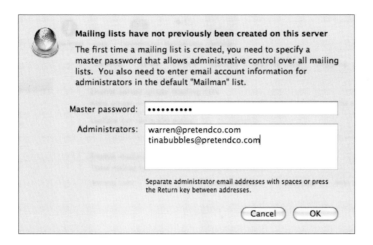

4   Click OK.

The Mailman master mailing list will be created. This is just a systemwide list for tracking the master password. We'll be creating our mailing list next.

5   Click the Add (+) button below the Mailing Lists list to create a new list.

6   A dialog will appear. Configure it as follows:

   ▶   List Name: *PretendcoWomen*

   ▶   Admin User: *tinabubbles@pretendco.com*

7   Click OK.

The new PretendcoWomen list has just been created. We'll add members to it now.

8   Click the Users & Groups button.

9   Drag the user names of all the women at Pretendco to the list of Email Address members of the PretendcoWomen Mailing List.

Note that Tina is already a member because she was designated as an administrator of that mailing list earlier.

10   Click Save.

Now any messages sent to PretendcoWomen@pretendco.com will be distributed to all of the women who were added to the mailing list.

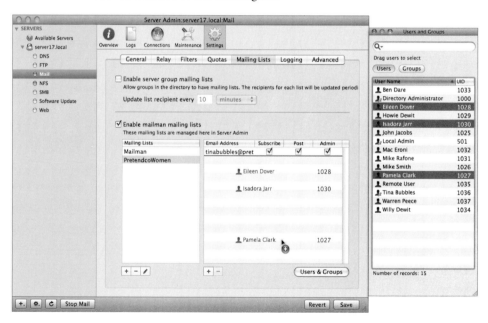

Configuring Mail Logs

As with all services, logs play a big part in diagnosing and troubleshooting any mail issues. In the case of email, logs may also be used for confirmation of message delivery if a dispute arises. Configuration of the Mail server logs is done through Server Admin. Depending on the scenario, you may be adjusting the various log levels. Because email is received in such great quantity, you probably don't want verbose mail-service logging when operating under normal conditions.

1 In Server Admin's Mail service Settings, click the Logging tab.

2 Set the "SMTP log level" to Warning.

3 Set the "IMAP/POP log level" to Warning.

4 Set the "Junk Mail/Virus log level" to Warning.

5 Select the option to "Archive logs every *1* day."

6 Click Save.

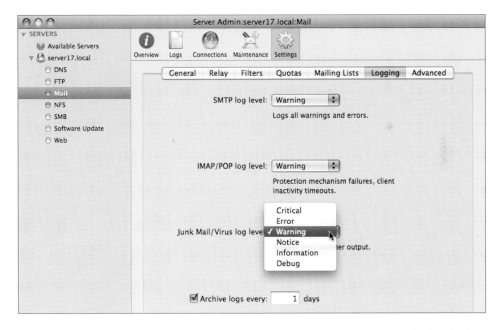

If you're having problems with message delivery, you may want to increase the level of SMTP logging to Information or Debug. If users are having problems with their mail clients, you'll want to increase the level of IMAP/POP logging to Information or Debug. Lastly, if messages are being mistagged as junk mail or virus containing, you can increase the logging level for that service.

Once your mail service is running, you can use your logs to diagnose problems that your users are having. The logs will be able to identify if email addresses are mistyped or if the user is over quota. If the user is having problems retrieving his or her mail, you'll recognize failed authentication attempts in the logs.

What You've Learned

▶   Mac OS X Server includes a robust email server that handles SMTP, IMAP, and POP communication.

▶   Internet email messages travel from server to server based on MX record information in DNS.

▶   Numerous mail authentication options are available and can be enabled or disabled as needed.

▶   You should configure your server so it does not act as an open-relay server.

▶   You can configure the mail service to filter spam and virus-infected messages.

▶   Quotas should be enabled to control disk consumption.

▶   You can create mailing lists to distribute a message to multiple recipients.

References

The following documents provide more information about installing Mac OS X Server. (All of these and more are available at www.apple.com/server/documentation.)

Administration Guides

Mac OS X Server Getting Started

Mail Service Administration

Network Services Administration

Apple Knowledge Base Documents

You can check for new and updated Knowledge Base documents at www.apple.com/support.

URLs

Clam AntiVirus: www.clamav.net

Cyrus: cyrusimap.web.cmu.edu

MacEnterprise: www.macenterprise.org

Mailman: www.list.org

Postfix: www.postfix.org

SpamAssassin: spamassassin.apache.org

SquirrelMail: www.squirrelmail.org

Review Quiz

1. What is an open relay?

2. What is an MX record?

3. What is SMTP?

4. What are the main differences between POP and IMAP?

5. What is a mail cluster?

6. What are the two methods to limit the amount of disk space used on a mail server?

Answers

1. An open relay is a mail server that allows anyone on the Internet to anonymously send email messages through it. It is the primary tool used by spammers on the Internet.

2. An MX record is a DNS record that indicates the priority and host name of a domain's email server.

3. Simple Mail Transfer Protocol defines how messages travel from one computer to another on the Internet.

4. IMAP maintains a persistent connection between the client and server, allows folder access, and supports higher security authentication methods. POP requires fewer server resources.

5. A mail cluster is a group of Mac OS X Server computers attached to a common Xsan file system to provide distributed and redundant mail services.

6. Two methods to control disk consumption by users are user quotas and maximum message size limits.

7

Time

This lesson takes approximately 3 hours to complete.

Goals

Define Mac OS X Server's web engine

Understand how to manage the web service

Configure multiple websites and locate site files

Examine website log files

Locate and use secure certificates for websites

Use WebDAV for users and groups

Understand the ramifications of folder listings on websites

Manage web service modules

Define realms as they relate to websites

Differentiate the various file-sharing protocols as they relate
to WebDAV

Lesson 7
Managing Web Services

This lesson helps you understand, manage, and secure the various aspects of Apple's web services, including managing high-bandwidth connections, sharing files, and locating log files for access, viewing, and troubleshooting.

Mac OS X Server's web service is based on Apache, open source software used on a variety of operating systems. Apache can be enhanced by the use of modules (think of them as plug-ins), and Apple has included several additional modules with Mac OS X Server to extend the abilities of Apache. The version currently installed on Mac OS X Server is Apache 2.2.6.

Understanding Basic Website Concepts

Before you manage any websites, it is important to know where critical Apache and website files are stored. All Apache and Apple configuration files for web services are located in /private/etc/httpd/, which is normally hidden from view in the Finder. Apache modules—including Apple-specific modules—are located in /usr/libexec/apache2/, which is also normally hidden from view in the Finder. The default location for Mac OS X Server's website is located in /Library/WebServer/Documents/, and each user added to Mac OS X Server, regardless of whether they are added to the local directory or the shared LDAP directory, has a home folder created and receives a folder with a default webpage that anyone can access when web services are enabled. The location of these individual websites resides inside the Sites folder in each user's home folder. The URL to reach a Mac OS X Server's webpage is its IP address or fully qualified domain name, such as http://10.1.17.1 or http://server17. pretendco.com. To access any user's website, a forward slash, a tilde (~), and the short name of the user are added to either the IP address or the FQDN.

Also, all website files and the folders in which they reside normally must be read only, otherwise, users won't be able to access the files displayed by their web browsers when they visit your site. Later in this lesson, there are examples of when restrictions should be placed on read-only access and how to implement this feature. Therefore, any location described in the preceding paragraph must have at the very least read-only access in order for the pages to be seen by all.

Enabling Websites

When managing websites on Mac OS X Server, you use the Server Admin tool. You also use the Server Admin tool to manage file and folder permissions, thus allowing or restricting access to folders that are to be seen by web browsers, such as Safari.

Because Mac OS X Server has preconfigured web services for the default website, all you need to do to start exploring is turn on the web service.

Enabling the Web Service in Server Admin

To start the web service, you must first enable it as a service in Server Admin.

1   Open Server Admin and select your server in the list of servers on the left.

2   Click the Settings button in the toolbar, click the Services tab, select the Web service, and click Save.

Starting the Web Service in Server Admin

Now that you have enabled the web service, you can simply start the service.

1   Select the Web service in the list of services displayed under your server on the left side of Server Admin.

2   Click the Start button in the lower left of Server Admin to start the web service.

3   Open Safari on Mac OS X and connect to http://10.1.17.1. Observe the page, and then enter the FQDN (http://server17.pretendco.com/) and ensure you can observe the page again. Refresh the page if necessary.

> **NOTE** ▶ Notice that you did not configure the website in any way. Mac OS X Server's web service is set to serve up the default webpages automatically.

4   Enter a tilde (~) and the name *john* after http://server17.pretendco.com/ and view john's personal default webpage. The entry should appear like this: *http://server17 .pretendco.com/~john*.

> **NOTE** ▶ Again, notice that you did not configure the personal website in any way. Mac OS X Server, like Mac OS X's web service, is set to serve up the default user web-pages automatically once the web service is started.

> **NOTE** ▶ It is important to note that the preceding exercises showcase the default behavior of Mac OS X and Mac OS X Server with respect to starting web services without any other configuration.

5   Quit Safari by using Command-Q or choosing Quit from the Safari menu.

You will now examine some basic options for managing websites on Mac OS X Server.

Managing Websites

You can manage many websites with Mac OS X Server. Each website can be distinguished by a different IP address, domain name, or port over which everyone accesses the site. Before you change any parameters on your existing site or add a new site, it is worthwhile noticing how Apple configures the defaults for the original site.

Viewing Default Website Parameters

Understanding what parameters Mac OS X Server sets for default websites is important, as you will often want to adjust or change some of these parameters.

1   Select the Web service in the list of services displayed under your server on the left side of Server Admin.

2 Click the Sites button in the toolbar, and then click the General tab to view the general parameters for the default website.

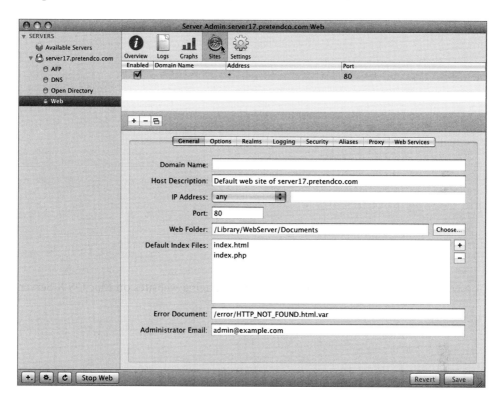

Notice the domain name is not listed, even though you were able to reach it with the FQDN.

3 Enter the fully qualified name, *server17.pretendco.com*, choose your IP address from the pop-up list beneath the domain name, and save the changes.

Notice the site is enabled via the Enabled checkbox in the Sites pane.

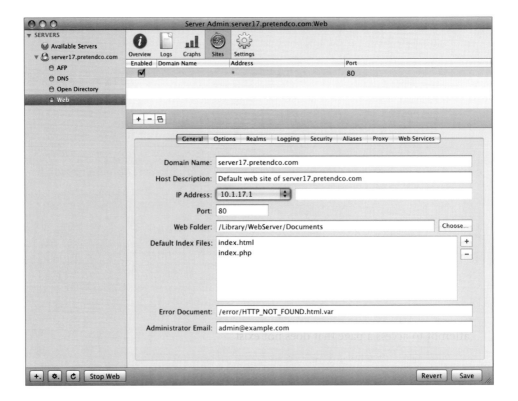

4   Open Safari on Mac OS X and connect to http://10.1.17.1. Observe the page, and then enter the FQDN (http://server17.pretendco.com/) and ensure you can observe the page again. Refresh the page if necessary.

> **NOTE ▶** All you did was specify a domain name and IP address. Mac OS X Server can have multiple IP addresses on a single interface, or, in the case of Mac Pros and Xserves, have more than one Ethernet interface. Therefore, it is important to distinguish IP addresses as mapped to certain sites. Entering this information limits the site to just the entered parameters.

5   View the other general parameters for websites managed under Mac OS X Server:

▶   Domain Name: Fully qualified domain name

▶ Host Description: Definition of the site

▶ IP Address: IP address of the site

▶ Port: Logical port value that users visiting the site may need to know in order to access the site. Ports 80 and 443 are known by most browsers and do not require additional typing when entering the address.

FQDN, IP address, and port are used to separate sites from one another. For example, you can have two sites on the same IP address as long as their ports are different. You can also have two sites with the same IP address and different domain names. By editing and ensuring one of these three parameters is unique, you are logically separating your sites.

▶ Web Folder: The location of the files served up by the selected site

▶ Default Index Files: Initial file that is loaded when a user visits the site. Depending on how complex the site is, the default file may be an executable file or code that interacts with a language, such as WebObjects, Hypertext Preprocessor (PHP), or Perl.

▶ Error Document: Path to the page that visitors see if they are misdirected or attempt to access a page that does not exist

▶ Administrator Email: Email address of the site administrator

Creating a Website

Now that you have viewed the general parameters, you will create a secondary website based on a second IP address.

1 On your server, use the Finder to navigate to /Library/WebServer.

2 Select the Documents folder and choose File > Duplicate to duplicate the folder. Rename it *MySite*.

3 Open the MySite folder and locate the index.html file, open it with TextEdit, change the first line, *Mac OS X Server* to *MySite*, save the change, and quit TextEdit.

You have now edited a file you will use for a second website.

4 Open Server Admin, select the Web service in the list of services, select the Sites button from the toolbar, and click the General tab.

5 Click the Add (+) button to create a new site, and enter the following information:

▶ Domain Name: *mysite.pretendco.com*

▶ Host Description: *This is my site.*

▶ IP Address: *10.1.17.1*

▶ Port: *8080*

▶ Web Folder: Click Choose and navigate to /Library/WebServer/MySite/.

This tells Apache to look in the chosen location for the files to be used on this particular site.

▶ Default Index Files: Because you edited the default line, leave this value alone.

▶ Error Document: Leave this value alone.

▶ Administrator Email: *john@pretendco.com*

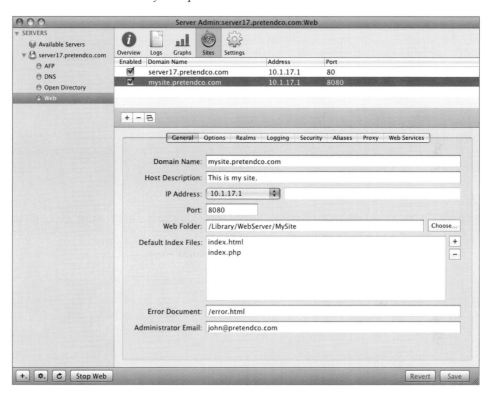

6 Enable the site via the checkbox and click Save.

7 Within Safari on your Mac OS X computer, enter *http://10.1.17.1:8080* in the address bar and press Return to contact the site.

You should see your edited webpage from your directory over the port you chose, 8080.

NOTE ▶ You will not be able to locate the site by using the fully qualified domain name because we did not add that record to your DNS entries.

8   If you try accessing http://www.pretendco.com, you will see it defaults back to the original Mac OS X Server default page, indicating that it has a DNS record (which you added in Lesson 2, "Providing Basic DNS Service"), whereas mysite.pretendco.com does not.

9 Within Server Admin, deselect the Enable checkbox for mysite.pretendco.com and click Save, thus disabling the site for maintenance, for example.

10 Attempt to contact http://10.1.17.1:8080 again. Notice you cannot access the site because you disabled it in Server Admin.

11 Attempt to contact http://server17.pretendco.com:8080.

Notice it goes to the MySite folder. This is because you are asking for this website over port 8080, not the standard port 80. You have two unique sites defined by the port over which they are accessed. The IP address is the same and the FQDN works for one of the sites, but not for the other at this time. It is therefore the port number that is the defining factor.

12 Quit Safari.

Verifying Folder Access

Most of the time, website administrators want users to view all of a website's content. So it's imperative that folder permissions (and file permissions, to some extent) be set up with adequate access as well as appropriate controls. At a minimum, the WWW group must have read access for Apache to serve the files.

Folder permissions are set up via Server Admin under the File Sharing button in the toolbar.

To check if permissions are read only for All:

1 Open Server Admin, select your server in the list of Available Servers, select the File Sharing button from the toolbar, and click the Volumes button.

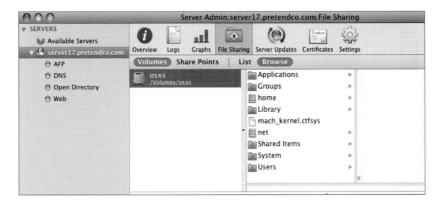

2 With your volume selected, navigate through /Library/WebServer/MySite/.

3 View the POSIX permissions on the MySite folder in the lower half of the window. Notice that for Others, permissions are set to Read Only.

This is why you were able to view your index.html page in your MySite folder.

Using Aliases

Website aliases are a way of having more than one name respond to the same site. This is often done when site administrators want to cover a gamut of names that lead back to one site.

Prior to enabling aliases, DNS should be configured to point the website to the aliased domains.

To enter a web alias:

1   Select the Web service in the list of services displayed under your server on the left side of Server Admin.

2   Click the Sites button in the toolbar, select the server17.pretendco.com site in the sites list, and then click the Aliases tab.

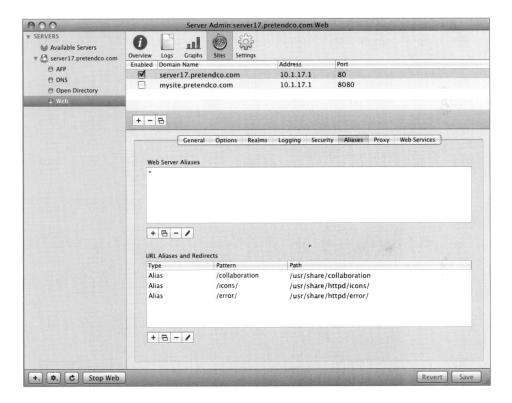

3   Select the asterisk and click the Minus (–) button to remove it from the list.

The asterisk is a wildcard that, when removed, permits the entry of additional names for your website.

4   Click the Add (+) button and enter *www.pretendco.com*, click OK, then click Save.

5   You can now test the alias from your Mac OS X computer. Because there is a DNS record for www.pretendco.com, the alias will work.

Redirects work by sending the visitor to a site, folder, or page that differs from the originally requested page. This is common when certain portions of a website are being upgraded. A redirect does not cause any other links on the site to break but instead silently forwards the visitor(s) to other locations.

Setting Advanced Website Options

There are additional options for websites on Mac OS X Server that can enhance file viewing, provide security, increase functionality, and handle file-sharing duties similar to those of other protocols, such as AFP or SMB. Secondly, when administering a website, it is important to understand how Mac OS X Server handles Apache log files, where they are stored, and how to view them.

Managing Apache Modules

Functionality is extended to Apache via modules, which can be enabled or disabled via Server Admin. Mac OS X Server ships with 67 modules, 40 of which are already enabled. Nine of these modules are Apple-specific modules. A module extends the capabilities of Apache by allowing interaction with the web browser and the web server. Some examples of this are allowing secure connections via the ssl_module, permitting Kerberos authentication via spnego_auth_module, or enabling execution of PHP code via the php5_module.

For security reasons, several modules that enable working with scripting languages are disabled by default in Mac OS X Server.

To enable, disable, or edit a module:

1   Select the Web service in the list of services displayed under your server on the left side of Server Admin.

2   Click the Settings button in the toolbar, and then click the Modules tab.

3   Click the Enable column header to sort the module list by those that are enabled and disabled by default.

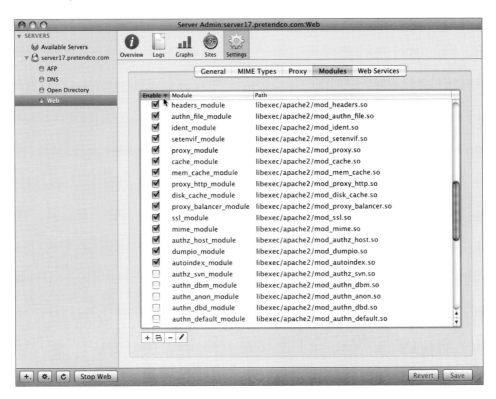

TIP ▶ It is important that you keep record of which modules Apple enables by default. This way you can quickly revert to the standard Apple default module set if necessary.

4   Select the checkbox adjacent to the module you wish to enable or disable.

5   To edit the name or path to a module, select the module in the list and click the Edit (pencil) button beneath the module list.

Managing Folder Listings

Websites are a collection of folders and files displayed via a browser window. The types of files vary, but in almost every case, a complex folder structure exists to restrict both web developers and visitors to the site to certain areas of the site. If the folder structure can be seen at any level, an attacker can decide which folders may merit further investigation. Conversely, a site that hosts files or applications for visitors to download may want its entire folder structure to be seen, which makes navigation of the site easier.

When deciding whether a folder listing is important for a given site, take into account the type of data stored in the folders and the names of the folders themselves. This will help in making the correct decision about folder listings.

Folder listings, unlike modules, are site-based, meaning they can be enabled or disabled per site, whereas modules are enabled or disabled for the entire web service.

To manage folder listings:

1   Select the Web service in the list of services displayed under your server on the left side of Server Admin.

2   Click the Sites button in the toolbar, select the server17.pretendco.com site from the sites list, and then click the Options tab.

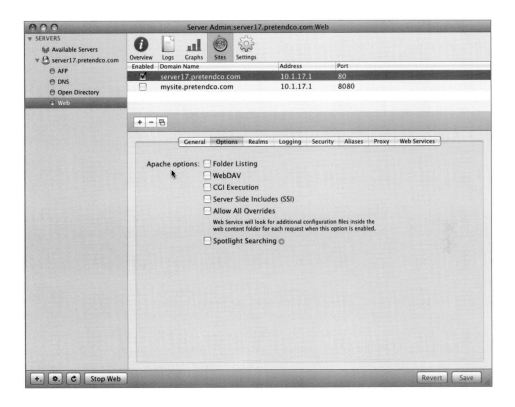

3 Select the Folder Listing checkbox and click Save.

4 From your Mac OS X computer, open Safari and enter *http://server17.pretendco.com/*.

You are presented with a folder listing instead of the standard index.html page.

Viewing Apache Log Files

Apache has excellent logging capabilities and uses two main files when logging website information: the Access log and the Error log. The log files can store all kinds of information, such
as the address of the requesting computer, amount of data sent, date and time of transaction,
page requested by the visitor, and a web server response code, just to name a few.

Log files, called access_log and error_log, are located inside /var/log/apache2/ and are readable via the Server Admin tool.

To view Apache log files for a given site:

1   Select the Web service in the list of services displayed under your server on the left side of Server Admin.

2   Click the Logs button in the toolbar and select the server17.pretendco.com Access log from the Domain Name list to view that log.

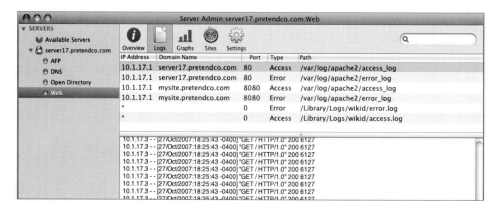

3   On your Mac OS X computer, open /Utilities/Terminal and type *ab −n 10000 −c 50 http://server17.pretendco.com/*, then press Return.

This is an Apache test tool that tells your Mac OS X computer to ask for 10000 (the −n parameter) requests run concurrently by 50 (the −c parameter) pretend users' concurrent connections.

4   Click the Refresh button to see the number of requests increase.

5   On your Mac OS X computer, open Safari and type *http://server17.pretendco.com/ hollyg.html*.

This page does not exist; therefore, it will log an error.

6   Using Server Admin, check the error_log for server17.pretendco.com. You will see an error generated by the bad request.

Disabling Apache Log Files

You can also disable and/or archive both the access and the error log for each website. To do so:

1   Select the Web service in the list of services displayed under your server on the left side of Server Admin.

2   Click the Sites button in the toolbar, select the server17.pretendco.com site in the sites list, and then click the Logging tab.

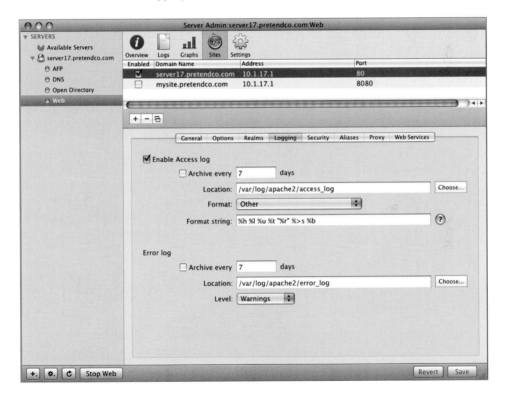

3   Notice the possible configurations for disabling and archiving the log files and the location and formatting for the access log. You can also change the level of logging for the error log, depending on the development and operational parameters of your site.

Graphing Web Traffic

Mac OS X Server permits you to view web traffic coming to your server. You can view both the number of requests and the throughput, although both are cumulative, not site-based. If your Mac OS X Server hosts many services, it is worthwhile to watch the traffic generated by your website(s) and compare that with the CPU and RAM usage on your server. It may be that your website(s) generate(s) enough traffic to warrant a server of their own. When viewing the graphs, you can choose a time for the x (horizontal) axis. It can be as short as one hour and as long as the past seven days of usage.

1 Select the Web service in the list of services displayed under your server on the left side of Server Admin.

2 Click the Graphs button in the toolbar and choose Throughput in the pop-up menu. Choose a time period in the adjacent pop-up menu.

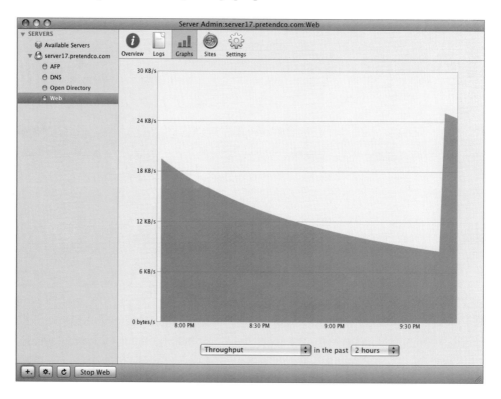

Managing Website Realms and WebDAV

Mac OS X Server makes use of another open standard called WebDAV, which allows sharing capabilities similar to that of other protocols. Additionally, Mac OS X Server provides realms, which are essentially directories or locations—such as other URLs—that can only be accessed by certain users or groups.

Using Realms

Realms are incredibly useful when dealing with websites that contain sensitive information or sections of a site that should only be accessible to one person or group. For example, you could set up a website so that only those users in a given group can access the site. You could also set up a realm on a portion of the site so that only a department has access to those particular pages. In most cases, realms are set up after users and groups are created, because the access to certain web directories is based on users and/or groups.

1 Select the Web service in the list of services displayed under your server on the left side of Server Admin.

2 Click the Sites button in the toolbar, select the server17.pretendco.com site in the sites list, and then click the Realms tab.

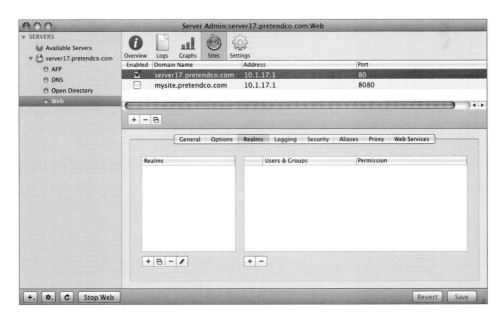

3 Click the Add (+) button under the Realms pane and give the realm a name. Then choose Digest as the authentication type. Leave the directory path at the default.

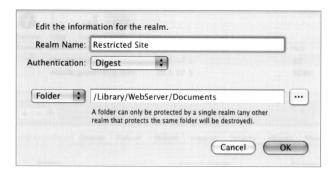

4 Click Save to save the realm. Click the realm to select it.

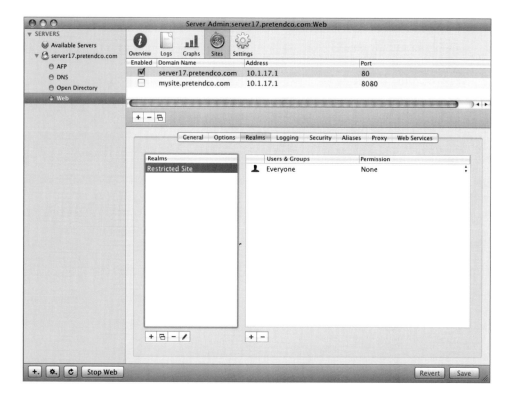

NOTE ▶ When you create a realm, no one has access to the realm by default. You must now add users and/or groups to have access to the realm.

5   Click the Add (+) button under the Users and Groups pane and add a group to the
    list. Once added, change the permissions to Browse Only for the group and click Save.

6   On your Mac OS X computer, open Safari and type *http://server17.pretendco.com/*.

    You are presented with an authentication dialog.

7   Enter a user within the group you added and click the Log In button.

You are now authenticated to use view the site.

Enabling WebDAV

Like realms, WebDAV restricts users and groups to certain directories with regard to web servers. However, WebDAV is a bit different in that a user or group can actually mount the directory of the web server on their desktop, allowing them to read and copy from the server or actually change files and write to the directory. WebDAV is extremely useful when using third-party web development applications that require the user of that application to upload files to the web server. Instead of transferring files back and forth, a WebDAV-enabled server and associated web development application work together to allow live editing of files directly on the server, without the need to download them and then subsequently upload them again. When using Connect to Server, Apple Filing Protocol uses afp:// as a precursor to the server address, and Samba uses smb:// as its precursor. WebDAV uses http://, just as it would if you were to type it in your browser.

1   Select the Web service in the list of services displayed under your server on the left side of Server Admin.

2   Click the Sites button in the toolbar, select the server17.pretendco.com site in the sites list, and then click the Options tab. Select the WebDAV checkbox and click Save.

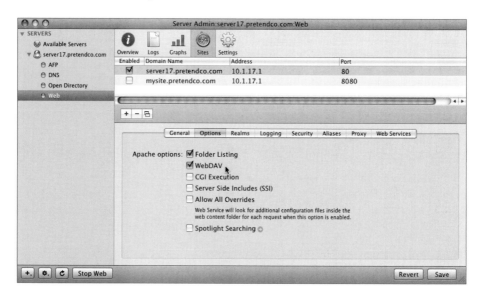

WebDAV is now enabled for that particular site.

Once you enable WebDAV, you must ensure that the folder within your website has the correct permissions for the user or group in your realm. Use Server Admin to check permissions and change them if necessary. If these files are going to be seen by all visitors to the site, it is important to allow read-only access for all other users.

> **NOTE ▶** Even though Server Admin allows you to change permissions on the WebDAV realm folder from within the Web service, ultimately it is still the effective permissions of the web server that determine what is accessible over WebDAV.

To check or change permissions on a folder for WebDAV usage:

1 Select the Web service in the list of services displayed under your server on the left side of Server Admin.

2 Click the Sites button in the toolbar, select the server17.pretendco.com site in the sites list, and then click the Realms tab.

3 Double-click the realm you created earlier and view the path to the folder that holds those documents. In this case, it is /Library/WebServer/Documents/.

4 Click the Ellipsis (...) button and change the realm path to /Library/WebServer/Documents/manual-1.3. Click OK.

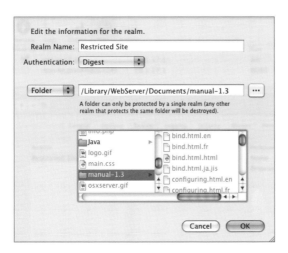

5 Click the realm to select it and edit the eng group's permissions to Browse and Read/Write WebDAV. Change the Everyone group's permissions to None.

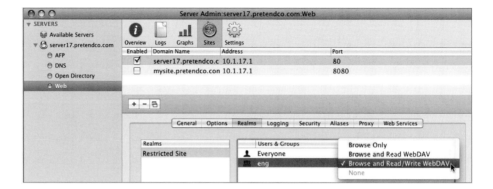

6 Click Save.

7 Select your server in the list of Available Servers, select the File Sharing button from the toolbar, and click the Volumes button.

8 Click Browse to navigate to the /Library/WebServer/Documents/ folder and view the POSIX permissions at the bottom of the window.

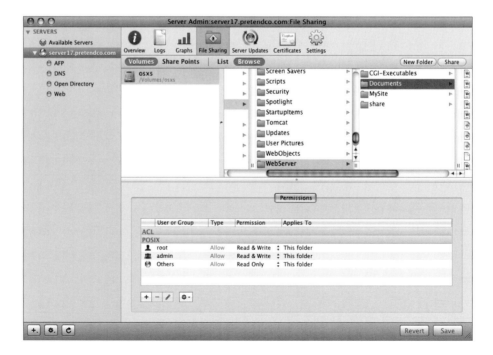

9 Within the Documents folder, scroll down and locate the manual-1.3 folder, select it, and view the permissions. This is the folder we want to restrict.

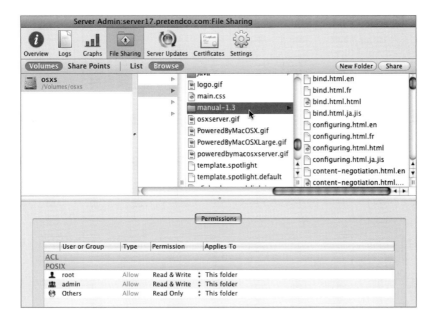

10 Change the POSIX permissions on the manual-1.3 folder as follows.

▶ root: Allow Read & Write, This folder

▶ eng: Allow Read & Write, This folder

You changed the group from admin to eng here.

▶ Others: Allow None, This folder

11 Click Save.

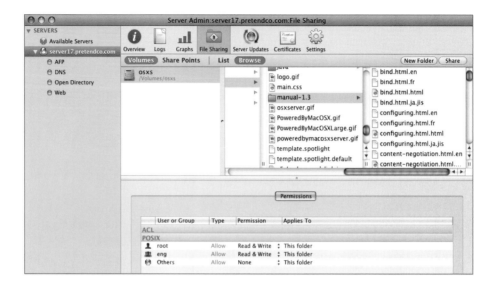

12 On your Mac OS X computer, open Safari and type *http://server17.pretendco.com/*.

You can access the main site.

13 Now type *http://server17.pretendco.com/manual-1.3/*.

You are presented with an authentication dialog.

Only the members of the engineering group have access to this portion of the site. Your realm is working correctly. Attempt a WebDAV connection.

14 Authenticate as a user in the Engineering group and click Log In to ensure you have access. Then quit Safari.

15 From the Go menu, choose Connect to Server and enter *http://server17.pretendco.com/ manual-1.3/*, then click Connect.

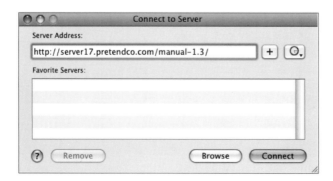

16 You are presented with a WebDAV authentication dialog. Enter the user name and password of a member of the Engineering group and click OK.

17 You are shown a Finder window that permits you to edit files, add files, and delete files from this folder, just like you would any other file-sharing protocol.

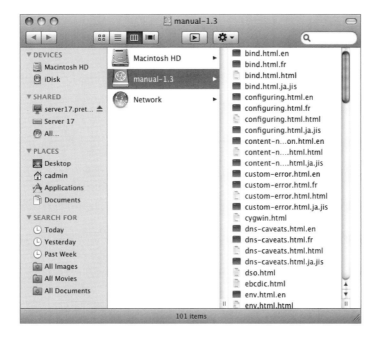

18 Eject the share point.

Comparing File Sharing

Now that you have learned how WebDAV can be implemented, you should understand the basic differences and uses of the other file-sharing protocols with respect to WebDAV.

Table 7.1 File-sharing comparison

	AFP	SMB	FTP	NFS	HTTP
Native platform	Mac OS X	Windows	Multiple	UNIX	Multiple
Security	Kerberos or standard	Kerberos or NTLMv2	Kerberos or clear text	Kerberos or none	Kerberos, digest, or basic
Browsable	Yes	Yes	No	Yes	No
Example URL	afp://server17.pretendco.com	smb://server17.pretendco.com	ftp://server17.pretendco.com	nfs://server17.pretendco.com	http://server17.pretendco.com

What You've Learned

▶   Mac OS X Server's web service is based on Apache, as is Mac OS X's web service.

▶   Apache uses modules to extend its functionality.

▶   Permissions on website folders are crucial to visitors gaining access to portions of the site.

▶   Realms can be used to restrict areas of a site to certain users or groups.

▶   Mac OS X Server can host multiple websites over a single IP address.

▶   Server Admin is used to manage both the Web Service and folder permissions.

▶   You can graph the throughput and number of requests for your websites.

References

The following documents provide more information about installing Mac OS X Server. (All of these and more are available at http://www.apple.com/server/macosx/resources/.)

Administration Guides

Web Technologies Administration (http://images.apple.com/server/macosx/docs/ Web_Technologies_Admin_v10.5.pdf)

File Services Administration (http://images.apple.com/server/macosx/docs/ File_Services_Admin_v10.5.pdf)

URLs

Apache Organization site: http://httpd.apache.org

Apache log formatting information: http://httpd.apache.org/docs/1.3/mod/ mod_log_config.html

Review Quiz

1. On what is Mac OS X Server's web service based?
2. What permissions are necessary on a web folder so visitors to the site can access the pages?
3. What are realms?
4. How do you enable folder listings and WebDAV, and can you do so for more than one site?
5. Where is the default location for the Apache log files?

Answers

1. Mac OS X Server's Web service is based on Apache, the open source web server software.
2. The WWW group must have read access to the web files.
3. Realms are paths to folders or URL locations that can be restricted based on user and/or group.
4. You enable folder Listings and WebDAV options by selecting your site and clicking the Options button. They can be enabled on a site-by-site basis. Modules are enabled or disabled for the entire web service.
5. The default location for Apache log files is /var/log/apache2/access_log and /var/log/ apache2/error_log.

8

Time   This lesson takes approximately 3 hours to complete.

Goals   Set up Mac OS X Server's Wiki service

Enable the iCal service

Allow groups to manage a Wiki

Secure an iCal service connection

Troubleshoot the iCal service

Use the iChat service on Mac OS X Server

Permit users and groups to use the iChat service

Log iChat service transcripts

Permit the joining of two iChat servers

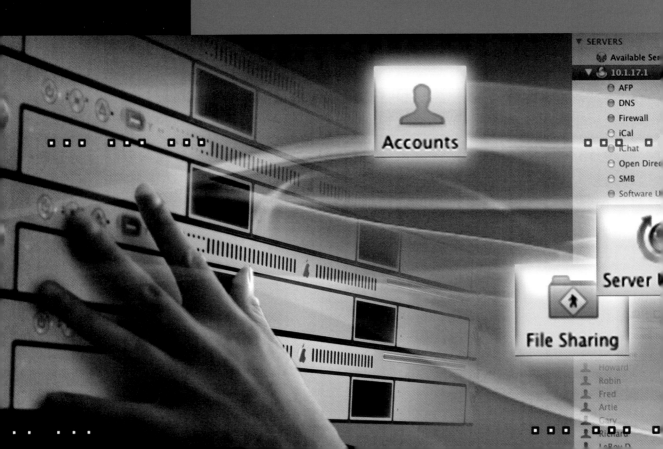

Lesson **8**
Using Collaborative Services

Mac OS X Server has several services that offer a true collaborative environment for users. These services allow for the posting of information, events, scheduling, chatting, and blogging. They comprise the core of what is known as collaborative services. They are the iCal service, iChat service, and Wiki service.

With these services, users can chat in approved groups in a secure environment about internal projects; schedule appointments and meetings and permit others to manage their calendars; set up a Wiki to document the progress of projects; and blog about certain aspects of their projects and other interests.

Understanding and Managing a Wiki

A Wiki is a collaborative web-based tool that allows users and groups to post information in a manner that promotes the logical progression of an idea, project, theme, or any other focal point of discussion within an organization. Wikis are central to the idea of all users within a given group being able to post, edit, review, and discuss material without interference from other groups or departments within an organization. This can benefit the group whose Wiki is hosting a secret project or sensitive information. Mac OS X Server Wikis also keep a detailed history of a group's Wiki, so retrieval of older information can be done if necessary.

Once groups are associated with a Wiki, they can post images and files for downloading, link pages together, and format the pages to their liking.

Similar to Wikis are blogs. Blogs permit users and groups to catalog their experiences surrounding a project or theme. Where Wikis are collaborative, blogs tend to be singular in nature and organized in a chronological format; however, with group blogging, shared experiences are posted together.

Enabling a Wiki in Server Admin

Enabling the Wiki on Mac OS X Server is a relatively simple task. In Lesson 7, "Managing Web Services," you enabled and started the Web service for server17.pretendco.com. Now, you will use Server Admin to enable a Wiki.

1 Open Server Admin and select your server in the list of servers on the left.

2 Select Web in the list of services under your server on the left side of Server Admin and ensure the service is running, as noted by the green button next to the service.

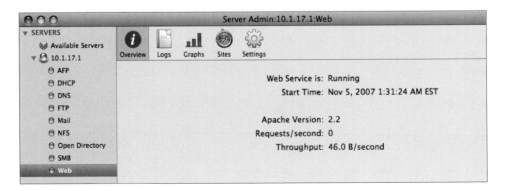

3   Click the Sites button in the toolbar, and then click the server17.pretendco.com site in the list. Ensure the site is turned on via the checkbox and that mysite.pretendco.com is not turned on.

4   Click the Web Services tab, enable the Wiki and blog via the checkbox from the window on the right, and click Save.

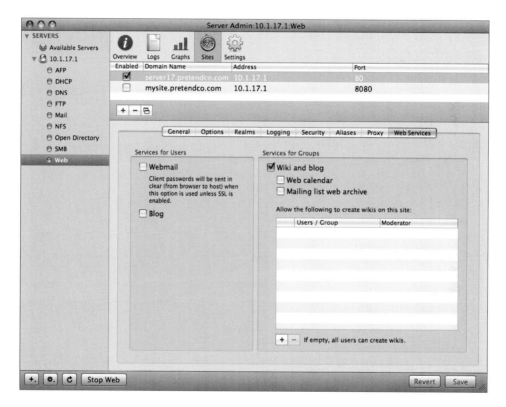

You have now enabled the option to allow users and groups to create Wikis.

Editing Wiki Services for Groups

Notice the text below the Users/Group box that states if the box is empty, all users can create Wikis. You will likely want to restrict who has access to creating Wikis. You may also want to add more services for users and/or groups, such as the web calendar or mailing list archive.

1   With Server Admin still open and Web Services selected, click the Add (+) button under the Users/Groups window, click the Groups button in the Users and Groups dialog, and select a group in the list.

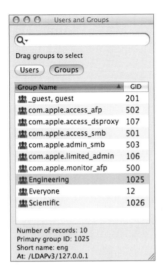

2 Drag the group from the list into the User/Group area in the Server Admin window, select the checkbox to enable the Web calendar, and click Save.

You have now restricted the creation of Wikis to a given group and permitted the use of web calendaring. You must now enable the group to utilize the Wiki and web calendaring.

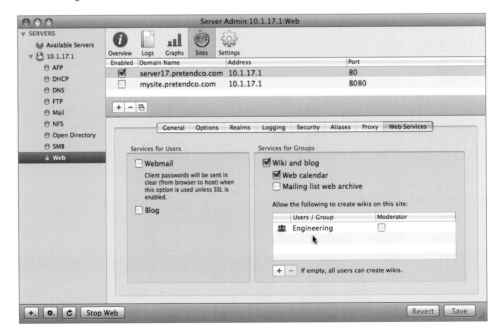

3 Open Workgroup Manager, located in the /Applications/Server folder, click the Accounts button in the toolbar, and select the Groups button in the accounts list.

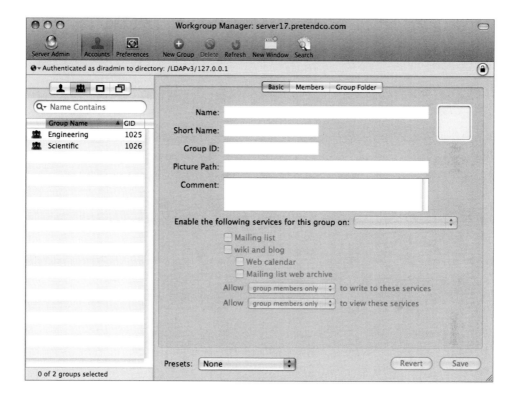

4 Select the group you added to the Wiki creation approval list in step 2, choose the default website from the "Enable the following services for this group on" pop-up menu, select the "wiki and blog" and "Web calendar" checkboxes, and click Save.

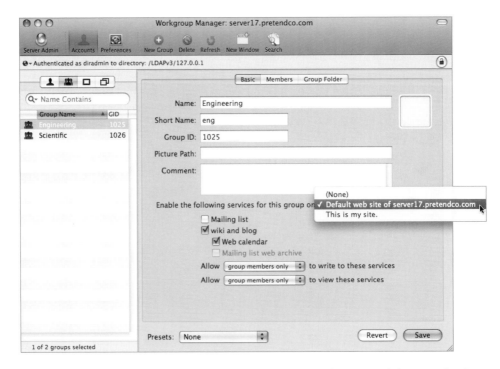

You have restricted the creation of Wikis to a given group and permitted the use of web calendaring to a selected group. You must now enable the group to use the Wiki and Web calendaring.

Creating Wikis

Once the Wiki has been authorized by the Mac OS X Server administrator, users and/or groups can begin the process of creating a Wiki. Because Wikis are web based, you can use any browser on any platform to authenticate users to begin the process of Wiki creation.

1 From your Mac OS X computer, open Safari and enter *http://server17.pretendco.com*, then press Return.

Your Mac OS X Server's default webpage appears.

2   Click the Groups button on the site and view the available groups authorized to create
a Wiki.

3   Click the group in the list and enter a user name and password for a member of the
group to log in. Click the Log In button.

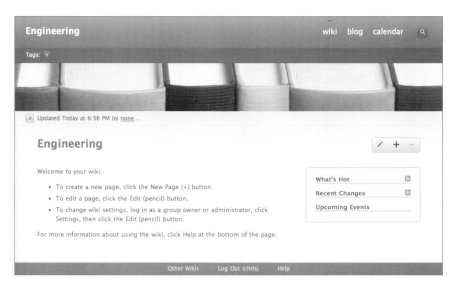

4   You will notice the main Wiki page appears. From here, you can navigate to the blog
or calendar, or create and edit new pages.

5   Click the Add (+) button to create a new page.

A dialog appears that allows you to enter the name for your new page.

6   Edit the text and format the new page to suit your liking and click Save. The results of the page now look something like this:

Once you are on your Wiki page, you can change several parameters by clicking the Edit (pencil) button on the webpage.

Using iCal Services

Mac OS X Server v10.5 contains a calendaring service based on several open-source initiatives, primary among them, the Calendar Server Extensions for WebDAV (CalDAV) open-source calendaring protocol. The iCal service uses the HTTP protocol for access to all of its files. Users who want to use the calendaring service can take advantage of several useful features:

▶   Scheduling rooms or items that can be checked out, such as projectors

▶   Integrating with Mac OS X Server's Open Directory

▶ Enabling access control for delegation of scheduling and/or restricted viewing of your calendar(s)

▶ Allowing multiple calendars per user

▶ Permitting the attachment of files to events

▶ Sending invitations to events

▶ Checking to see if users or meeting locations are available for a certain event

Once the iCal service is started, users can use iCal from Mac OS X v10.5 and the Wiki calendar pages to manipulate events and schedules. There are third-party applications that also work with the iCal service, and those can be located by doing a web search for CalDAV support.

Managing the iCal Service

You use Server Admin to start and manage the iCal service. The parameters that you can adjust are:

▶ Path to location of calendaring files

▶ Maximum attachment size and quota

▶ Name of calendaring server (if you have more than one name for your server in DNS)

▶ Port for access to service

▶ Ability to use Secure Sockets Layer (SSL)

▶ Authentication for service that can be Kerberos (tried first if you choose Any Method from the menu) or Digest

Starting the iCal Service

You will be enabling the iCal service to permit users in groups to create events and ultimately to add resources and locations. To enable the iCal service:

1 Open Server Admin and select your server in the list of servers on the left.

2   Click the Settings button in the toolbar, click the Services tab, select the iCal service, and click Save.

3   Select the iCal service in the list of services under your server on the left side of Server Admin.

4   Click the Settings button in the toolbar to view the options.

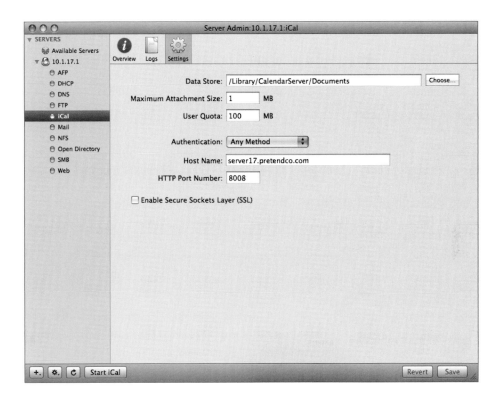

5   Change the user quota to *20* MB and click Save.

You set user quotas to prevent users from attaching extremely large files to every event they have. For example, if a user attaches a 900 KB file to one event, they are under the maximum attachment size. However, if they have more than 20 events, they may run into the user quota limit, thus preventing them from attaching any more files to events.

6   Click the Start iCal button to start the service.

Permitting Users to Create Events

Now that you have enabled the iCal service, you will use Workgroup Manager to enable a user to add events to the iCal service.

1 Open Workgroup Manager, click the Accounts button in the toolbar, click the Users button, and select a user in the list.

2 Click the Advanced tab, select the "Enable calendaring" checkbox, and choose server17.pretendco.com from the calendar host pop-up menu. Click Save.

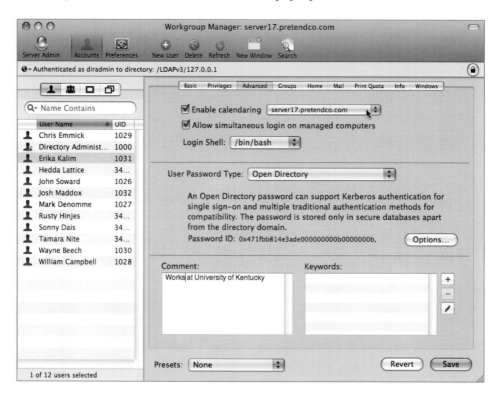

3 From your Mac OS X computer, open the iCal application, choose Preferences under the iCal menu, and click the Accounts button in the toolbar.

4 Click the Add (+) button to add an iCal service (called CalDAV) account and enter the following:

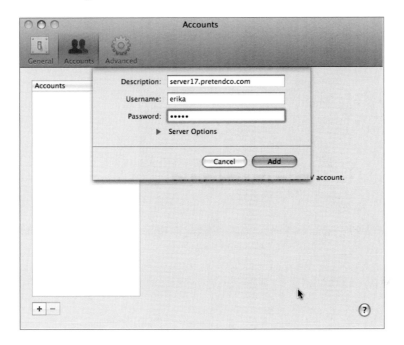

▶ Description: *server17.pretendco.com*

▶ Username: Enter a user of your choice.

▶ Password: Enter the user's password.

After you click the Add (+) button, a dialog may appear asking if you want to connect in an insecure fashion. This indicates you are not using Kerberos at this time. You may continue to connect.

5 You will now see the calendar in your list on the left of iCal. You can rename the calendar and you can add an event like you normally would using the iCal application

> **NOTE** ▶ This is only possible because the client has been integrated with the Open Directory Master (the Mac OS X Server as it is configured at this time). If this were not the case, the calendar would not be automatically found.

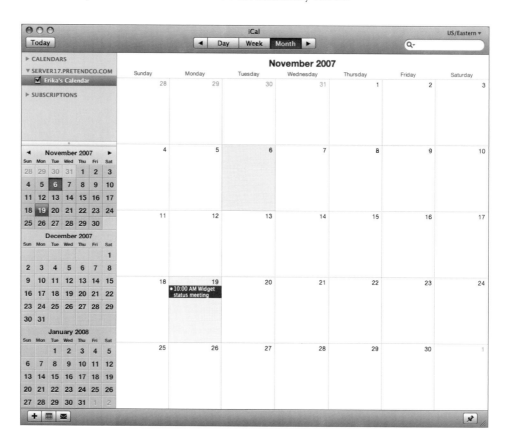

6 You can now edit the event by Control-clicking it to make changes.

Using Directory to Add Resources and Locations

Directory is a utility that allows users to browse a company phone book of sorts. It views certain records in the Open Directory database and allows users to search Directory for certain criteria that matches what they seek. It not only shows users, but groups, locations, and resources, such as projectors, meeting rooms, and conference phones. You add items to the Directory to allow those items to be used by those scheduling events in iCal.

You add locations and resources to Directory; you add users and groups with Workgroup Manager.

To add locations to a Directory:

1   On your Mac OS X Server, navigate to the /Applications/Utilities/ folder and double-click Directory.

2   Click the Add (+) button in the lower-left corner and select New Location in the list. Authenticate as one of your users in the Kerberos authentication dialog and click OK.

3   Enter and/or change the following data for your new resource:

▶   Change Untitled Location to *GarageA*.

▶   Enter Building *3* for the Building.

▶   Enter *2* for the Floor number.

▶   Enter *200* for the capacity.

▶   Do not change the owner. This is who you authenticate as.

▶   There are no maps to choose from at this point.

▶   Enter a phone number and address information to your liking.

4 Click the Scheduling tab and check reservable and auto-accept invitations, then click Save.

You have now added a location that you will see when you add an event with iCal.

5 On your Mac OS X computer open iCal, double-click the event you added, and click the Edit button.

6 You can now enter GarageA under the location menu. You'll notice the information will autofill for you. When you are finished, click Done.

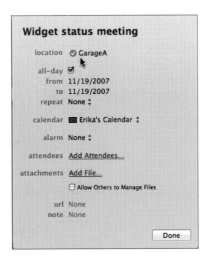

You have now added a location to your meeting. You can also edit your events using your Wiki calendar.

Enabling iCal Service Options

Once you begin using iCal, you may wish to enable some of the options, such as securing your iCal traffic against anyone who may be watching network traffic, looking for meetings to monitor, or changing the default storage locations for your iCal events—such as placing them on another drive or Xserve RAID. You can also use the log files associated with the iCal service to troubleshoot when users cannot connect, find a resource, or authenticate.

1   Select the iCal service in the list of services under your server on the left side of Server Admin.

2   Click the Settings button in the toolbar and click the Choose button next to the Data Store location. If you have an external drive or second partition, you can navigate to that drive or partition and choose to save the iCal event files there.

3   To secure your iCal service, select the Enable Secure Sockets Layer (SSL) checkbox and choose the Default certificate from the pop-up menu. Note that the iCal service will now use port 8443.

4   Try to access your iCal service from your Mac OS X computer using the iCal application. You will note that you cannot connect.

> **TIP** ▶ To ensure secure communications, you must either transfer the certificate from your Mac OS X Server to your Mac OS X computer or accept a dialog that may appear asking you to always trust the certificate.

5 In Server Admin, select the iCal Service and select the Logs button in the toolbar.

6 Choose the Calendar Server Log from the pop-up menu at the bottom of the window and view any errors that may have occurred during this exercise.

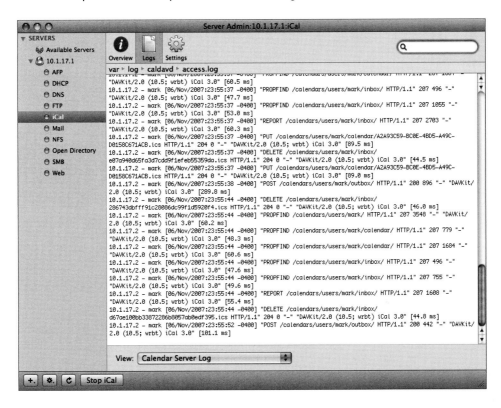

Managing the iChat Service

Users who chat with each other can use Mac OS X Server's iChat service to keep those chats within their organization and control the text of the chats. Like many other services on Mac OS X Server, the iChat service can be restricted to certain users or groups, permitting chats to be private and controlled. Chats can also be secured through encryption and logged, permitting them to be searched later. The iChat service is based on the open source Jabber project. The technical name for the protocol used is the Extensible Messaging and Presence Protocol (XMPP).

Setting Up iChat Service

You use Server Admin to enable the iChat service like all other services in Mac OS X Server. Once enabled, the service is managed in a fashion similar to other services. Options are available that permit iChat services located on other servers to work in concert with your iChat service. Those options will be discussed later in this lesson.

1 Open Server Admin and select your server in the list of servers on the left.

2 Click the Settings button in the toolbar, click the Services tab, select the iChat service, and click Save.

3 Select iChat in the list of services displayed under your server on the left side of Server Admin.

4 Click the Settings button in the toolbar to view the iChat service options.

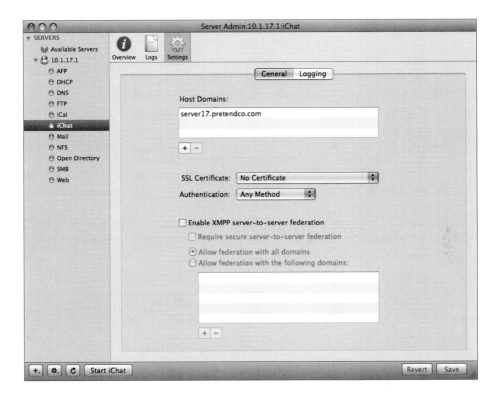

5 Click the Add (+) button under the Host Domains. You can add any other domains that your Mac OS X Server hosts.

You can also secure the text, audio, and video of all chat participants by using a secure certificate. As with the Mail, Web, iCal, Open Directory, RADIUS, and VPN services, the iChat service can use Mac OS X Server's Default certificate (or any certificate you create or purchase) to encrypt data pertaining to the service between the client and the server.

6 Choose No Certificate from the SSL Certificate pop-up menu.

7 Choose Any Method from the Authentication pop-up menu. By designating Any Method, when users join the iChat service, Kerberos will be tried first, then Digest. You can also specify that just Kerberos or Digest authentication will be used.

8 Start iChat by clicking the Start iChat button in the lower left of Server Admin.

Configuring iChat Service Users

After the iChat service has been set up, you can permit users to join the iChat service (called Jabber in the interface). The iChat service user's name is their short name followed by their domain. For example, the user erika would set up her iChat application as erika@server17.pretendco.com.

To enable an iChat account to use the iChat (Jabber) service:

1 On your Mac OS X computer, select the iChat icon in your Dock and click past the introduction screen.

2 Choose Jabber Account from the Account Type pop-up menu. Enter the name of one of your *users*@server17.pretendco.com and his or her password.

3 Click Continue, and then click the Done button.

iChat will open, and you will see your iChat (Jabber) service buddy list.

You can add buddies (other users with whom you wish to chat and have their names appear in a list so you can frequently open a chat with them) to your buddy list as you normally would when using iChat for any other account. You can optionally add a buddy who exists in your Open Directory database. Be sure to include the full name when adding an iChat (Jabber) service buddy.

Once you add a buddy, that person receives a notice when he or she logs in to iChat (Jabber) asking if he or she would like to be added to your buddy list.

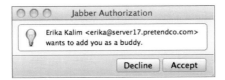

Once you have authorized the listing of your name in that person's buddy list, he or she will see you every time you log in to the iChat (Jabber) service.

You can of course communicate back and forth using iChat.

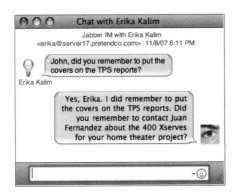

Managing iChat Service Logs

The iChat service can be used for all sorts of purposes, among them group chatting related to projects. Often, a member of the group may wish to review the chat logs of a conversation, perhaps to follow up or for notes relating to future meetings.

The iChat service can log all chat messages and save them in a directory of your choosing. The default directory is located in /var/jabberd/message_archives/.

To enable iChat service logging and to change the location of those logs:

1   Select iChat in the services listed under your server on the left side of Server Admin.

2   Click the Settings button in the toolbar and click the Logging tab.

3   Select "Automatically save chat messages."

4   You can also change the location of the log by clicking the Choose button next to the log path.

5   Enter 7 as the number of days designating the frequency for archiving logs.

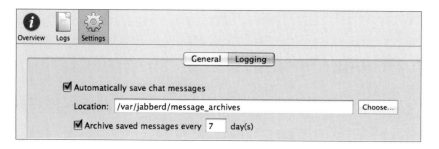

6   Click Save. You are then asked if you want to restart the iChat service. Click the Restart button.

7   You can now log back in to the iChat (Jabber) service with your Mac OS X computer and relay messages, knowing they will be logged.

To view any logged messages, you must be the root user and navigate to /var/jabberd/ message_archives. You can then use any text editor to view the log files and search them for relevant keywords.

Restricting iChat Service Users

You can also restrict who is permitted to use the iChat service by using service access controls. Like many other services discussed in this book, you restrict user and/or group access for various services.

To restrict users or groups from chatting with others on the iChat service:

1   Open Server Admin and select your server in the list of servers on the left.

2   Click the Settings button in the toolbar, click the Access tab, and select the Services tab.

3   Select the "For services selected below" option and select the iChat service.

4   Select "Allow only user and groups below."

5   Click the Settings button in the toolbar, click the Access tab, and select the Services tab.

6   Click the Add (+) button and drag over any users or groups you want to use the iChat service, then click Save.

Using iChat Federation to Join Services

Your organization may have more than one Mac OS X Server. If both of those servers use the iChat service, it is possible to join them together, allowing users and groups in both Open Directory Masters to engage each other in instant messaging. The process of joining different iChat service servers together is called federation. Federation not only allows two Mac OS X Servers running iChat services to join, it also allows any other XMPP chat service to join as well, such as GoogleTalk.

To enable the iChat service federation feature:

1   Select iChat in the services listed under your server on the left side of Server Admin.

2   Click the Settings button in the toolbar and click the General tab.

3   Select the "Enable XMPP server-to-server federation" checkbox and click Save.

4   Restart the service when prompted.

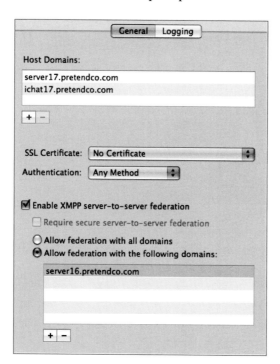

NOTE ▶ You can enable secure encryption for the federation if you are already using an SSL certificate. This forces all communications between the servers to be encrypted, similar to the way the communication between iChat and the iChat server are encrypted when using that certificate. For archiving purposes, messages are always decrypted on the server.

By default, you allow federation with any other iChat service running on any other Mac OS X Server. However, you can restrict the iChat service federation to approved iChat servers only. To do so, select the "Allow federation with the following domains" option and click the Add (+) button to add only those domains that you want to participate within the federation.

Viewing iChat Service Logs

As an administrator, you have access to various iChat service log files. These files permit you to see who is currently logged in to the iChat service, any errors that may occur, and the ports used during an iChat session. These parameters are logged into the iChat Service log, which can be accessed by choosing that log file from the pop-up menu under the Logs button in the toolbar after selecting the iChat service in the services list of Server Admin. Once there, simply type *session started* in the search box and you will see all users, dates, and times that sessions have begun.

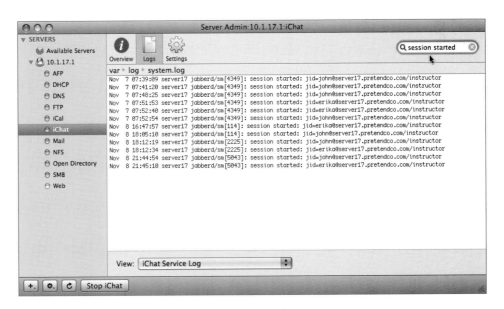

The iChat service log can also log any errors that may occur, and those can be searched for using the Search bar in the toolbar and located in a fashion similar to that of locating users who have started an iChat session. Typical troubleshooting involves ensuring valid DNS entries, network configuration, Network Address Translation (if the servers are on NAT'd networks), and Firewall configuration.

What You've Learned

▶   The iCal service is based on CalDAV, an open-source initiative.

▶   The iChat service uses the XMPP protocol and is also based on an open-source initiative, in this case Jabber.

▶   Setting up a Wiki service involves running the Web service with at least one web server running on Mac OS X Server.

▶   Workgroup Manager is used to allow users to manage events on their iCal service accounts.

▶   iChat service servers can be joined together in a process called federation.

▶   A Wiki can contain files, graphics, text, and links.

References

The following documents provide more information about installing Mac OS X Server. (All of these and more are available at http://www.apple.com/server/macosx/resources/.)

Administration Guides

Web Technologies Administration
(http://images.apple.com/server/macosx/docs/Web_Technologies_Admin_v10.5.pdf)

User Management
(http://images.apple.com/server/macosx/docs/User_Management_v10.5.mnl.pdf)

iCal Service
(http://images.apple.com/server/macosx/docs/iCal_Service_Admin_v10.5.pdf)

iChat Service
(http://images.apple.com/server/macosx/docs/iChat_Service_Admin_v10.5.pdf)

URLs

Jabber site: http://www.jabber.org

CalConnect site: http://www.calconnect.org

Wiki site: http://www.wiki.org

Review Quiz

1. What protocol is used for the iChat service?

2. How would you enable a Wiki on Mac OS X Server?

3. Can you enable users, groups, or both to create events in a calendar using the iCal Service, and if so, where are those options located?

4. How would you enter the iChat name for the user Holly Gleason (short name holly) on server17.pretendco.com?

5. What application do you use to create resources and locations for use in iCal events?

Answers

1. The iChat service uses Extensible Messaging and Presence Protocol (XMPP).

2. The following steps are executed to enable a Wiki:

    1. Authenticate to Server Admin.

    2. Enable the Web Service.

    3. Select the Sites button.

    4. Select the appropriate web site.

    5. Click the Web Services tab.

    6. Enable Wiki and blog under the Services for Groups pane.

3. Using Workgroup Manager, you can enable calendaring for users under their name by selecting the Advanced tab and enabling that option. You enable the calendaring for groups by clicking the Group button, selecting the group, and enabling the calendar under the Basic tab.

4. The iChat name format for Holly Gleason on server17.pretendco.com is holly@server17.pretendco.com.

5. The Directory application, located in the /Applications/Utilities folder, is used to create resources and locations for use in iCal events.

9

Lesson Files	Mac OS X Install DVD
Time	This lesson takes approximately 6 hours to complete.
Goals	Learn the advantages of Apple's network-based deployment solutions
	Create NetBoot and Network Install images
	Configure the server to allow NetBoot and Network Install
	Boot from a NetBoot image

Implementing Deployment Solutions

Knowing how to use time efficiently is a very important aspect of an administrator's job. When managing several hundred Mac OS X computers, an administrator needs a solution that is both speedy and flexible for performing day-to-day management of computers. When computers need to be set up for the very first time, what software should be installed? Should they have the latest software updates? Should they have a full complement of non-Apple software, such as Adobe Creative Suite or Microsoft Office? What about shareware programs and the necessary work-related files? Safety videos? Mandatory PDFs?

Before you can push out data to a computer, you must decide *how* to push out that data and in what state. Apple has several applications to assist you with this process, and there are several third-party tools that also complete the tasks of image creation and deployment. Apple has several applications—including System Image Utility, Apple System Restore (ASR), Apple Remote Desktop (ARD), and NetBoot—to help you with this process.

There are also some third-party tools that perform image-creation and deployment tasks. These include:

▶   Carbon Copy Cloner (Mike Bombich Software)

▶   NetRestore (Mike Bombich Software)

▶   Radmind (University of Michigan)

With the advantage of these and other deployment software tools, you can build an automated system that needs very little user interaction to function. This lesson will focus primarily on the NetBoot service provided by Mac OS X Server.

Creating NetBoot images can be a lengthy process, but most of it is just waiting for the image to be processed. Because this lesson includes creation of two images, you may wish to split this lesson over a couple days or over a dinner break at either of the two image creation steps.

Deployment Issues

One significant challenge for Mac OS X administrators today is the deployment of software to multiple computers. Whether it is operating system (OS) releases and updates or commercial applications, installing the software manually is a labor-intensive process. Mac OS X Server provides services and technologies to aid in this deployment. NetBoot and Network Install simplify OS rollout and upgrades.

Managing Computers with NetBoot

Think about the ways you boot your computer. Most often, your computer starts up from system software located on the local hard drive. This local startup provides you with a typical computer experience of running applications, accessing information, and accomplishing tasks. Sometimes when you perform OS installations or system upgrades, you need to boot from a CD-ROM or DVD-ROM disc.

Managing a single standalone computer isn't much of an inconvenience. However, imagine managing a lab of computers. Every time you need to upgrade the operating system or install a clean version of Mac OS X, you would need to boot each computer in the lab from the installation CD or DVD disc. Even with a set of installation discs for each computer, it would still be time-consuming to update or refresh the entire lab.

Mac OS X Server provides a service called NetBoot, which simplifies the management of operating systems on multiple computers. With NetBoot, client computers start up using system software that they access from a server instead of from the client's local hard drive. With NetBoot, the client obtains information from a remote location. With other startup methods, the client is booting off a local source, such as the internal hard drive, DVD, or other device.

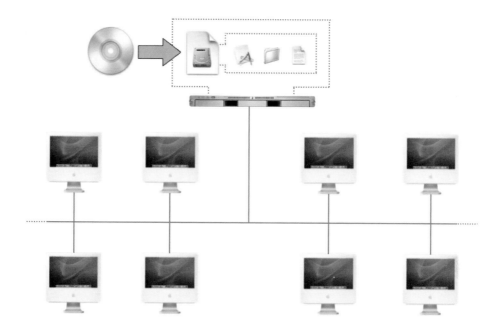

NetBoot is most effective in situations where there is a high frequency of user turnover and where a large number of computers are being deployed with a common configuration. The ability to deploy standard configurations across multiple computers makes NetBoot ideal for computing environments such as:

▶ Classrooms and computer labs: NetBoot makes it easy to configure multiple identical desktop systems and repurpose them quickly. With NetBoot, you can reconfigure systems for a different class simply by restarting from a different image.

▶ Corporate workstations: Using NetBoot to install system software allows you to reimage, deploy, and update workstations very quickly by not having to use a DVD to load each workstation individually. Also, because installation is done over the network, it can even be done in place at the user's desk. A creative way to take advantage of this technology is to create a NetBoot image with various computer diagnosis and disk recovery software. NetBooting into such a rescue image at a user's desk could save a lot of time for a frustrated user.

▶   Kiosks and libraries: With NetBoot, you can set up protected computing environments for customers or visitors. For example, you can configure an information station with an Internet browser that connects only to your company's website, or set up a visitor kiosk that runs only a database for collecting feedback. If a system is altered, a simple restart restores it to its original condition.

▶   Computational clusters: NetBoot is a powerful solution for data centers and computational clusters with identically configured web or application servers. Similarly purposed systems can boot from a single NetBoot image maintained on a network-based storage device.

The requirements for NetBoot to function vary slightly. To boot Mac OS X using NetBoot or to use Network Install, the client computer must have a minimum of 512 MB of RAM and 100Base-T Ethernet or faster network connections. For NetBoot deployments of 10 to 50 clients, a 100Base-T switched network is required. Gigabit Ethernet is required for booting more than 50 clients (although Apple has no official test results for configurations beyond 50 clients). Apple does not support the use of AirPort wireless technology with NetBoot clients.

Understanding NetBoot Startup Types

There are two types of NetBoot startup:

▶   A standard NetBoot startup (using a NetBoot boot image) provides a fairly typical computing experience, because clients start up using software that they access from a server.

▶   A Network Install startup sequence (using a NetBoot Install image) enables you to quickly perform fresh installations of your operating system (much like installing from a DVD-ROM), install applications or updates, or install-configured disk images.

Keep these two types of NetBoot startup in mind while you work through the remainder of this lesson.

With NetBoot, you create disk images on the server that contain Mac OS X or Mac OS X Server system software. Multiple network clients can use each disk image at once. Because you are setting up a centralized source of system software, you need to configure, test, and deploy only once. This dramatically reduces the maintenance required for network computers.

When you start up from a NetBoot image, the startup volume is read-only. When a client needs to write anything back to its startup volume, NetBoot automatically redirects the written data to the client's shadow files (which are discussed later in this lesson, in the section "Understanding Shadow Files"). Data in shadow files is kept for the duration of a NetBoot session. Because the startup volume is read-only, you always start from a clean image. This is ideal in lab and kiosk situations where you want to ensure that users never alter the startup volume.

Stepping Through the NetBoot Client Startup Process

When a client computer boots from a NetBoot image, it performs a number of steps to start up successfully:

1   The client places a request for an IP address.

    When a NetBoot client is turned on or restarted, it requests an IP address from a DHCP server. While the server providing the address can be the same server providing the NetBoot service, the two services do not have to be provided by the same computer.

2   After receiving an IP address, the NetBoot client sends out a request for startup software. The NetBoot server then delivers the boot ROM (read-only memory) file ("booter") to the client using Trivial File Transfer Protocol (TFTP) via its default port, 69.

3   Once the client has the ROM file, it initiates a mount and loads the images for the NetBoot network disk image.

    The images can be served using Hypertext Transfer Protocol (HTTP) or network file system (NFS).

4   After booting from the NetBoot image, the NetBoot client requests an IP address from the DHCP server.

    Depending on the type of DHCP server used, the NetBoot client might receive an IP address different from the one received in step 1.

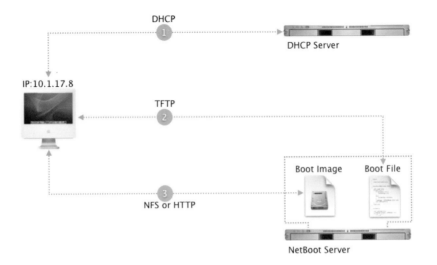

NOTE ▶ Previous versions of NetBoot server that used AFP to deliver network disk images could potentially run into AFP license restrictions. If you purchased the 10-client version of Mac OS X Server, your AFP license restricted you to supporting no more than 10 AFP clients. This would not affect your Mac OS X NetBoot clients, because they use NFS or HTTP and are unrestricted even with the 10-client version of Mac OS X Server.

Using Home Folders with NetBoot

When you restart a client computer from a NetBoot image, the client computer receives a fresh copy of the system software and the startup volume. Users cannot store documents or preserve preferences on this startup volume because it is a read-only image. If the administrator denies access to the local hard drive or removes the hard drive, users might not have any place to store documents. However, if users log in using a network user account, they can store documents and preserve preferences in their network home folders.

When a user logs in to a NetBoot client computer using a network user account, the client computer retrieves his or her home folder from a share point. Typically, this share point resides on a server other than the NetBoot server, although with a small number of clients, one could perform both duties from the same server.

TIP ▶ NetBoot service places high demands on a server. To prevent performance degradation, store home folders on a different server.

Creating Images with System Image Utility

System Image Utility is the tool you use to create Mac OS X NetBoot and Network Install images. It replaces the Network Image Utility of previous releases. Located in the /Applications/Server folder on your Mac OS X Server computer, System Image Utility uses files on a Mac OS X Install DVD, mounted volume, or disk image to create a NetBoot image.

Each image requires an image ID, or index, which client computers use to identify similar images. When a client lists the available NetBoot images in the Startup Disk pane of System Preferences, and if two images have the same index, the client assumes that the images are identical, so it displays only one entry. If only one server will serve an image, assign it a value between 1 and 4095. If multiple servers will serve the same image, assign it a value between 4096 and 65535. In the System Image Utility that comes with Mac OS X Server v10.5, the index is chosen automatically for you unless you customize the install.

When creating an image, you also specify where to store it. For the NetBoot service to recognize the image, it must be stored in /Library/NetBoot/NetBootSP*n*/*imagename.nbi*, where *n* is the volume number and *imagename* is the image name you entered when you created the image. If you have already configured the NetBoot service, the Save dialog includes a pop-up menu listing the available volumes. If you choose a volume from that pop-up menu, the save location changes to the NetBootSP*n* share point on that volume.

> **TIP** In a NetBoot environment, several clients booting from the same NetBoot server can place high demands on the server and slow down performance. To improve performance, you can set up additional NetBoot servers to serve the same images.

System Image Utility also enables you to customize your NetBoot or Network Install configurations by instituting the following:

▶ Add Packages and Post-Install Scripts, which allows you to add third-party software, or make virtually any customization you desire automatically.

▶ Add User Account will include additional users in your image. These users could include accounts such as system administrator accounts or teacher accounts.

▶ Using the Apply System Configuration Settings option, you can automatically bind computers to LDAP Directory servers, along with applying basic preferences such as the computer's host name.

▶ Automated Installation can assist in doing speedy deployments where you're dealing with identical configurations and want to do hands-off installations.

▶ Boot Camp support is built in to System Image Utility so you can add a Boot Camp partition automatically in your deployments.

System Image Utility contains a feature called Filter Computer Models that enables you to determine which system the image will boot. You can specify which model of hardware will be booted off which image. For example, if you wanted to configure a portable or desktop image, you could choose those models from a list for each image.

Creating NetBoot Image Types

With System Image Utility, you can create two distinct types of NetBoot images:

▶ A *boot image* is a file that looks and acts like a mountable disk or volume. NetBoot boot images contain the system software needed to act as a startup disk for client computers on the network. When creating a boot image, you can specify a default user account that the client can use to access the network disk image. You must specify a user name, short name, and password.

▶ An *install image* is a special boot image that boots the client long enough to install software from the image, after which the client can boot from its own hard drive. Just as a boot image replaces the role of a hard drive, an install image is a replacement for an installation DVD.

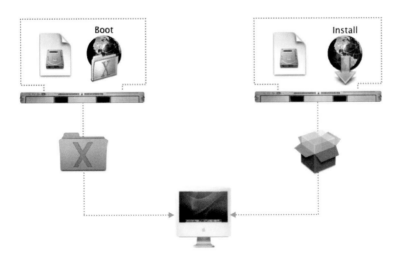

NOTE ► There is no real difference between the NetBoot and Network Install processes: A boot image starts up and runs either the Finder or the Installer. The distinction is how the image file is tagged. The tag allows the user to visually differentiate between image file types in utilities such as Startup Disk in System Preferences.

Using Network Install

Like a bootable DVD-ROM, Network Install is a convenient way to reinstall the OS, applications, or other software onto local hard drives. For system administrators deploying large numbers of computers with the same version of Mac OS X, Network Install can prove very useful. Network Install does not require the insertion of a DVD-ROM into each NetBoot client, because all startup and installation information is delivered over the network. You can perform software installations with Network Install using a collection of packages or an entire disk image (depending on the source used to create the image).

TIP ► For installing small packages and not entire disks, using ARD to install the packages might be easier because not all packages require a restart. If NetInstall is chosen to deploy a package, the client system has already been restarted once to actually boot off the NetBoot server.

While creating an install image with System Image Utility, you have the option to automate the installation process to limit the amount of interaction from anyone at the client computer. Keep in mind that responsibility comes with this automation. Because an automatic network installation can be configured to erase the contents of the local hard drive before installation, data loss can occur. You must control access to this type of Network Install disk image and must communicate to those using these images the implications of using them. Always instruct users to back up critical data before using automatic network installations. When configuring your NetBoot server, you will be warned about this even if you aren't doing automated installs.

NOTE ► Set the default NetBoot image on every server. Images that normal users can select should probably be NetBoot images, not Network Install images.

Creating NetBoot Images

When creating NetBoot images, specify a source for the image in System Image Utility. System Image Utility can only build images of Mac OS X v10.5. If you wish to make images of earlier Mac OS X versions, you should use the respective version of Mac OS X Server to build the image. You can create images using installation DVDs, hard drives, or disk images as sources:

▶   DVDs: You can use System Image Utility to build a new NetBoot image from a Mac OS X Install DVD. Startup images created using installation discs contain a "clean" version of the operating system and require minimal configuration. Install images created using the install disc replicate the experience of starting from the install disc to install the OS.

▶   Mounted volumes: When a mounted volume is selected as a source, the entire contents of the volume—including the operating system, configuration files, and applications—are copied to the image. When a client computer starts up from an image created from a mounted volume, the boot experience is similar to that of starting up from the original source volume. When a client computer starts up from an install image created from a mounted volume, a copy of the source volume is written to the client computer's disk drive. A benefit of using volumes for image sources is that the image creation is much faster than when using discs. In addition, installations that use images created from volumes are faster than installations that use disc-created images.

▶   Disk images: Instead of using a configured hard drive as a source, you can use Disk Utility to create a disk image of a configured hard drive, and then use the disk image as a source for creating NetBoot images.

When creating the images, you have the option of adding additional software to the image. For example, you may need to include an update to the operating system with an image created from the installation discs. You specify additional software to be installed, in the form of an installer package, in the Other Items field.

TIP ▶ Use the latest version of the operating system when creating NetBoot images to ensure backward compatibility.

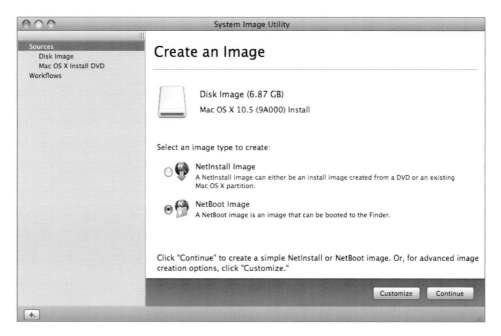

When adding new computers to the NetBoot environment, you may need to update the NetBoot image to support them. Check the OS software version that accompanied the new computer.

To create a Network Install image from a Mac OS X Install DVD, follow these steps:

1 Insert the Mac OS X Install DVD in your Mac OS X computer.

   You could also create your image on your server, but we'll perform these steps from your client machine instead.

2 Launch /Applications/Server/System Image Utility.

3 In the Sources list on the left, select Mac OS X Install DVD.

4 Select the NetInstall Image radio button.

5 Click Continue.

6 Change the Image Name to *My Install.*

7 Change the Description to *This is the network install image created for lesson 9.*

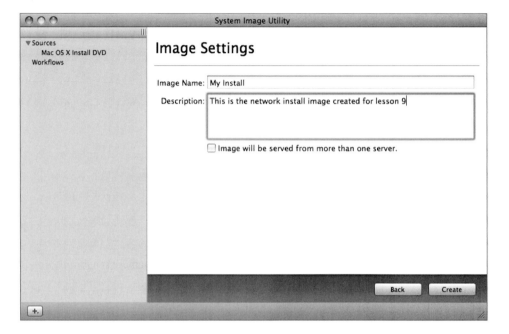

8 Click Create.

9 Agree to the software license agreement.

10 When prompted where to save the image, select your Desktop and click Save.

Creating an image can take from 15 minutes to a few hours depending on the size of the source image and the speed of the computer you're creating the image on. In the meantime, we'll continue by configuring your server.

Specifying a Default Image and Protocol

The NetBoot service is configured in Server Admin. Within Server Admin, the Images pane lists the available NetBoot images on the server, which can host up to 25 different disk images. Each image can be enabled, allowing client computers to use the image to boot, or each image can be disabled, preventing client computers from accessing the image. While you can have several images, you must specify one of the NetBoot images as the default image. When you press the N key on a client computer at startup, and the client has never started up from that NetBoot server before, the server will provide the default image to start up the client.

For each image, you can also specify which protocol, NFS or HTTP, is used to serve the image. NFS continues to be the default and the preferred method. HTTP is an alternative that enables you to serve disk images without having to reconfigure your firewall to allow NFS traffic.

> **TIP** ▶ Remember that image files can be very large and can take up a large amount of disk space on the server.

Understanding Shadow Files

Many clients can read from the same NetBoot image, but when a client needs to write any-thing (such as print jobs and other temporary files) back to its startup volume, NetBoot auto-matically redirects the written data to the client's *shadow files*, which are separate from regular system and application software files. These shadow files preserve the unique identity of each client during the entire time the client is running off a NetBoot image. NetBoot also trans-parently maintains changed user data in the shadow files, while reading unchanged data from the shared system image. The shadow files are recreated at boot time, so any changes that the user makes to the startup volume are lost at restart.

This behavior has important implications. For example, if a user saves a document to the startup volume, after a restart that document is gone. This preserves the condition of the environment the administrator set up, but it also means that you should give users accounts on a network server if you want them to be able to save their documents.

For each image, you can specify where the shadow file is stored using the Diskless check-box in the NetBoot image configuration in Server Admin. When the Diskless option for an image is disabled, the shadow file is stored on the client computer's local hard drive at /private/var/netboot/.com.apple.NetBootX/Shadow. When the Diskless option is enabled, the shadow file is stored in a share point on the server named NetBootClients*n* in /Library/ NetBoot, where *n* is the number of the client using the shadow file. With the Diskless option enabled, NetBoot enables you to operate client computers that are literally diskless.

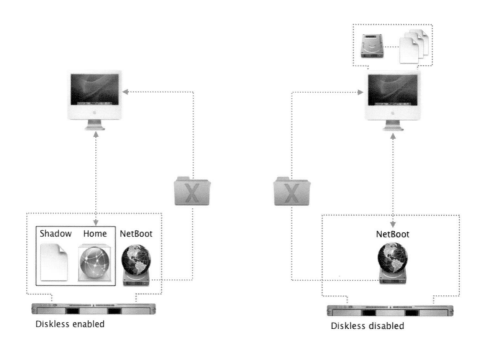

Diskless enabled   Diskless disabled

TIP ▶ Make sure you consider the storage need for shadow files when configuring your server. When running diskless, users may experience delays, since writes to the shadow files take place via the network and not locally.

Configuring a NetBoot Server

We need to configure your server to offer NetBoot images to your client computers. This, like many other services, is done through Server Admin.

1 Open /Applications/Server/Server Admin and connect to your server.

2 Select the NetBoot service in the left column.

   If the NetBoot service isn't visible, add it by choosing the Add Service option from the Add (+) button in the lower-left corner of Server Admin.

3 Click the Settings button in the toolbar.

4 In the General pane, enable the Ethernet port.

5 Select your server's hard drive to serve both Images and Client Data.

6 Click Save.

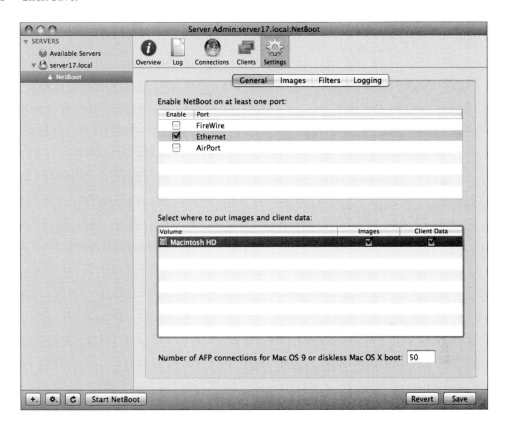

Verifying the Share Points

Your NetBoot service is now partially configured. The action of selecting a hard drive to serve the images from should have automatically configured two share points for you. You should verify this now.

1 Select your server name in the left column of Server Admin.

2 Click the File Sharing button in the toolbar.

3 Click the Share Points button just below the toolbar.

You should notice the addition of two share points, NetBootClients0 and NetBootSP0. These share points are used for the shadow files and NetBoot images, respectively. However, only the NetBootClients0 share is available over AFP by default. Additionally, this process does not start the file-sharing services, so you should do that now.

4   Select the NetBootSP0 share.

5   Select the Share Point tab in the bottom half of Server Admin.

6   Click the Protocol Options button.

7   Click the checkbox to "Share this item using AFP." Click OK, then click Save.

8   Select the AFP service in the left column.

   If the AFP service isn't visible, add it by choosing the Add Service option from the Add (+) button in the lower-left corner of Server Admin.

9   Click the Start AFP button in the lower-left corner of Server Admin.

Configuring NetBoot to Serve an Image

Before we can start the NetBoot service, it has to have an image it can serve, and be configured to use it.

1   From your Mac OS X computer, connect to the NetBootSP0 share of your server using AFP.

2   After the image is created, copy your My Install NetBoot image (NBI) to the NetBootSP0 share. Do so by dragging the entire My Install.nbi folder to the NetBootSP0 folder.

3   After it has copied over, return to Server Admin.

4   Select the NetBoot service in the left column.

5   Click the Settings button in the toolbar.

6   Click the Images tab.

You should see your My Install image listed. Note when you select it that it was assigned an image ID index, and that the description you typed when creating the image is visible in the bottom pane. This is the only place where the description is shown, and it can be useful to describe certain aspects of the image. Users will not see this description.

7 Enable the image by selecting the Enable and Default checkboxes.

8 Click Save.

9 Click the Start NetBoot button.

The NFS service will start automatically if it isn't already running. You may have to wait a few seconds and click the Refresh button to see this.

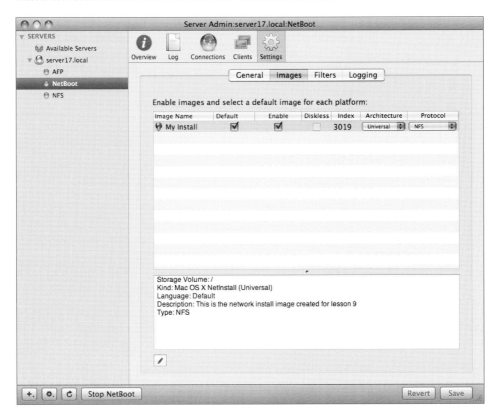

Configuring a NetBoot Client

As long as your client computer has the latest version of its firmware and is a supported client computer, you don't need to install any other special software. The Extensible Firmware Interface (EFI) (Intel) or Open Firmware (PowerPC) boot code contains the software used to boot a computer using a NetBoot image.

There are three ways to cause a computer to use NetBoot at startup:

▶ Press the N key on the keyboard until the blinking NetBoot globe appears in the center of the screen. This method allows you to use NetBoot for a single startup. Subsequent reboots return the computer to the previous startup state. Your client machine will then boot from the default NetBoot image hosted by the NetBoot server.

▶ Select the desired network disk image from the Startup Disk pane in System Preferences. The version of the Startup Disk pane included with Mac OS X v10.2 and later presents all available network disk images on the local network. Notice that NetBoot and Network Install disk images maintain unique icons to help users differentiate between the two types of images. With the desired network disk image selected, you can reboot the computer. The computer then attempts to use NetBoot on every subsequent startup.

▶ Hold down the Option key on the keyboard during startup. This invokes the Startup Manager, which presents an iconic list of available system folders as well as a globe icon for NetBoot. Click the globe icon and click the advance arrow to begin the NetBoot process. This option doesn't allow you to pick which image you want to boot from. Like holding down the N key, you will get the default image.

It is important to note a couple of things that can upset the NetBoot process:

▶ If no network connection exists, a NetBoot client will eventually time out and look to a local drive to start up. You can prevent this by keeping local hard drives free of system software and denying users physical access to the Ethernet ports on a computer.

▶ Zapping the parameter random-access memory (PRAM) resets the configured startup disk, requiring you to reselect the NetBoot volume in the Startup Disk pane of System Preferences.

We'll try NetBooting your client computer now.

1 Shut down your Mac OS X computer.

2 Turn on the computer while holding down the N key on the keyboard until the blinking NetBoot globe appears.

It should boot into the Mac OS X Installer from the NetInstall image you just created and enabled. Because we don't actually want to reinstall your computer, just shut down the computer. We'll be booting the computer into Target Disk Mode in the next section, so just leave it turned off.

Configuring NetBoot Images

The NetInstall image you created is a very basic image used for the same purpose as the Mac OS X installation media. In most NetBoot situations where people are working off the network image, you will probably want to create a customized environment for them. In our example, we'll take the Mac OS X client computer you've been working on, and use that as our template machine for creating a NetBoot image that hundreds of computers could boot and operate from.

1 Hold the T key on your client computer, and power it on. Release the T key once you see a FireWire logo on the screen.

This boots your client computer into Target Disk Mode, effectively turning the computer into an external FireWire disk enclosure.

2   Plug a FireWire cable between your client and server computers.

You should see your client computer's hard drive appear on your server's desktop.

3   On your server, open System Image Utility.

4   Click the Customize button.

This opens a window containing Automator Library actions related to System Image Utility. This is a new feature with Mac OS X Server v10.5 in that you can create complex workflows for creating NetBoot images, and save them for later repeated use if desired.

5   In the Define Image Source action that should already be in the window, select NetBoot, with the Source being your client computer's hard drive.

6   Drag the Add User Account action to the workflow.

7   Configure the Add User Account action as follows:

  ▶ Name: *NetBoot Admin*

  ▶ Short Name: *nbadmin*

  ▶ Password: *appleNB*

  ▶ Allow user to administer this computer.

  If desired, you could add additional local accounts by adding more Add User Account actions to the workflow.

8   Drag the Apply System Configuration setting action item to the workflow and configure it as follows:

  ▶ Generate unique Computer Names starting with *Lesson9*.

  ▶ Change ByHost preferences to match client after install.

  This last setting may or may not be desired in your environment. Certain settings are saved in preference list (plist) files that include the MAC (Media Access Control) address of your computer in the filename. If you'd like those files to be renamed to the MAC address of the target machine, you should use this option.

9   Drag the Create Image action to the bottom of the workflow and configure it as follows:

  ▶ In: NetBootSP0. Because we're on the server and it already knows we're running NetBoot, it allows you to save the image directly in the correct location, /Library/NetBoot/NetBootSP0.

  ▶ Named: *The Boot*

  ▶ Volume Name: *The Boot*

  ▶ Description: *This is the boot image made from a target mode computer.*

  ▶ Index: Pick a number below 4095 that is different from the index of your first image.

10   Click Run.

  If you'd like to see more information about what is happening, you can choose View > Show Log.

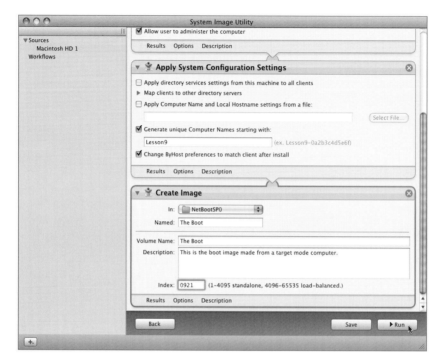

After the image is created, you must enable it. We'll do that in the next section.

Filtering NetBoot Clients

The NetBoot Filters pane permits you to allow or deny access to NetBoot services based on the client computer's hardware, or MAC, address. Once you enter a list of hardware addresses, you can either limit NetBoot access to just the listed computers or prevent the listed computers from using NetBoot (and allow all others to use it). This allows NetBoot and non-NetBoot clients to coexist in harmony. Filtering removes the risk of allowing non-NetBoot clients to access unlicensed applications or to accidentally perform a network installation. By maintaining accurate Filters settings, you can seamlessly integrate NetBoot into traditional network configurations.

NetBoot access is controlled through a list of hardware addresses. If you know a computer's hardware address, you can click the Add Hardware Address (+) button and type it in. Alternatively, if you enter a computer's DNS name in the Host Name field and click the Find button, Server Admin retrieves the hardware address, which you can add by clicking the Add (+) button next to the Hardware Address field.

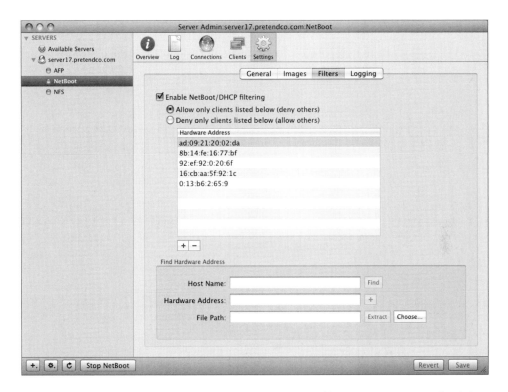

New in Mac OS X Server v10.5 is the ability to set NetBoot filters on a per-image basis in addition to the per-server filters. This could be particularly useful if you have one server for multiple Mac classrooms. Each classroom could be configured with its own NetBoot image, and use per-image filters to limit which classrooms can access which image.

We'll now try out the new image we just created.

1   Open Server Admin on your Server computer.

2   Click the checkbox to enable your new The Boot image.

3   Click the checkbox to make The Boot the default image.

   This determines which image a machine boots from when it is booted while holding the N key.

4   For the Protocol menu, leave it set to NFS.

HTTP is also an option here if your security policies prohibit the use of NFS.

5   Click the Edit Image (pencil) icon at the bottom of the Images pane.

This pane allows you to perform per-image filters based on hardware type and/or specific Ethernet hardware addresses. It's important to differentiate between the per-image filters and the NetBoot servicewide filters.

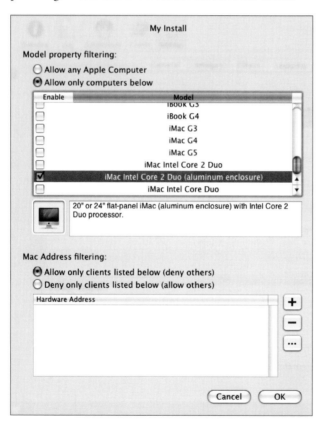

6   Select "Allow only clients listed below," and select your client computer hardware type in the list.

7 Click OK to dismiss the Edit Image dialog.

8 Click Save.

9 Drag your client computer's drive icon to the Trash to eject it from your server.

10 Turn off your client computer and remove the FireWire cable attaching it to your server.

11 Boot your client computer normally and log in.

12 Open System Preferences.

13 Click Startup Disk.

14 Select The Boot.

15 Restart your client computer.

It should boot from the NetBoot image you just created. Try logging in using the nbadmin account you specified when creating the image.

Monitoring NetBoot Clients

You can monitor NetBoot usage with Server Admin. The NetBoot Clients pane provides a list of client computers that have booted from the server. Note that this is a cumulative list—a list of all clients that have connected to the server—not a list of currently connected computers only. By selecting a given computer in the list, you can also see additional information about that client, such as its system type, client name, the name and index of the NetBoot image it booted from, and the last time it booted.

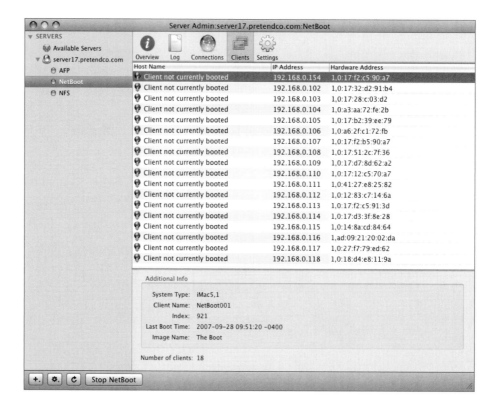

Additionally, the NetBoot logs can be useful when monitoring the progress of a NetBoot in action. You can access your NetBoot server logs using these steps:

1 Open Server Admin and connect to your server.

2 Select the NetBoot service on the left.

3 Click the Log button in the toolbar.

Troubleshooting NetBoot

NetBoot is a fairly straightforward process. If a client does not successfully start up from a NetBoot server, you can troubleshoot the issue by looking into the following areas:

▶ Check the network. The client needs an IP address obtained through DHCP.

▶ The underlying process that serves NetBoot is bootpd, so you can check the server logs for bootpd messages. These logs can also identify if you mistyped an Ethernet hardware address or selected the wrong type of hardware for a filter.

▶ Press and hold the Option key as you boot the client, which will indicate if you have a firmware password configured for the computer.

▶ Check the disk space on the server. Shadow files and disk images may be filling the server's hard drive disk space. You may want to add bigger hard drives or more of them to accommodate these files.

▶ Check for server filters. Do you have filters enabled for IP address, hardware address, and model type? If you do, you should disable the filters to allow all computers on the network to NetBoot or NetInstall.

▶ Check your server firewall configuration. NetBoot requires that a combination of DHCP/Bootp, TFTP, NFS, AFP, and HTTP ports be open. Temporarily disabling the firewall or adding a rule to allow all traffic from the subnet you're NetBooting will indicate if you have a firewall configuration problem.

What You've Learned

▶ Deployment options are available to keep multiple desktops up-to-date.

▶ NetBoot and Network Install is a server-based method of deploying.

▶ You can create images from optical media, hard drives, or disk images.

▶ You can add servicewide or per-image filters based on hardware type or Ethernet hardware address.

References

The following documents provide more information about installing Mac OS X Server. (All of these and more are available at www.apple.com/server/documentation.)

Administration Guides

Mac OS X Server Getting Started

System Imaging and Software Update Administration

Deploying Mac OS X Computers for K-12 Education

Apple Knowledge Base Documents

You can check for new and updated Knowledge Base documents at www.apple.com/support.

URLs

Mike Bombich, Mac OS X Deployment: www.bombich.com

MacEnterprise: www.macenterprise.org

Review Quiz

1. What are the advantages of using NetBoot?

2. What are three ways to configure the network startup disk?

3. What network protocols are used during the NetBoot startup sequence? What components are delivered over each of these protocols?

4. What is a NetBoot shadow file?

Answers

1. Because NetBoot unifies and centralizes the system software that NetBoot clients use, software configuration and maintenance is reduced to a minimum. A single change to a NetBoot image propagates to all client computers on the next startup. NetBoot also decouples the system software from the computer, decreasing potential time invested in software troubleshooting.

2. A client must have selected a network disk image via the Startup pane within System Preferences, or the user must hold down the N key at startup to boot from the default NetBoot image, or use Remote Desktop Admin.

3. NetBoot makes use of DHCP, TFTP, NFS, and HTTP during the NetBoot client startup sequence. DHCP provides the IP address, TFTP delivers the boot ROM ("booter") file, and NFS or HTTP is used to deliver the network disk image.

4. Because the NetBoot boot image is read-only, anything that the client computer writes to the volume is cached in the shadow file. This allows a user to make changes to the boot volume, including setting preferences and storing files; however, when the computer is restarted, all changes are erased.

10

Time   This lesson takes approximately 4 hours to complete.

Goals   Create and configure home folders for network user accounts

Create and manage access to shared group folders

Manage user, workgroup, and computer preferences

Create mobile accounts and configure Mac OS X Server for
mobile home folders

View and edit an application's preferences

Configure a local Software Update server

Managing Accounts

If you run an organization with several hundred users, how can you make sure they all have the same items in their Dock? Printers? The Finder interface? In previous lessons, you learned management techniques involving the user name, password, and home folder. There are many other aspects to user account management, and it is important to understand how these various aspects interact with each other. When applying other types of management to your user and group accounts, consider that there are also two other types of management—computer and computer group accounts—to add to your options. Careful planning will reveal the best way to implement your management, whether it is based on user accounts, group accounts, computer accounts, computer group accounts, or a combination of all four.

This lesson covers the following areas of account management:

▶ Concepts and tools—Describes account management and its main tool, Workgroup Manager.

▶ User, group, computer, and computer group accounts management—Describes how to use Workgroup Manager to manage users, groups, and computers.

▶ Preference management—Describes how to use Workgroup Manager to customize and control the Mac OS X user experience.

▶ Software Update server—Describes how to get better network utilization and control over which updates are available to your users.

▶ Mobile accounts and mobile users—Describes challenges and solutions for home folders of users who work at multiple computers and those that aren't always attached to the network.

▶ Troubleshooting preferences—Lists the top issues that cause problems with managed accounts.

Introducing Account Management

Account management encompasses everything from setting up accounts for network access and creating home folders to fine-tuning the user experience by managing preferences and settings for users, groups, and computers. The term "managed client" refers to a user, group, or computer whose access permissions and preferences are under administrative control.

With effective account management, you can:

▶ Provide users with a consistent, controlled interface while allowing them to access their documents from any computer

▶ Control permissions on mobile computers

▶ Restrict certain resources for specific groups or individuals

▶ Secure computer use in key areas such as administrative offices, classrooms, or open labs

▶ Customize the user experience using group folders

▶ Customize Dock settings

▶ Control access to software updates

Workgroup Manager

Workgroup Manager is an account-management tool that, among other capabilities, provides centralized, directory-based management of users, groups, and computers from anywhere on your network. You can create standardized desktop configurations, set system preferences, establish and enforce password policies, and control access to hardware, software, and network resources. Your settings are automatically cached so the preferences and user permissions you've defined remain in effect even when computers are offline. These caches are stored at /Library/Managed Preferences/ on a managed computer.

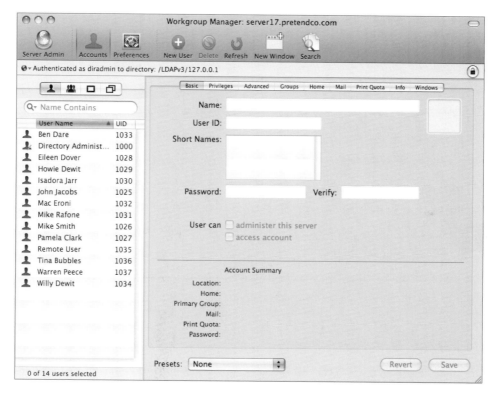

You can also configure systems to open predefined applications, mount resources on the desktop, and provide users with network-based home folders, allowing them to access their own personalized desktop, applications, and files from any computer on the network.

Workgroup Manager stores preferences and policies for users, groups, and computers in an LDAPv3 directory server using Apple's Open Directory architecture. Naturally, you can use the existing hardware and directory domains you already have (such as another server on your network providing user directory information). Based on open standards, Open Directory works with any LDAPv3 server, thereby protecting your investment in standards-based network resources. Also, Open Directory works with other directory technologies such as Microsoft's Active Directory.

Workgroup Manager Inspector

Workgroup Manager is a directory-services editor and the user interface is customized for entering data specific to managing user, group, computer, and preference records. The Workgroup Manager application enters the data into the directory in a known format, and other applications and utilities may also save data in the directory. Applications may also store preference-type XML data, which could be added to the attributes of user records, for example. When you need to dig deeper into the attributes and associated values of those attributes, Workgroup Manager provides the Inspector for viewing and editing this raw data. The Inspector is enabled as a Workgroup Manager preference so that once it's enabled, you can click any specific record and select the Inspector to bring up the XML data stored for that entry.

Basic type casting is handled for you in the editor, and there is minimal error checking at this level. Manual editing using the Inspector is a power-user option. As a read-only tool, the Inspector is a powerful debug tool.

Enable the Inspector now in Workgroup Manager:

1   Launch /Applications/Server/Workgroup Manager and connect to your server.

2   Choose Workgroup Manager > Preferences from the menu bar.

3   Select "Show 'All Records' tab and inspector."

4   Click OK.

   The Inspector is now visible as a new bull's-eye icon above your user list. Click it and explore the contents of various records. User records are shown by default, but others can be viewed using the pop-up menu above the user list. Be sure not to change any values here at this time.

Managing User, Group, Computer, and Computer Group Accounts

Mac OS X saves settings for four different types of accounts:

▶ Users: Usually relates to a specific person. This is the account that the person identifies himself or herself with when logging in to the machine. A user's short name or UID number uniquely identifies the user on a system.

▶ Groups: Represents a group of users, a group of groups, or a mixture of both

▶ Computers: Similar to a user account, it's the singular entity that represents a given piece of hardware. Computer accounts are uniquely identified by their Ethernet ID.

▶ Computer Groups: Represents a group of computers, a group of computer groups, or a mixture of both

When you log in to a Mac OS X system using a local user account, both the user account information and the home folder are stored on that computer. This arrangement is difficult for an administrator to manage, because the user configuration on each computer has to be managed individually and locally. With Workgroup Manager, Mac OS X Server provides two additional types of user accounts with different user configurations:

▶ Network: A Mac OS X Server user account with the following characteristics:

The account information can reside in any Open Directory domain accessible from the Mac OS X Server that needs to use the account. A directory domain can reside on a Mac OS X computer (for example, the LDAP directory of an Open Directory master) or it can reside on a non-Apple server (for example, an LDAP or Active Directory server). The user's home folder can be stored on the same server as the directory domain that contains the user's account, or it can be stored on another file server.

▶ Mobile: A Mac OS X Server user account with the following characteristics:

Two synchronized accounts. The main account resides in a shared directory domain. The second account is a copy of the main account and resides in the local domain of the user's computer. The user's home folder resides locally, on the user's computer, or, in the case of external accounts, on a removable drive.

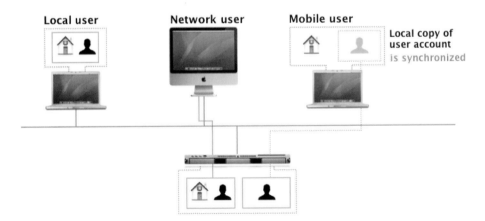

Setting Up a Network Home Folder Review

As discussed in Lesson 5, "Using File Services," you also use Workgroup Manager to set up a network home folder for a network user. The user's home folder can reside in any AFP or NFS share point that the user's computer can access. The share point must be automountable—it must have a network mount record in the directory domain where the user account resides. An automountable share point ensures that the home folder is visible in /Network/Servers automatically when the user logs in to a Mac OS X computer configured to access the shared domain. Apple recommends storing home folders in AFP share points, because AFP provides better security.

> **NOTE ▶** The home folder doesn't need to be stored on the same server as the directory domain containing the user's account. In fact, distributing directory domains and home folders among various servers can help balance the workload among servers.

When a network user logs in to a Mac OS X computer, the computer retrieves the account information from a shared directory domain on the accounts server. The computer uses the location of the user's home folder, stored in the account, to mount the home folder, which resides physically on a home folder server. Conversely, if you don't set up a home folder for a network user account, any changes the user makes to preferences are lost after logging out.

To set up a home folder for a network user in Workgroup Manager:

1   Select the user in the user list.

2   Click Home to set up the selected user's home folder.

3   In the share points list, select the previously set automounted share point you want to use.

   The list displays all the automountable network-visible share points in the search path of the server to which you are connected. If the share point you want to select is not listed, click Refresh. If the share point still does not appear, it might not be automountable. In this case, you need to set up the share point to have a network mount record configured for home folders.

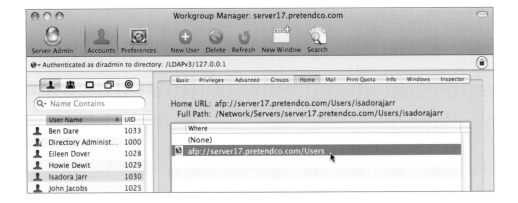

4   Click the Create Home Now button, and then click Save.

If you do not click the Create Home Now button before clicking Save, the home folder is created the next time the user restarts the client computer and logs in remotely. The name of the home folder has the same name as the user's first short name. When having Windows users connect, the home folder should be created in advance of the Windows user's initial log in.

Optionally, you can use the Disk Quota field in the Home pane to limit the disk space a user can consume to store files in the partition where the user's home folder resides.

Setting Home Folders Simultaneously for All Users

Now, you will set and create home folders for all users who do not yet have home folders.

1   On your Mac OS X computer, open Workgroup Manager and authenticate as necessary.

2   Click the Accounts button in the toolbar, and then click the globe icon below the toolbar. Choose /LDAPv3/127.0.0.1 from the pop-up menu.

3   Select all the users and deselect the Directory Administrator account.

4   Click the Home tab.

5   Select the path of afp://server17.pretendco.com/Users.

6   Click the Create Home Now button, and then click Save.

Even if you already have home folders for some of the users, this will not change those settings.

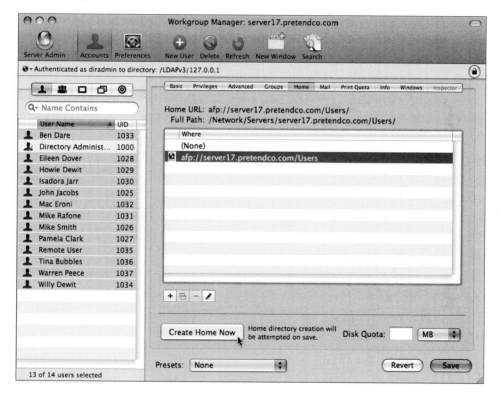

7   On your server, navigate to the /Users folder and verify that all the home folders were created.

8   Verify you have a home folder for Pamela by logging in as Pamela from your Mac OS X computer, then log out and log in as your local administrator.

Managing Preferences for Users in a Workgroup

Although you can set up preferences individually for users with network accounts, it's more efficient to manage preferences for the workgroups to which they belong. Using workgroups allows you to manage users regardless of which computers they use. Using Workgroup Manager, you can provide all users in a workgroup with the same access permissions for media, printers, and volumes.

> **NOTE ▶** It is important to note the difference between a workgroup and a group. A group is a file-system designation. It is used to handle access to the file system (as in owner, group, others). It is specific to the file system, server, or computer. A workgroup is a directory-service record separate from any specific file system or server. It is used as a method of associating similar preferences for sets of user records.

A user can be assigned to one or more workgroups, and during login, the user is presented with a list of the workgroups to which he or she belongs. At login he or she can select which workgroup's settings should preside over that login session. The user then has all the permissions and access privileges assigned to that workgroup.

> **TIP ▶** Administrative users are given an option to disable management. Once selected, this option is hidden but is visible again if the Option key is pressed during login.

Setting Up a Group Folder

You can use Workgroup Manager to set up a group folder for use by members of a particular workgroup. A *group folder* offers a way to organize documents and applications of special interest to group members and gives group members a way to pass information back and forth among them.

To set up a group folder in Workgroup Manager (you will do this in a later exercise):

1 Select the group and click the Group Folder tab.

2 Select a listed share point in which to set up a group folder.

 If the predefined Groups share point or any other existing share point is not listed in the Group Folder pane, create an automount record for it in the File Sharing window in Server Admin.

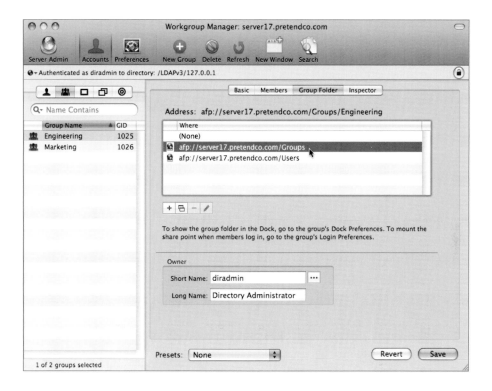

3   In the Short Name field, click the Browse (…) button to select an owner (Directory Administrator) from a list of users in the current directory domain.

A common mistake is to not assign an owner to the folder. This will result in errors. The group folder owner is given read/write access to the group folder.

4   Click Save.

5   Create the group folder using the sudo CreateGroupFolder command in Terminal on the server.

NOTE ▶ You need to run CreateGroupFolder manually on the server containing the groups, because it is not automatically executed.

TIP ▶ There are at least two ways in which you can facilitate a group member's access to the group folder when the user logs in. You can set up Dock preferences to make the group folder visible in the Dock, or you can set up login preferences so that the share point in which the group folder resides appears on the desktop.

Managing Computer Group Accounts

A *computer group account* is a group of computers that have the same preference settings and are available to the same set of users and groups. You create and modify these computer groups in Workgroup Manager. Computer groups that you set up appear in the searchable list on the left side of the window. Computer group settings appear in the List, Access, and Cache panes on the right side of the window.

When you set up a computer group, make sure you have already determined how computers are identified. Use descriptions that are logical and easy to remember (for instance, the description might be the computer name). You must use the built-in Ethernet address for a computer's address information. This information is unique to each computer. The client computer uses this data to find preference information when a user logs in. An easy way to add computers to a group is to use the Browse (…) button. When you select a computer from the browse list, Workgroup Manager automatically enters the computer's Ethernet address and name for you. It is best to use a computer group for resources in a specific area as well as computers of a specific type, such as portables. For example, all kiosk computers might have the same login preferences, or all computers in a lab might have the same default printer preferences. Where preferences are associated with users, workgroups are more efficient.

When a computer starts up, it checks directory services for a computer record that contains its Ethernet address. If it finds one, it checks to see if that computer record is a member of any computer groups, and if so, it uses settings for that computer group. If no record is found, the computer uses settings for the default Guest Computer computer account. You can add up to 2000 computers to a computer group. New in Mac OS X Server v10.5 is the ability to have a computer belong to more than one group. You can even have computer groups that contain other computer groups.

NOTE ▶ Computer groups are not part of any ACLs. They should not be confused with user groups.

TIP ▶ Although you can add different types of computers to computer groups (for example, iMac and MacBook computers), in some cases it is more effective to create homogeneous computer groups (for example, create one list for iMac computers and another for MacBook computers). In this way, you can avoid hardware incompatibilities when you configure computer groups.

Creating a Computer Account

The way to set up a computer account in Workgroup Manager is to follow these generic steps (you'll execute these steps in an exercise later):

1   Click Accounts.

2   Click the globe icon below the toolbar and select the directory domain where you want to store the new account.

3   If the selected directory domain is still locked as shown by the lock icon, click the lock and enter your user name and password.

4   Click the Computer button (the square icon).

5   Choose Server > New Computer or click the New Computer button in the toolbar.

6   Type a computer name in the Name field.

7   Type a short name in the Short Name field.

8   Type a comment and assign keywords if desired.

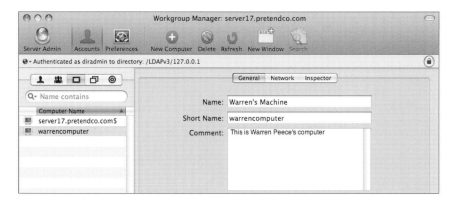

9   Click the Network tab.

10   Type the Ethernet hardware address in the Ethernet ID field.

11   Click Save.

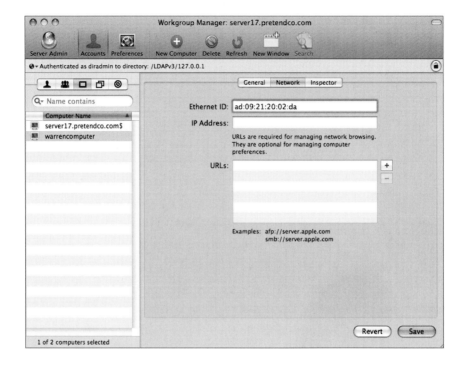

Creating a Computer Group

The generic steps for setting up a computer group account in Workgroup Manager are as follows (you'll execute these steps in an exercise later):

1   Click the Accounts button.

2   Click the globe icon below the toolbar and open the directory domain where you want to store the new account.

3   If necessary, click the lock and enter your user name and password.

4   Click the Computer Group Name button (the multisquare icon).

5   Choose Server > New Computer Group or click the New Computer Group button in the toolbar.

6   Type a group name in the Name field.

A default Group ID and Short Name that is a derivative of the long name will be automatically inserted, but can be changed if desired.

7 Click Save.

Adding Computers to a Computer Group

When adding computers to an existing computer group in Workgroup Manager, follow these steps each time (you'll execute these steps in an exercise later):

1 Select the computer group in the left column to which you want to add computers.

2 Click the Members tab.

3 Click the Add button (+) to add a computer to the list, and drag the desired computer into the Members list.

> If the computer you're looking for is not in the list, you must either add a computer account for it, or you may be able to browse for it by clicking Browse (…). If Workgroup Manager can see the computer in its browse list, you simply need to click the computer to create a computer account for it.

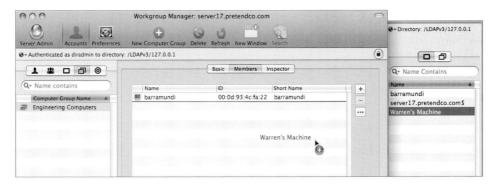

4   Click Save.

> **TIP** ▶ When there are only a few computers to manage, it is useful to enter them into a computer group or groups. In this way, they are accessible via group accounts, user accounts, and computer group accounts. This list is also less likely to change frequently.

Creating a Guest Computer Account

If an unknown computer (one that isn't already defined with a computer account) connects to your network and binds to your Open Directory server, that computer is treated as a guest. Settings chosen for the guest computer account apply to these unknown or guest computers. Using the guest computer's account (or just a single computer group) is not recommended for large numbers of computers. Most of your computers should belong to regular computer groups. This makes managing them easier.

To manage guest computers in Workgroup Manager, choose Server > Create Guest Computer. After the account is created, "guest" appears in the list of computer accounts. Each directory domain can have only one guest computer account. Depending on network organization and setup, you may not be able to create a guest computer account in certain directory domains.

NOTE ▶ You cannot change the Name, Short Name, Ethernet ID, IP Address, or URLs associated with the guest computer account.

Managing Workgroups and Computer Accounts

Once you have computers assigned to your computer groups, you can limit which workgroups can access computers in each of the computer groups. Different sets of users may access the same sets of computers (for example, different shifts in a workplace or different classes in a computer lab, or any time you have multiple-use computers).

In the following figure, only members of the Marketing and WidgetMaster 3000 groups can access computers in the Marketing Computers list, which have sensitive information and special applications that no one else should have access to.

Similarly, only members of the WidgetMaster 3000 and Engineering groups can access computers in the Engineering Computers list.

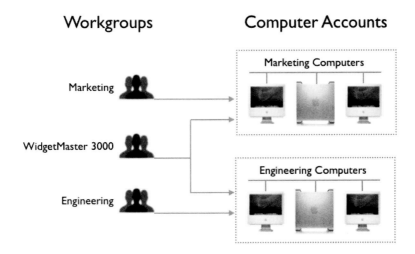

Managing Preferences

When you manage preferences, you centrally control the configuration of specific system settings. You also control users' ability to change those settings, as well as their ability to access applications, printers, removable media, or even certain computers. Information about preferences and their settings in user, group, computer, or computer group records is stored in a directory domain accessible to Workgroup Manager, such as the LDAP directory of an Open Directory master. In addition, a copy of group preferences is stored in the workgroup's folder and, at login, user preferences are stored in the local directory domain.

After user, group, computer, and computer group accounts are created, you can start managing preferences for them using the Preferences pane in Workgroup Manager. To manage preferences for Mac OS X clients, you should make sure that each user you want to manage has either a network or local home folder.

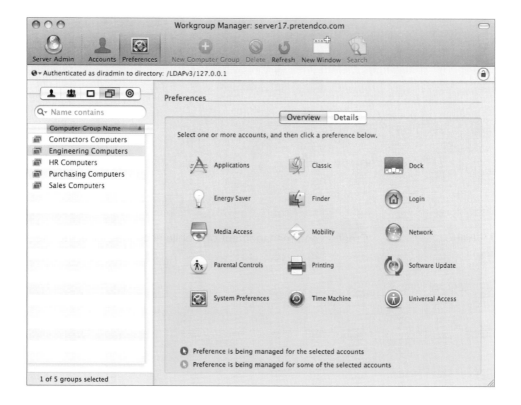

Which Preferences Can Be Managed?

In addition to various other settings for user, group, computer, and computer group accounts, Workgroup Manager provides control over these preferences:

Preference	What You Can Manage
Applications	Applications and widgets available to users
Classic	Classic startup settings, sleep settings, and the availability of Classic items such as control panels

Preference	What You Can Manage
Dock	Dock location, behavior, and items
Energy Saver	Available only for computers and computer groups; sleep configuration for the computer
Finder	Finder behavior, desktop appearance and items, and availability of Finder menu commands
Login	Items that open automatically when a user logs in and automatically mounted volumes; additionally, for computers and computer groups, login window appearance, login and logout scripts, auto logout, login access, including guest and external account availability
Media Access	Settings for CDs, DVDs, and recordable discs, plus settings for disk images, and internal and external disks such as hard drives
Mobility	Creation and management of mobile accounts, including their synchronization and file vault configurations
Network	Configure proxy settings for Internet services; for computers and computer groups, disable Internet sharing, AirPort, or Bluetooth
Parental Controls	Website and time limits
Printing	Available printers and printer access
Software Update	Software Update server to connect for Software Update service
System Preferences	System preferences available to users
Time Machine	Available only for computers and computer groups; backup server and Time Machine configuration
Universal Access	Settings to control mouse and keyboard behavior, enhance display settings, and adjust sound or speech for users with special needs

When you manage preferences for a user, group, computer, or computer group, an arrow icon appears next to the managed preference in the Preferences pane to indicate that you're managing that preference. If the arrow is dimmed, it means that you have selected two or more accounts in the list at the left of the window, and that for some of the selected accounts this item is managed, while for others it is not.

When Do You Want to Manage Preferences?

In Workgroup Manager, you have three options for managing a preference:

▶ If you don't want to manage settings for a particular preference, select Never in the management bar. If you provide users with access to an unmanaged preference, they can change settings as they want. Never is the default management setting for all preferences.

> NOTE ▶ Even if you select Never, it is possible these settings may still get managed at a different level, such as if the user is a member of a workgroup for which these settings are managed.

> TIP ▶ If you do not manage a particular preference, the user and system preferences are set to default values until changed by the end user. For example, if you do not set any managed preferences for Dock placement, the Dock uses the default location at the bottom of the screen.

▶ If you want to manage a preference initially for accounts but allow the user to make changes if they have that privilege, select Once in the management bar. When a user logs in, preference files in his or her home folder are updated and time-stamped with any preferences that are managed once. If you update settings for a preference that is managed once, Workgroup Manager applies the most recent version to the user's preference files the next time the user logs in. For some preferences, such as Classic preferences or Media Access preferences, Once is not available. You must select Never or Always.

▶ You can force preference settings for an account by selecting Always in the management bar. The next time the user logs in, the preference settings are those selected by the administrator. A user cannot change a preference that is Always managed, even if the user is allowed access to that preference. In that case, the changes will just not be saved.

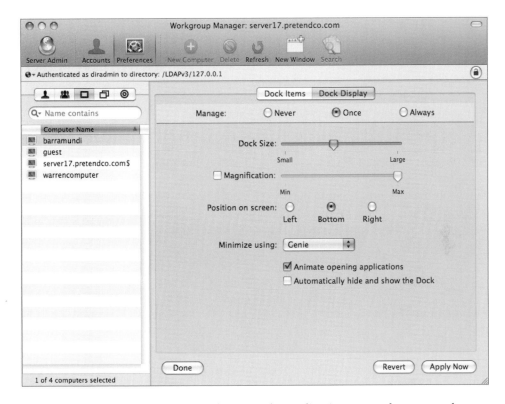

Not all settings make sense in all cases (for example, application access does not make sense in the Once setting, because Once is essentially the same as Always). Mac OS X v10.4 also introduced the notion of Often. This persistent setting allows the user to change the preferences but resets them the next time the computer boots or a user logs in.

NOTE ► The Often option is only available via the Preference Manifest screen. This is available by selecting Details on the main preference screen.

Managing User, Group, and Computer Preferences

You might want to manage preferences at the user level only for specific individuals, such as directory domain administrators, teachers, or technical staff. You should also consider which preferences you want to leave under user control. For example, if you aren't concerned about where a user places the Dock, you might want to set Dock Display management to Never.

Follow these steps to manage user, group, computer, and computer group account preferences with Workgroup Manager:

1   Click Preferences.

2   Click the globe icon below the toolbar and open the directory domain where you want to store the new account.

3   If necessary, click the lock and enter your user name and password.

4   Select the user, group, computer, or computer groups you want to manage.

5   Click the icon for the preference you want to manage.

6   In each pane for that preference, select a management setting (Never, Once, or Always), then select preference settings or fill in the information you want to use.

7   Click Apply Now.

A more efficient way to manage user preferences is to do it at the workgroup level. Workgroup preferences are shared among all users in the group. Setting some preferences only for groups instead of for individual users can save time, especially when you have large numbers of managed users. In some cases, it may be more efficient to manage preferences for computers instead of for users or groups. These options are all part of proper planning when preparing to manage accounts.

Managed Preference Precedence—Inherit

If you manage the same preference for user, group, computer, and computer group accounts, which preference setting takes precedence? This can be a complicated question, because in some cases the preferences override each other, while in others they are combined.

To simplify preference management, you might decide to manage certain preferences at only one level. For example, you could set Login preferences only for workgroups, set

Dock preferences only for computers, set Finder preferences only for computer groups, and Application preferences only for users. In such a case, if a user logs in at a managed computer with a managed user account that is a member of a workgroup, the user will inherit each of the managed preferences from each of the managed accounts.

	Login	Dock	Finder	Applications
Workgroup	Address Book launch at login	"Not Managed"	"Not Managed"	"Not Managed"
Computer Group	"Not Managed"	"Not Managed"	✅ Snap to grid	"Not Managed"
Computer	"Not Managed"	◉ Right	"Not Managed"	"Not Managed"
User	"Not Managed"	"Not Managed"	"Not Managed"	Chess Allowed
Result:	Address Book launch at login	◉ Right	✅ Snap to grid	Chess Allowed

Managed Preference Precedence—Override

In cases where you have set managed preferences at more than one level, and the preference setting can only have one value, the override rule applies: Managed user preferences override managed computer preferences, which override managed computer group preferences, which in turn override workgroup preferences. For example, if you are managing Dock preferences and decide to set the Dock position to the right for the workgroup the user belongs to, to the left for the computer the user is logging in at, and at the bottom for the computer group that computer belongs to, what does the user get when using one of the managed computers? Because computer preferences override computer group and workgroup preferences, the user will see the Dock on the left.

	Dock
Workgroup 👥	⊙ Right
Computer Group	⊙ Bottom
Computer	⊙ Left
User 👤	"Not Managed"
Result:	⊙ Left

TIP ▶ In general, it's most efficient to manage preferences at the group level. Then you can use the override rule to grant additional privileges to specific users, or to set specific preferences on certain computers.

Managed Preference Precedence—Combine

If a preference can have more than one value, and you set different values for it at the user, computer, computer group, and workgroup levels, Workgroup Manager combines these values. For example, suppose you configure managed Application preferences to allow a workgroup to launch the Address Book application, the user to launch Safari, the computer the user is logging in at to launch Preview, and the computer group that contains that computer to launch Chess. When the user logs in, he or she will be able to launch all four of the applications because the rules are combined.

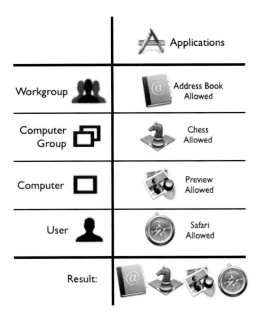

Managing Preference Manifests

Applications store their preference data in specific formats, which are known only to the application developers. Therefore, Workgroup Manager has no way of determining or decoding these formats. In Mac OS X v10.4, Workgroup Manager introduced the notion of *preference manifests*, which are built into the application and list various options that can be managed for that application.

Applications that adhere to the manifest format can have their preference data imported and stored with user, group, computer, and computer group accounts. When the manifest settings are saved, the application preferences will also be managed. This allows you to manage preferences for items other than those that are already defined in Workgroup Manager, as long as the developer of that application provides a preference manifest. Workgroup Manager will do simple checking for the manifest format when you click Add in the Details pane.

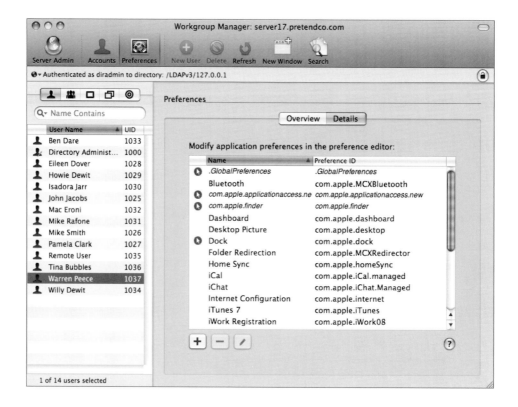

Edit Preference Manifests

All Workgroup Manager preferences (such as Dock, Finder, or System Preferences) are editable using the preference manifest edit function once they have been initially managed. Select the preference you want to view or edit and an XML editor appears. You can edit entries here and set them to be managed always, often, or once. This is the only place where the Often setting is available. Workgroup Manager will make a best effort to display record types in known formats. Not all the options configurable may be displayed. Only those settings with values are displayed, and no error checking is applied to the fields (for example, it would be possible to set a font size to 240 instead of 24).

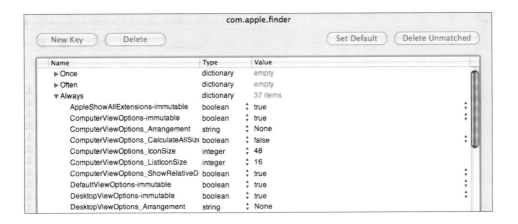

Restrict Access to Applications

Now, you will use the Applications pane in the Preferences pane to specify which applications Pamela Clark can open.

1   Open Workgroup Manager on your Mac OS X computer and authenticate if necessary.

2   Select Pamela Clark in the Accounts list and click the Preferences button in the toolbar.

3   Click the Applications tab in the Preferences pane and select Always as the management choice.

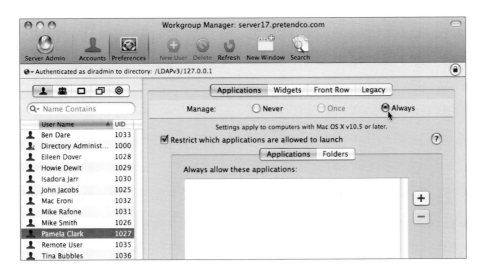

4   Select "Restrict which applications are allowed to launch."

5   Click the Add (+) button to add applications.

6   Select Calculator, Dictionary, Font Book, Mail, and Preview, and then click Add.

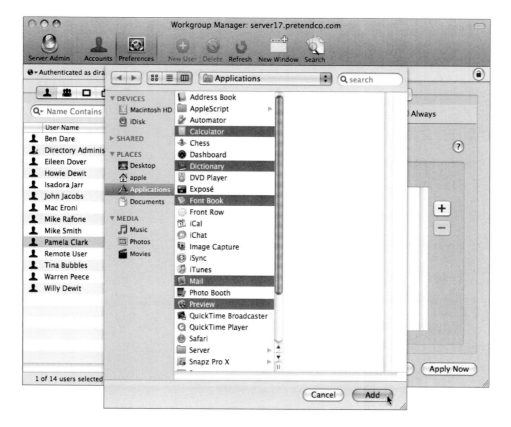

NOTE ▸ The applications listed are those found on your local computer, therefore it's best to do this from a computer configured similarly to your users' computers so you have the same third-party applications available to select.

7   Click Apply Now.

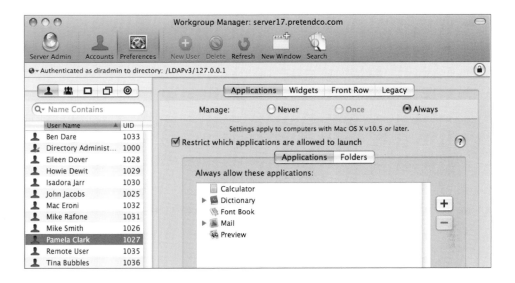

8 Log out of your Mac OS X computer and log back in as Pamela. (You can use Fast User Switching for this if you want.)

9 Go to the Applications folder and double-click Dictionary. What happens?

10 Click System Preferences in the Dock. What happens?

Go to the Applications folder and double-click System Preferences. What happens? In both instances, you can't launch System Preferences.

NOTE ▶ System Preferences is an application. By not allowing access to this application, you have prevented Pamela from viewing or changing any system preferences.

11 Attempt to open Directory Utility located in the Utilities folder within the Applications folder.

You cannot launch Directory Utility.

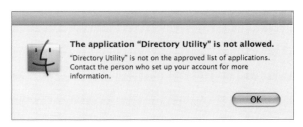

12 Log out as Pamela.

> **NOTE** ▸ Do not use Fast User Switching to log out of the managed user's account during these exercises because updated preferences take effect only when a user logs in, not when a Fast User Switching session is restored.

Restrict Access to Selected System Preferences

In the following steps, you will enable Pamela to access a selected number of system preferences.

1 Log in as your local administrator, open Workgroup Manager, and select Pamela Clark. Click the Preferences button in the toolbar, and click the Applications tab. (This view will still be open if you just used Fast User Switching in the previous exercise.)

2 Click Add, select System Preferences from the list of applications, click Add again, and click Apply Now.

You must add the System Preferences application back to the list of applications that the user can manage. If you don't do this, then attempting to manage various system preferences is a moot point.

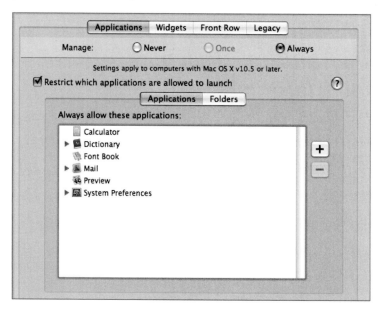

3   Click the Preferences button in the toolbar, and click the System Preferences icon in the Preferences pane.

4   Select Always as the management choice and deselect the Accounts and Energy Saver preferences.

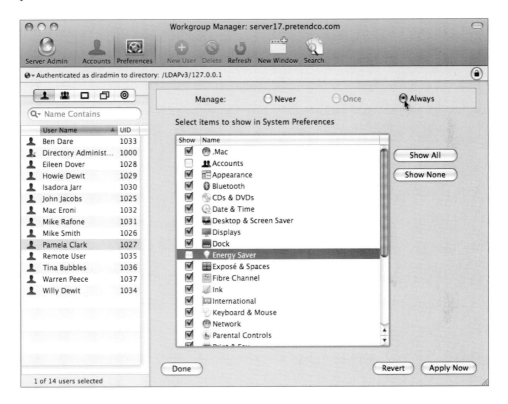

5   Click Apply Now.

6   Log out or use Fast User Switching and log back in as Pamela.

This will reset the preferences for the user Pamela. Preferences are configured when the user logs in to the system.

7 Open System Preferences.

In the System Preferences window, the Accounts and Energy Saver preferences are dimmed and cannot be changed by Pamela.

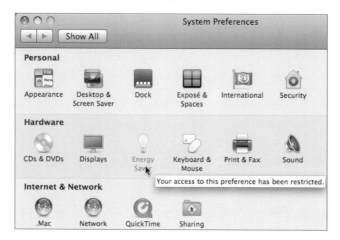

8 Log out as Pamela and log back in as your local administrator.

Restrict Access to Selected Dashboard Widgets

In the following steps, you allow Pamela to access a selected number of Dashboard widgets.

1 Log in as your local administrator, open Workgroup Manager, and select Pamela Clark. (This will already be done if you're using Fast User Switching.)

2 Click the Preferences button in the toolbar, followed by the Applications icon in the Preferences pane.

3 Select the Widgets tab, and then select Always as the management choice.

4 Remove all of the widgets from the list except the Calculator, iCal, Stickies, Weather, and World Clock widgets.

If you need to add back a widget after removing it, they can be found at /Library/ Widgets.

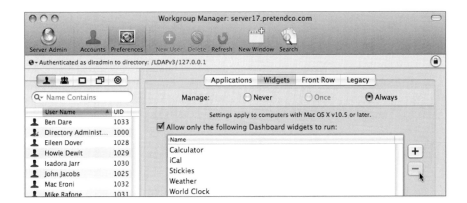

5   Click Apply Now.

6   Log out or use Fast User Switching and log back in as Pamela.

This will reset the preferences for the user Pamela. Preferences are configured when the user logs in to the system.

7   Press the F12 key to display the Dashboard. What happens?

The Dashboard displays the default widgets because they are allowed.

8   Click the Add (+) button in the lower-left corner.

9   Drag the Stickies widget onto the Dashboard.

If you don't see the Stickies widget at the bottom of your screen in the list of available widgets, click the arrow button at the edge until you find the Stickies widget.

The Stickies widget appears on the Dashboard after you drag it because it is an allowed widget.

10   Drag the Stocks widget onto the Dashboard. What happens?

Because the Stocks widget isn't allowed, an error message displays.

11 Log out as Pamela and log back in as your local administrator.

> **NOTE** ▶ The default widget layout for a new user contains Calculator, iCal, Weather, and World Clock. If you remove any of these from the allowed list, the user will be shown an error message similar to the one shown in the previous figure the first time he or she displays the Dashboard.

Managing Preferences on a Network

Next, you will use Workgroup Manager to manage Login, Dock, Finder, and Printer preferences for given accounts.

Configure Login Preferences

These steps show you how to use the Login pane under Preferences in Workgroup Manager to make the Mail application open the first time a user logs into a Mac OS X computer.

1 Back in your local administrator account's session, open Workgroup Manager if it's not already open.

2 Select the user Mike Smith, and then click the Preferences button in the toolbar.

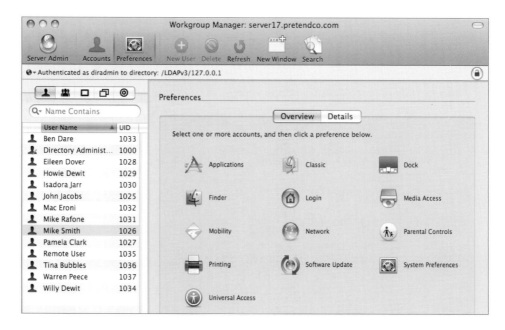

3 Click the Login icon in the Preferences pane.

4 Click the Items tab and select Once as the management choice in the Items pane. Click the Add button to add the Mail application (located in /Applications), and then click Apply Now.

The Mail application will always open automatically when Mike logs in, unless he changes his login options and removes Mail from the list of applications that open automatically at login.

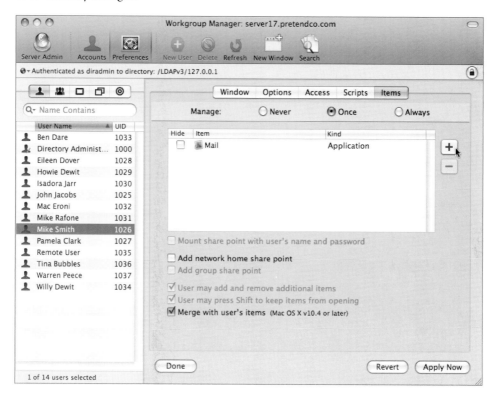

5 Open System Preferences on your Mac OS X computer, click the Accounts preferences pane, click Login Options, and select the "Enable fast user switching" checkbox if you have not already done so.

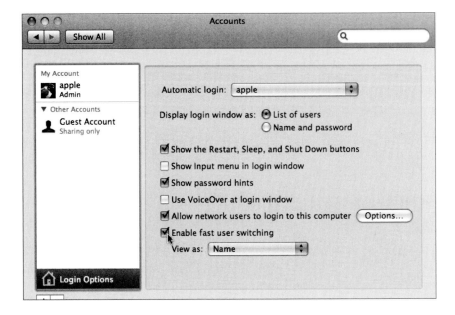

6   Use Fast User Switching to switch to the login window and log in as Mike Smith.

    Notice that Mail starts automatically.

7   Quit Mail by clicking the Cancel button.

8   Open the Accounts pane in System Preferences, select the Mike Smith account, and
    click Login Items.

    Notice that Mail has been added to the list of items that open automatically when
    Mike logs in.

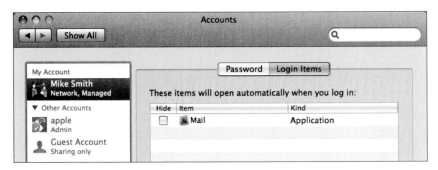

9 Select Mail from the Login Items list and click the Delete (–) button.

Mail will not start the next time Mike logs in because the preferences were set to Once. Therefore, Mike has the freedom to choose whether to keep Mail as a login item or not.

10 Log out as Mike Smith and log back in as the local administrator.

You *must* log out as Mike Smith so the next preference changes will take effect. Just doing Fast User Switching from Mike to your local administrator will not show the newer preferences.

Because you are using Fast User Switching, Workgroup Manager is still running.

Configure Dock Preferences

Use the Dock preferences pane to add three applications (Calculator, Stickies, and TextEdit), to add the Applications folder to Mike Smith's Dock, and to set the size of the Dock.

1 In Workgroup Manager, select the Mike Smith account, and then click the Preferences button in the toolbar.

Notice that because you previously managed Login preferences, it has an arrow next to the icon.

2 Click the Dock in the Preferences pane, select Always as the management choice, click the Add button next to the Applications list, and add the following applications:

▶ Calculator

▶ Stickies

▶ TextEdit

3 Click the Add button next to the Documents and Folders list, navigate to the Applications folder, click Add, make sure "Merge with user's Dock" is selected, and click Apply Now.

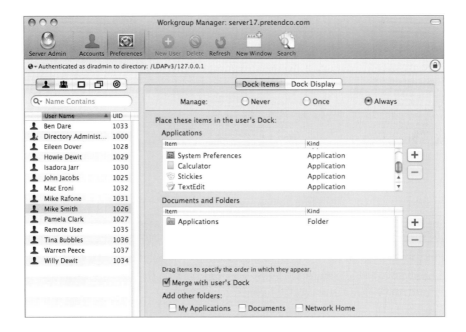

4 Click the Dock Display tab, select Always as the management choice, set the Dock Size to Large, select "Automatically hide and show the Dock," and click Apply Now.

When Mike logs in, the Dock will contain Calculator, Stickies, and TextEdit; it will be large; and it will be hidden until the pointer is moved to the bottom of the screen.

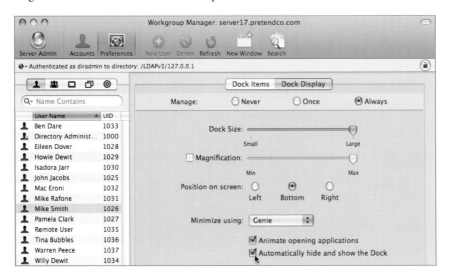

5   Use Fast User Switching and log back in as Mike Smith.

Verify that the Dock settings you just defined in Workgroup Manager have taken effect. Verify that the change is persistent and that Mike can't remove the contents of the Dock.

6   Log out as Mike Smith and log back in as the local administrator.

Because you are using Fast User Switching, Workgroup Manager is still running.

Configure Finder Preferences

Next, you will use Workgroup Manager to configure Finder preferences to restrict the views and remove some menu item commands.

1   In Workgroup Manager, select the Mike Smith account and click the Preferences button in the toolbar.

Notice that because you previously managed Login preferences and Dock preferences, they have arrows next to the icons.

2   Click the Finder icon in the Preferences pane.

3   Click the Views tab, and select Always as the management choice.

4   Set the Icon Size to Large in three places: Desktop View, Default View, and Computer View.

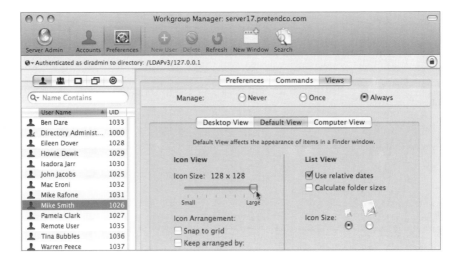

5   Click the Commands tab, select Always as the management choice, and deselect the following checkboxes:

▶   Go to iDisk

▶   Burn Disc

▶   Go to Folder

▶   Restart

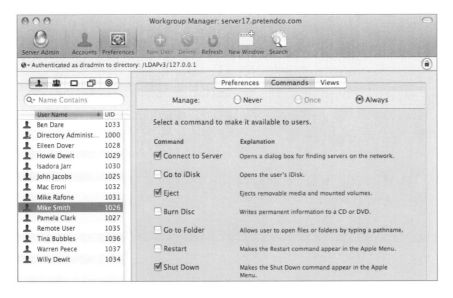

6 Click Apply Now.

7 Use Fast User Switching to log back in as Mike Smith and verify the following:

► The hard disk icon is extremely large.

► The Restart option is missing from the Apple menu.

► The "Go to My iDisk" option is disabled, and the "Go to Folder" option is removed from the Go menu.

► The Burn Disc option is missing from the File menu.

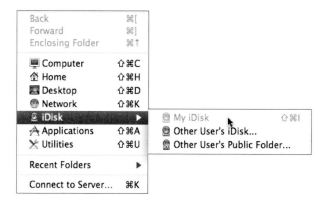

8 Log out as Mike Smith and log back in as the local administrator.

Because you are using Fast User Switching, Workgroup Manager is still running.

Managing Workgroup Accounts

You will use Workgroup Manager to configure Application preferences, Dock preferences, and Finder preferences for a group. You will then log in to the Mac OS X computer and observe how group preferences work with user preferences.

Create Groups with Workgroup Manager

First, you will create a group to share preferences.

1 In Workgroup Manager on your Mac OS X computer, select the /LDAPv3/127.0.0.1 domain from the Directory pop-up menu.

2 Click the Accounts button in the toolbar, and then click the Group button to verify the two groups you previously created:

▶ Engineering

▶ Marketing

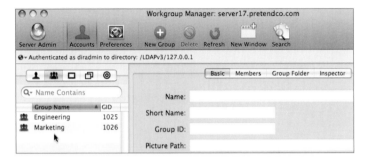

3 Confirm that the Engineering group contains three members:

▶ Warren Peece

▶ Mike Smith

▶ Pamela Clark

Add those who are missing, and remove those who shouldn't be members.

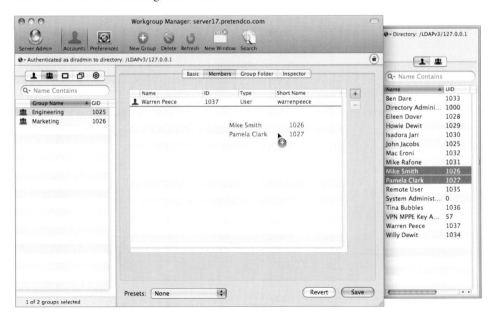

Specify Preferences for Groups

Configure preferences for the Engineering group.

1   Select the Engineering group in Workgroup Manager, click the Preferences button in the toolbar, and then click the Applications icon in the Preferences pane.

2   Select Always from the Manage options and select "Restrict which applications are allowed to launch."

3   Click the Add button and add the following applications to the approved list:

   ▶   Image Capture (located in /Applications)

   ▶   Console (located in /Applications/Utilities)

   ▶   Kerberos (located in /System/Library/CoreServices)

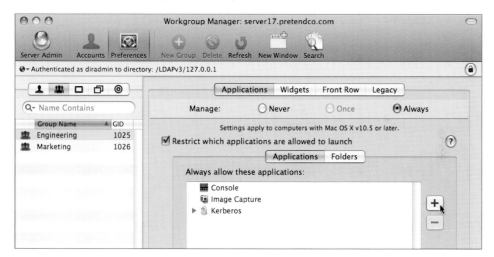

4   Click Apply Now.

5   In Workgroup Manager, click the Preferences button in the toolbar and click the Dock icon. Click the Dock Items tab.

6 Select Always from the Manage options and click the Add button to add the following applications to the Dock:

▶ Image Capture (located in /Applications)

▶ Console (located in /Applications/Utilities)

▶ Kerberos (located in /System/Library/CoreServices)

7 Click Apply Now.

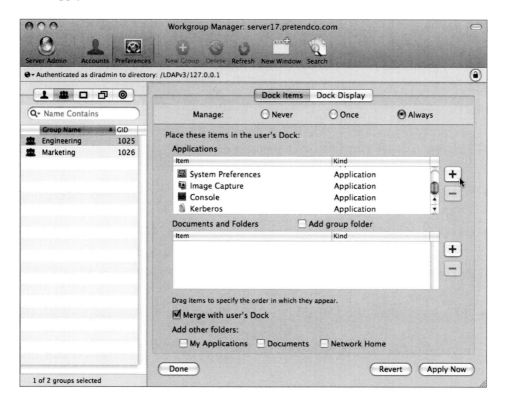

8 Click the Preferences button in the toolbar in Workgroup Manager and click the Finder preferences. Click the Preferences tab that is in the Finder Preferences pane, select Always from the Manage options, and select the "Always open windows in column view" checkbox.

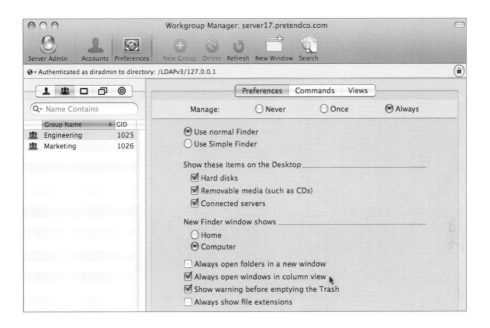

9 Click the Views tab, select Always from the Manage options, click Desktop View, and set Icon Size to Small.

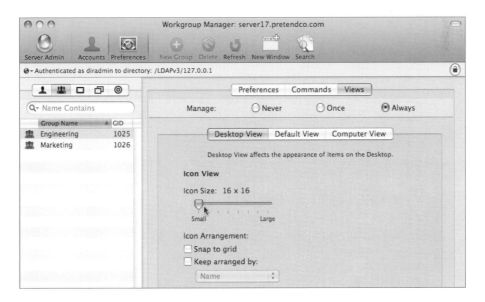

10 Click Apply Now.

Check Group Preferences Against User Preferences

Now, you will now learn how group preferences work with user preferences.

1 Use Fast User Switching to log back in as Mike Smith.

Recall that Mike is a newer member of the Engineering group.

Notice how Mike's Finder preferences, which specify large icon size, took precedence over the group's preferences. Also, notice that Mike's Dock has both Mike's applications and the Engineering group's applications. Verify that Mike also still does not have access to the Restart option under the Apple menu and his Go menu remains altered.

2 Log out as Mike and log in as Warren Peece (another member of the Engineering group).

Notice that Warren's hard drive icon is small and the Image Capture application has been added to the Dock in addition to the other applications that were specified by the Engineering group. Verify that Warren does, however, have access to the Restart option under the Apple menu as well as access to the other Go menu options.

3   Log out as Warren and log back in as the local administrator.

Because you are using Fast User Switching, Workgroup Manager is still running.

Create Group Folders

Now, you will use the CreateGroupFolder command to manually create group folders.

1   Open Server Admin and connect to your server.

2   Click the File Sharing button, click the Share Points button, and select the Groups folder from the list. In the Share Point pane, click the checkbox to Enable Automount.

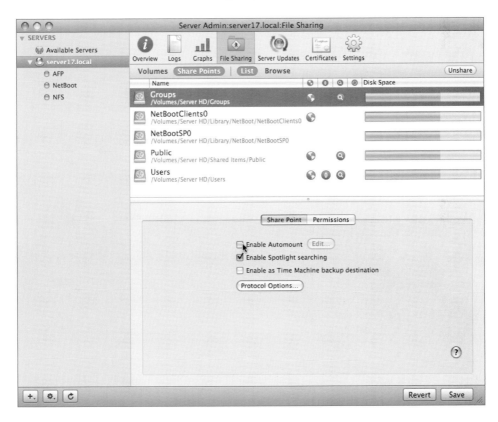

3   Set the Protocol to AFP, and select "Use for: User home folders." Click OK, then Save.

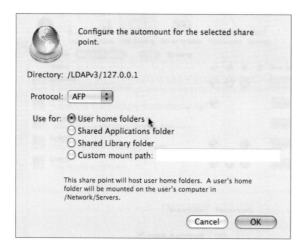

4 Open Workgroup Manager and connect to your server.

5 Click the Accounts button in the toolbar, click the Group button, and select the Engineering group.

6 Click the Group Folder tab and select afp://server17.pretendco.com/Groups from the list of share points shown. Click the Browse (…) button to select mikesmith in the Owner Short Name field, and then click Save.

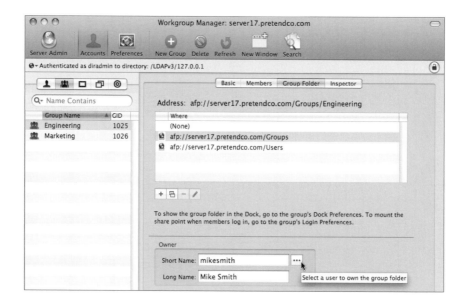

7   On your Mac OS X computer, open the Terminal application (located in /Applications/ Utilities) and type *ssh 10.1.17.1* and press Return.

If this is the first time you have connected to your server via the Terminal (exactly what you are doing here), type *yes* at the prompt about the RSA Fingerprint and press Return.

8   Enter the password for ladmin (root's password on Mac OS X Server is initially the same as the administrator's account during the setup process).

9   Type *sudo CreateGroupFolder* and press Return.

In the Finder on your server, notice that a new group folder is created in /Groups called Engineering.

10   Type *exit* in the Terminal and press Return to exit the ssh connection, and then quit the Terminal application.

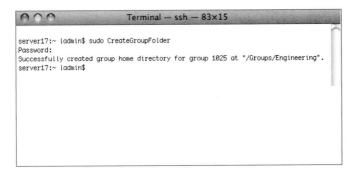

Configure the Group Folder to Be Available to Members
You can make the group folder automatically available to members of the group when they log in to their computers by changing the Login and Dock preferences.

1   In Workgroup Manager on your Mac OS X computer, choose the /LDAPv3/127.0.0.1 domain from the Directory pop-up menu.

2   Select the Engineering group in Workgroup Manager, click the Preferences button in the toolbar, and click the Dock icon in the Preferences pane. Then click the Dock Items tab, select the "Add group folder" checkbox, and click Apply Now.

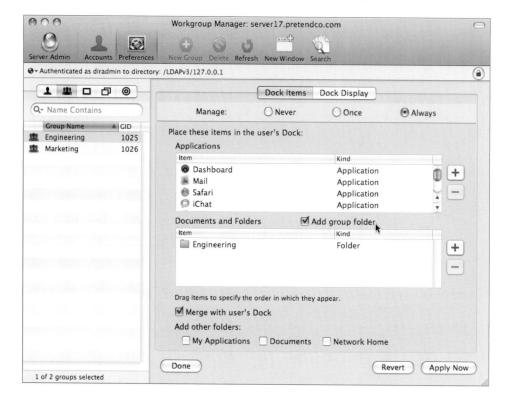

3   Click the Preferences button in the toolbar and click the Login icon to reveal the Login preference options, then click the Items tab.

4   Select Always from the Manage options and select "Add group share point." Then select the share point "Groups" from the Login Items window and place a checkmark in the "Mount share point with user's name and password" checkbox. Click Apply Now.

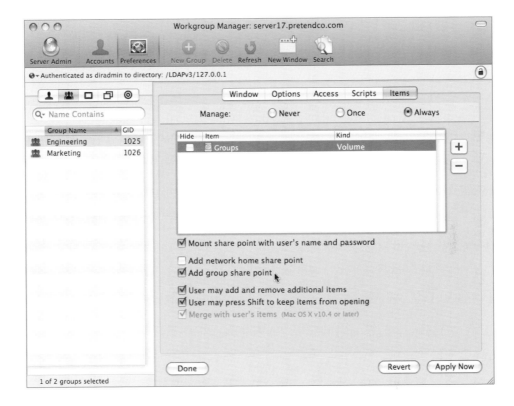

5   Use Fast User Switching to log back in as Mike Smith. Verify that the Engineering folder is in the Dock, the Groups share point is mounted on the desktop, and that you have access to the Engineering group folder.

6 Log out as Mike Smith and log back in as the local administrator.

Because you are using Fast User Switching, Workgroup Manager is still running.

Creating Computer Accounts

Now you will create some computer accounts, which will later be added to a computer group. Preferences can be assigned to individual computers, or to computer groups, just like they can be assigned to individual users or workgroups. Similarly, it's usually best to make use of computer groups that mimic your organizational structure so you only have to manage the group membership rather than reassigning all of the preferences to each computer as it enters service.

1 In Workgroup Manager on your Mac OS X computer, choose the /LDAPv3/127.0.0.1 domain from the Directory pop-up menu.

2 Click the Accounts button in the toolbar and click the Computer button.

3 Click the New Computer button in the toolbar.

4 In the Name field, type *Warren's Machine*.

5 In the Short Name field, type *warrencomputer* and click Save.

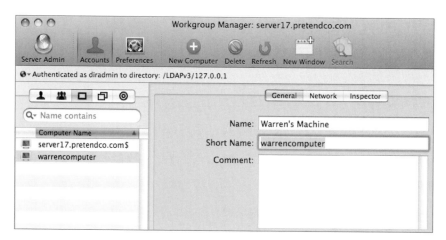

6 Click the Network tab.

7 In the Ethernet ID field, type *ad:09:21:20:02:da* and click Save.

This Ethernet ID is a fictitious one used for this exercise. Normally, you would use the actual Ethernet ID for the computer for which you're creating a computer account.

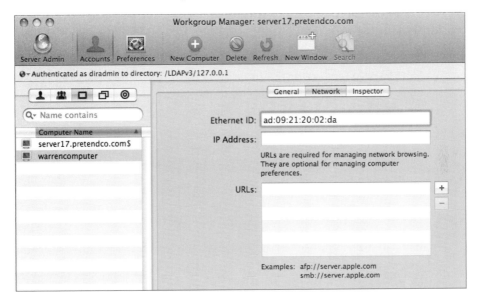

8 Repeat these steps to create another computer with these attributes:

▶ Name: *Pamela's Machine*

▶ Short Name: *pamelacomputer*

▶ Ethernet ID: *ed:ea:15:aa:be:ef*

Managing Computer Access

Now you will create a computer account and computer group, and configure its Application, Dock, and Finder preferences. You will then log in to the client and observe how computer preferences work with group and user preferences. Finally, you will enable Auto Log-Out for the computer group.

> **WARNING** ▶ While this lesson is non-destructive, if you do not follow the steps exactly, you will not be permitted access to your applications again. If you have not already backed up, do so now.

1   In Workgroup Manager on your Mac OS X computer, choose the /LDAPv3/127.0.0.1 domain from the Directory pop-up menu.

2   Click the Accounts button in the toolbar and click the Computer Group button.

3   Select all of the computer groups and click the Delete button in the toolbar.

4   Click New Computer Group in the toolbar, and in the Name field, type *XSE Course*. Leave the other fields at their default settings. Click Save.

5   Click the Members tab, then click the Browse (...) button, select your Mac OS X computer from the list, and click Add.

6 Click Save.

7 Click the Preferences button in the toolbar and select the Finder preferences. Click the Preferences tab located in the Finder Preferences pane, select Always from the Manage options, and then select the "Always open folders in a new window" checkbox.

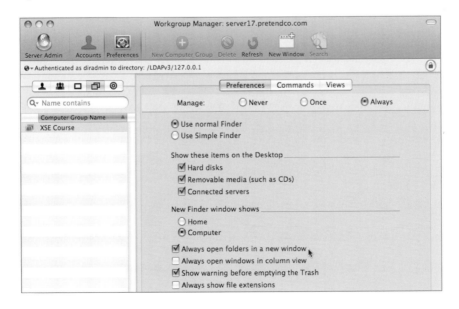

8   Click Apply Now.

9   Click the Preferences button in the toolbar and select the Login preferences.

10   Click the Access tab located in the Login preferences pane, then select Always from the Manage options.

11   Click the Add (+) button and add the Engineering group to the Access Control List. Click Apply Now.

Only members of the Engineering group have access to the Mac OS X computer.

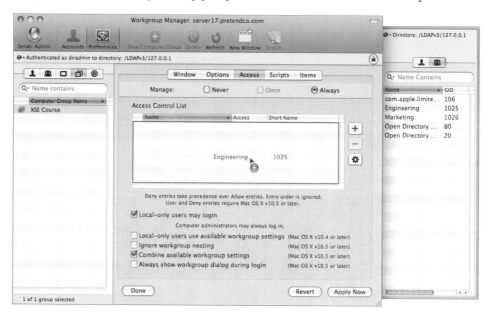

12   Use Fast User Switching and attempt to log in as Tina Bubbles.

You cannot log in because Tina is not part of the Engineering group.

13   Attempt to log in as Mike Smith and verify that restricted access allows Mike to log in because he is part of the Engineering group.

14   Log out as Mike and log back in as the local administrator.

Because you are using Fast User Switching, Workgroup Manager is still running.

Configuring Computer Group Preferences

Configure the Application preferences for the XSE Course computer group to allow users to open the Chess application.

1   In Workgroup Manager on your Mac OS X computer, choose the /LDAPv3/127.0.0.1 domain from the Directory pop-up menu.

2   Select XSE Course from the Computer Group list and click the Preferences button in the toolbar.

3   Click the Applications icon in the Preferences pane, select Always from the Manage options, and allow users to only open the Chess (located in the Applications folder) and Workgroup Manager (located in the Server folder inside the Applications folder) applications.

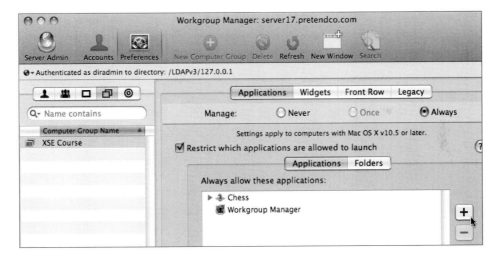

4   Click Apply Now and then click Done.

Clicking the Done button is another way to get back to the main Preferences pane of Workgroup Manager. It is not a requirement that you use this button—it's an optional step.

5   Click the Dock icon in the Preferences pane and then click the Dock Items tab. Select Always from the Manage options, and click the Add button to add Chess to the list of applications in the Dock.

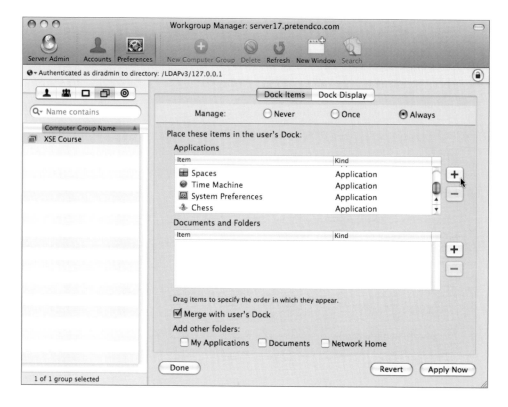

6   Click Apply Now and then click Done.

7   Click the Finder icon in the Preferences pane and then click the Preferences tab located in the Finder Preferences pane. Select Always from the Manage options and select the following:

▶   "Always open folders in a new window"

▶   "Always open windows in column view"

▶   "Show warning before emptying the Trash"

▶   "Always show file extensions"

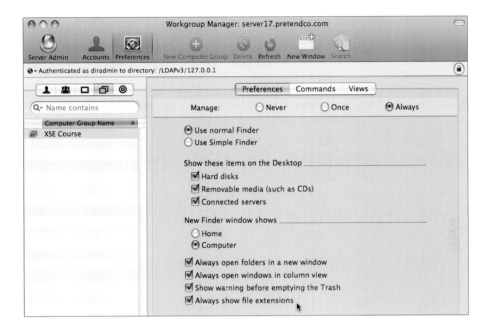

8   Click Apply Now and then click Done.

9   Click the Login icon in the Preferences pane, and then click the Options tab. Select
Always from the Manage options and select the "Log out users after x minutes of
inactivity" checkbox (where x is 5 minutes).

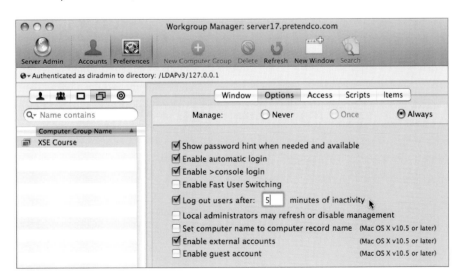

10 Click Apply Now, and then click Done.

11 Use Fast User Switching to log back in as Mike Smith and observe how computer group preferences interact with group and user preferences.

Notice that Mike's Finder preferences, which specify that the desktop icons be set to large, take precedence over the Group preferences, which are set to small. Also notice that Mike can open only the Chess application, which now shows up in his Dock, and the Workgroup Manager application (although Mike cannot actually use Workgroup Manager, he can launch it). Along with Chess, the three applications we specified for the Engineering group account preferences, Image Capture, Kerberos, and Console, also show up in the Dock and can be launched because the Applications preferences for the Engineering group also allow launching these applications.

12 Log out as Mike and log in as Warren Peece (another member of the Engineering group).

Notice how Warren's Finder preferences, which specify that the desktop icons never be managed, has the icon size for the desktop set to small by his group association. Also notice that Warren can open only the Chess application, which now shows up in his Dock, and the Workgroup Manager application (although Warren cannot actually use Workgroup Manager, he can launch it), as well as the three applications we specified for the Engineering Group account preferences, Image Capture, Kerberos, and Console. The restriction to launch Chess and Workgroup Manager is a computer group account preference combined with the Engineering workgroup preference.

13 Log out as Warren and log in as Pamela Clark (another member of the Engineering group).

Notice how Pamela's Finder preferences, which specify that the desktop icons never be managed, has the icon size for the desktop set to small by her group association. Also, notice that not only can Pamela launch Chess and Workgroup Manager, she can also launch System Preferences, which was specified by her user account application preferences. However, she cannot access the Accounts and Energy Saver preference panes, as specified by her System Preferences preference management.

14 Log out as Pamela and log back in as the local administrator.

Customizing the Preference Choices

You can use preference manifests to add additional preference management choices to Workgroup Manager. For example, if you wanted all of the users of your company to have their Safari homepages set to http://www.pretendco.com/, you would follow these steps:

1   In Workgroup Manager on your Mac OS X computer, choose the /LDAPv3/127.0.0.1 domain from the Directory pop-up menu.

2   Select XSE Course from the Computer Group list and click the Preferences button in the toolbar.

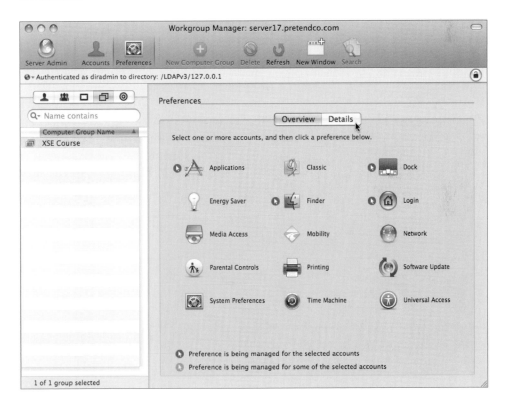

3   Click the Details tab.

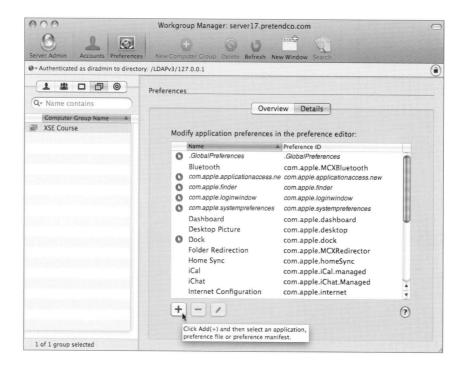

4   Click the Add (+) button at the bottom of the window.

5   Navigate to and select the Safari application.

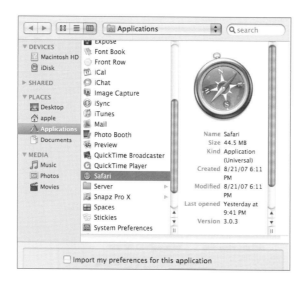

6 Deselect the option to "Import my preferences for this application."

This option would be used in cases where you want to preconfigure an entire user experience for an application by configuring the application to your liking, and then importing your preferences.

7 Click Add.

8 Find Safari in the list, select the com.apple.Safari entry, then click the Edit (pencil) icon.

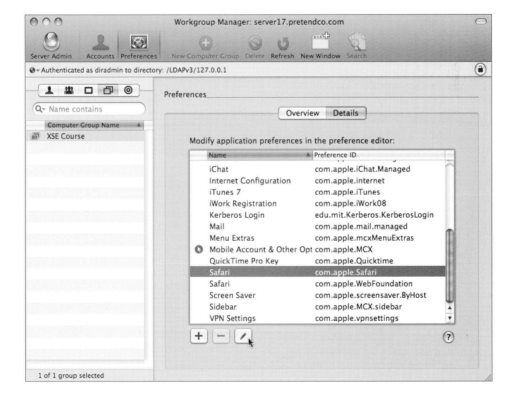

9 Click the disclosure triangle next to Once.

10 Select the Once entry so it's highlighted.

11 Click the New Key button.

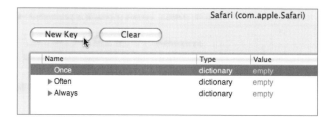

12 Click the New Item that appears. When you do so, a menu appears with the preference choices for Safari found in its preference manifest.

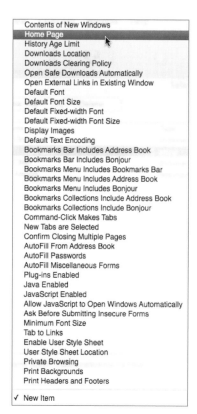

13 Choose Home Page from the menu.

Notice that the Value field is prepopulated with an example setting.

14 Double-click the value field and change it to *http://www.pretendco.com/*.

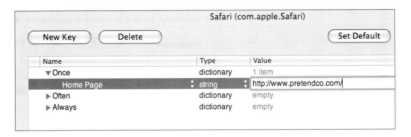

15 Click Apply Now followed by Done.

16 Click the Overview tab to return to the main Preferences pane.

17 Click the Applications icon and add Safari to the list of allowed applications for the XSE Course computer group.

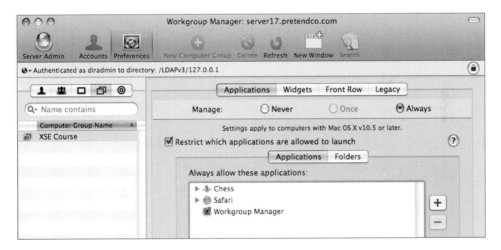

18 Use Fast User Switching to log back in as Mike Smith and launch Safari. Notice how it attempts to load http://www.pretendco.com/ as its homepage.

19 Log out as Mike Smith, and log in as your local administrator.

Managing Software Updates

With Mac OS X Server, you have the option of mirroring Apple's Software Update Servers on your local server. This has two distinct advantages. The first advantage is that you can save Internet bandwidth. All of your client computers will retrieve their software updates from the server on your local network rather than over the Internet, which will also result in faster downloads for your users. The second advantage is that you can control which updates are downloaded and which are available to your users. This can be particularly useful when a software update might be incompatible with some software you're using.

Setting up your Software Update server is easy. Here's how:

1   From your Mac OS X computer, open Server Admin and connect to your server.

2   Click the Add (+) button in the lower-left corner and choose Add Service to add the Software Update service on your server. Click Save.

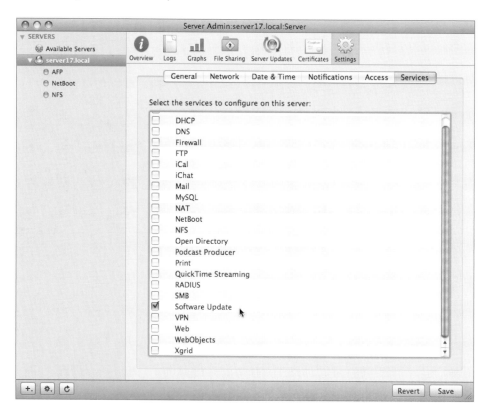

3 Click the Software Update service on the left side of the Server Admin window, and click the Settings button in the toolbar.

4 Click the General tab.

5 Configure the settings as follows:

▶ "Provide updates using port:" *8088* (the default)

▶ "Automatically copy *all* updates from Apple"

▶ "Automatically enable copied updates"

▶ "Purge unused/legacy software update packages automatically"

▶ Do not select "Limit user bandwidth for updates to"

TIP If you have a slow network between your client and server machines, or if you have a large number of clients, you may wish to limit the user bandwidth.

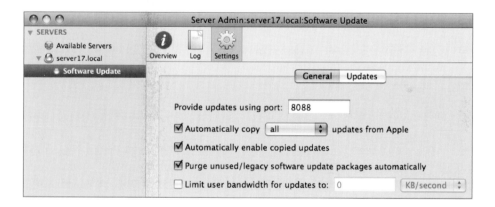

6 Click Save.

7 Click the Start Software Update button at the bottom of Server Admin.

8 Click the Updates tab.

9 Click the Update List button.

This will begin mirroring the software updates from Apple. If you have a slow Internet connection, this initial sync will take quite some time, possibly a number of hours.

Enabling Individual Updates

You can select which updates you wish to be available to enable for your users from within the list of updates.

1   In Server Admin, select the Software Update service on the left.

2   Click the Settings button in the toolbar.

3   Click the Updates tab.

This screen lists all of the updates currently available from Apple's servers.

4   Select which updates you wish to be enabled.

If the list of updates is empty, it is still being copied down from Apple.

NOTE ▶ The update must have been copied down before you can enable it.

5   Click Save.

If you aren't copying all of the updates automatically, this is the same screen where you would choose which updates you want to copy.

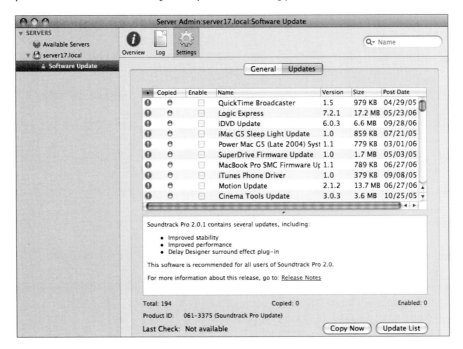

Configuring Clients for Your Software Update Service

As with other settings, you'll be using Managed Preferences to tell your machines to utilize your local software update server instead of Apple's.

1 Open Workgroup Manager and connect to your server.

2 Select Tina Bubbles in the Accounts list.

> **NOTE ▶** You could also assign this preference to a workgroup, computer, or computer group.

3 Click the Preferences button in the toolbar.

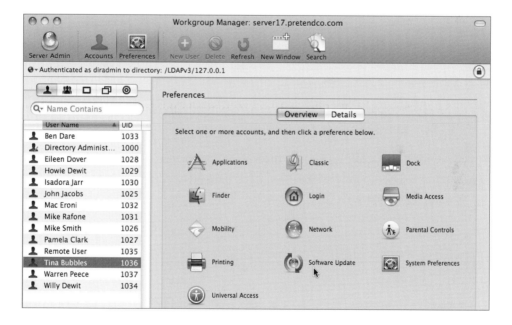

4 Click the Software Update icon.

5 Select the Always management setting.

6 In the "Software Update server to use" field, type: *http://server17.pretendco.com:8088/index.sucatalog.*

7 Click Apply Now.

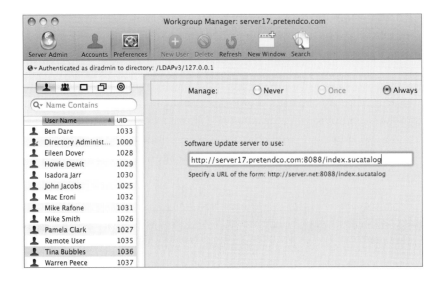

Restoring the Default Settings

We want to make sure to undo the managed preferences we set up in these exercises, so follow these steps.

1   Log in as the local administrator, then launch Workgroup Manager. Select the Engineering Computers account list, click the Preferences button in the toolbar, click the Applications icon, and click the option to Never manage applications again for this computer group. Click Apply Now. If any other management arrows exist next to preference management icons, click those icons and set the manage option to Never, and then click Apply Now.

2   Select XSE Course from the Computer Groups list, and click the Delete button in the toolbar.

3   Restart the Mac OS X computer, log in as the local administrator, and confirm you can access all applications.

Managing Mobile User Accounts

Network user accounts provide a great deal of administrative control, but they are useful only for computers that are constantly connected to the network. If a computer is disconnected from the network, it no longer has access to network user accounts or home folders.

To help manage accounts on computers that are not always connected to the network, such as portables, Mac OS X Server v10.3 and later provides the Mobile Accounts managed preference, which allows you to create mobile user accounts.

A mobile user account is a Mac OS X Server user account that resides in a shared domain but is copied to the local computer. This allows a user to log in to a portable computer using the network account even when the computer is not connected to a network. Mac OS X Server v10.4 added the ability to do file synchronization with the server account. Files can be set through Workgroup Manager to be automatically copied from the user's network home folder.

When a computer is connected to the network and the mobile user logs in, the operating system authenticates the user using the account information stored in the shared domain to which the computer is bound. The mobile account on the computer is updated automatically, including any managed preferences. When the computer is disconnected, the user logs in using the local account, which provides the same level of administrative control as that of the network account. In either case, whether the computer is connected to the network or not, the home folder is stored locally on the computer.

Because this will also work if a mobile user logs in to multiple computers, it's possible that the user may get a mobile account created on dozens of computers. Mac OS X Server v10.5 added account expiry as an option to help clean up stale mobile accounts.

Mac OS X Server v10.5 also added a new type of mobile account, known as an external account. This type of account stores the user's account information and files on a removable drive such as a FireWire drive. This allows users to take their accounts with them, rather than relying on a network connection to the main server to copy everything down each time mobile users log in to a new computer.

Creating and Deleting Mobile User Accounts

After creating an account, you can follow these generic steps to convert it into a mobile account. This option, like other account management options, is set through Workgroup Manager's Preferences options.

1 Open Workgroup Manager, select a network user account, and then click Preferences in the toolbar.

2 Click Mobility and set the management setting to Always.

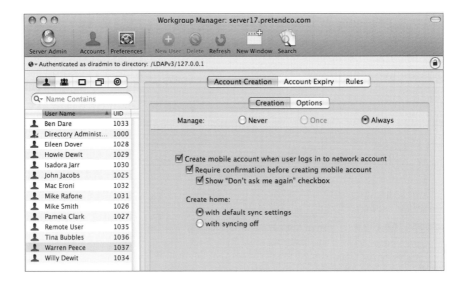

3 Select "Create mobile account when user logs in to network account."

4 Select "Require confirmation before creating mobile account" if you want to allow the user to decide whether to create a mobile account at login.

If this option is selected, the user sees a confirmation dialog when logging in. The user can click Create to create the mobile account immediately or click Continue to log in as a network user without creating the mobile account.

5 Click Apply Now.

> **TIP** ▶ If you manage only the creation of a mobile account for a network user, the user's local home folder becomes the default home folder. Any files that were stored in the network home folder are not copied to the local home folder. There is no file synchronization unless you set up rules for automatically copying files.

You can also create mobile user accounts by managing the Mobility preference for a workgroup, computer, or computer group. For example, if you manage the Mobility preference for a workgroup, all members of the workgroup become mobile users. This can be very useful in a large setting of portables, such as a school full of MacBook computers. Similarly, if you manage this preference for a computer group, all users of the computer become mobile users.

If a user no longer requires a mobile account, you should select Never as the Mobility preference in Workgroup Manager. In addition, you might want to delete the local copy of the account. Both the mobile account and its local home folder are deleted. You must have a local administrator account and password to delete a mobile account.

When you wish to delete a mobile account from a computer where they have logged in before:

1   Open System Preferences on the client computer.

2   Click Accounts.

3   Select the account you want to delete.

The mobile account should have the word "Mobile" beneath it.

4   Click the Delete (–) button, and then click OK.

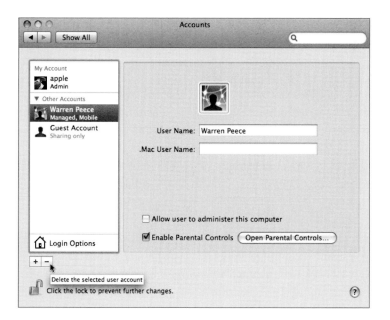

Synchronizing Accounts

Creating a mobile account is useful because a user can authenticate with the network information, and the owner of the files on the local and network folders is the same. You can set up rules for automatically copying files. For each preference set, you can establish which files can be synchronized at login and logout. These files are currently copied only from the home folder path.

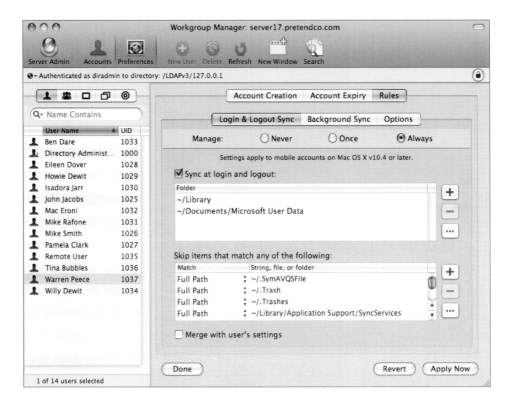

NOTE ▶ While you can set up mobile accounts for your Mac OS X v10.3 users, only users of Mac OS X v10.4 or newer can take advantage of the synchronization rules.

Synchronizing Account Home Folders

The Rules pane lets you designate which files you want synchronized. These files will be synchronized with the corresponding folder on the server. Because the mobile account is a duplicate of the Network account, all the permissions and ownership are identical. You can set up folders to copy and decide whether the copy takes place in the background. You can also determine which files should not be copied.

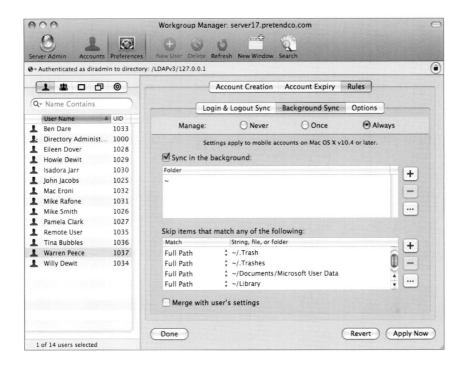

TIP ▶ Cache files, temporary files, and settings specific to the mobile account such as printer settings can be set to never be cached. Limit what is synchronized to essential files and important data. Network administrators may want to preclude music and photos as a rule.

Setting Account Synchronization Options

The Options tab lets you set the timing for the synchronization of files. This can be done on a set time interval or manually. This option is only for the file synchronization and does not affect preferences if they have been selected.

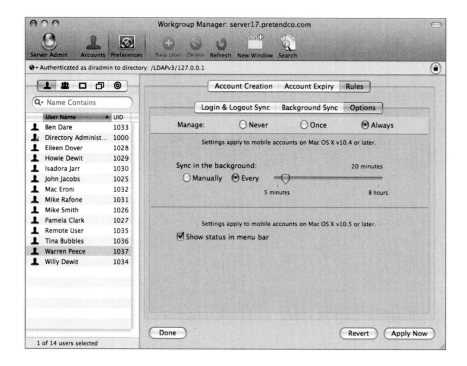

Configuring Mobile Computing

Now, you will use one of the accounts you set up previously and set up a synchronized mobile user account for that person.

1 In Workgroup Manager on your Mac OS X computer, choose the /LDAPv3/127.0.0.1 domain from the Directory pop-up menu.

2 Select Ben Dare from the Accounts list and click the Preferences button in the toolbar.

3 Click the Mobility icon. In the Account Creation pane, select Always from the Manage options, and select the following checkboxes:

▶ "Create mobile account when user logs in to network account"

▶ "Require confirmation before creating mobile account"

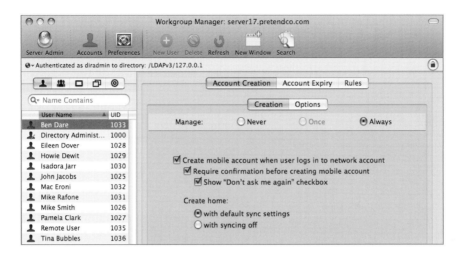

4   Click the Rules tab, click the Background Sync tab, and select Always from the Manage options. Delete the tilde (~) from the "Synchronize in background" list by selecting it and clicking the Delete (–) button.

The default is to copy the entire Home Directory path except those folders listed in the Skip pane. We'll configure it to synchronize only the Documents folder.

5   Click the Add (+) button and enter ~/Documents so you are synchronizing just the Documents folder.

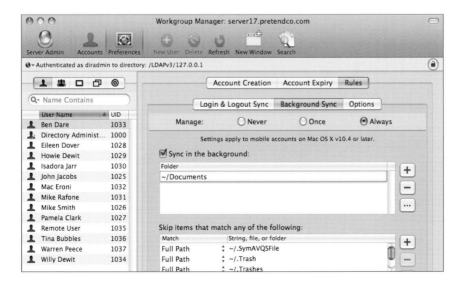

6 With the Documents folder configured, set the synchronization schedule. For this lesson, the schedule should be minimal.

7 Click the Options button, select Always from the Manage options, and verify the timing slider is set to 5 minutes. Click Apply Now.

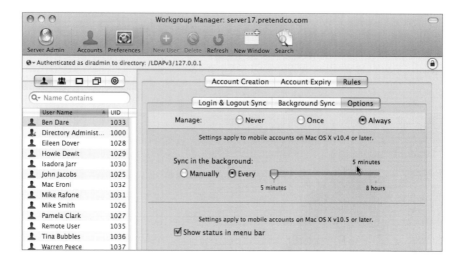

Configuring Account Expiry

1 Click the Account Expiry tab.

2 Select Always from the Manage options.

3 Select "Delete mobile accounts: 2 Days after user's next login."

4 Leave "Delete only after successful sync" selected.

This option ensures that there's no data loss from data that may not have been synchronized back to the server prior to the account's deletion.

5   Click Apply Now.

6   Quit Workgroup Manager and restart your Mac OS X computer.

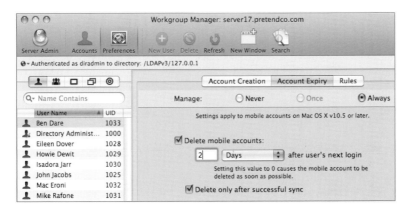

Verifying Mobile Account from the Client

The Ben Dare account is now configured to exist locally on each system he successfully logs in to, and files stored in ~/Documents will be synchronized with the Network account.

1   On the Mac OS X computer, log in as Ben.

2   Click the Create Now button when the confirmation dialog asks if you want to create a portable home directory.

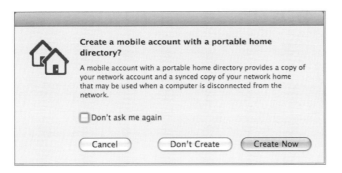

3 Open TextEdit, create a text file, and save it to the ~/Documents folder.

4 Wait 5 minutes.

5 On the server, view Ben's Document folder type with the Terminal by typing *sudo ls -al /Users/ben/Documents/*.

6 Enter the ladmin password when asked.

This will show all of Ben's documents without actually logging in as Ben on the server. The file should appear after about 5 minutes.

7 On your Mac OS X computer, log out as Ben, and then log in as the local administrator.

Configure External Accounts

You will use one of the accounts you set up previously and set up an external user account for that person.

1 In Workgroup Manager on your Mac OS X computer, choose the /LDAPv3/127.0.0.1 domain from the Directory pop-up menu.

2 Select Howie Dewit from the Accounts list and click the Preferences button in the toolbar.

3 Click the Mobility icon. In the Account Creation pane, select Always from the Manage options, and select the following checkboxes:

▶ "Create mobile account when user logs in to network account"

▶ "Require confirmation before creating mobile account"

4 Click the Options tab and select Always from the Manage options.

5 Set the Home folder location to "user chooses: any external volume."

6 Click Apply Now.

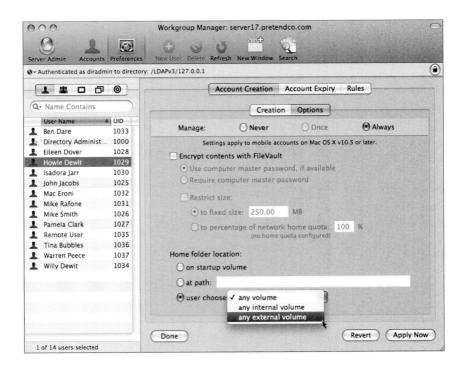

Verify External Account from the Client

The Howie Dewit account is now configured to exist on an external drive. If you have an HFS+ formatted external drive available to you, you can try logging in as Howie Dewit with the drive attached.

1   In System Preferences > Accounts > Login Option, set your login window to display as List of Users.

2   Log out, and then log in as Howie.

3   If the desired external device isn't already chosen, select it in the pop-up menu.

4   Click the Create Now button when the confirmation dialog asks if you want to create a portable home directory.

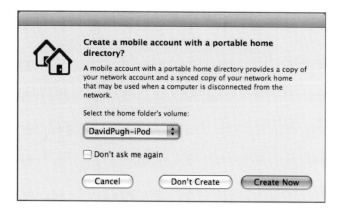

5 After Howie is logged in, shut down your Mac OS X computer.

6 Disconnect the external drive you saved the account on.

7 Disconnect the network cable on your Mac OS X computer.

8 Start your Mac OS X computer.

9 After the login window appears, plug in the external drive. What happens?

Because all of Howie's account information and files are stored on the external drive, his account appears in the list when you connect the drive. Because the account information, including his password, are stored on the drive, you can log in without a network connection.

10 On your Mac OS X computer, log out as Howie, and then log in as the local administrator.

11 Plug your network cable back in, and eject your external drive.

Troubleshooting

The majority of problems encountered initiate from users not being able to connect. This happens primarily at login. Check the following issues when troubleshooting account management:

▶ Check that the client bound to the correct directory.

▶ Check that the user and/or group home directories exported correctly.

▶ Check the user, group, computer, and computer group settings. Are the settings too restrictive? For example, is guest access denied and a new computer online?

▶ Check the preferences by logging in as a similar user. This works best if preferences are shared by a group.

▶ Use the Inspector in Workgroup Manager to view the raw preferences. It is especially useful if settings are set manually and copied into the user records. The Details functionality can also serve as a quick check for a set of preferences.

What You've Learned

▶ Account management encompasses everything from setting up accounts for network access and creating home folders to fine-tuning the user experience by managing preferences and settings for users, groups, and computers.

▶ Workgroup Manager is an account-management tool. It provides centralized directory-based management of users, groups, and computers—from anywhere on your network.

▶ The account information for a network user resides in a shared domain, and the user's home folder resides on a home folder server. Network users can log in from any client on the network and have access to their home folders.

▶ A group folder offers a way to organize documents and applications of special interest to group members, and gives group members a folder where they can pass information back and forth.

▶ A computer group is a list of computers that have the same preference settings and are available to the same users and groups. You can create and modify groups in Workgroup Manager.

▶ Preferences can be set for many built-in Mac OS X options for users, workgroups, computers, or computer groups. Other preferences can be managed if a preference manifest is provided with an application.

▶ Running a local software update server can control what updates are available to users and make more efficient use of the network for downloading software updates.

▶ A mobile user has many synchronized accounts. The main account resides in a shared domain, and a copy of the main account resides locally on the user's computer or an external disk. You can configure the user's files to be synchronized.

References

The following documents provide more information about managing accounts on Mac OS X Server. (All of these and more are available at www.apple.com/server/documentation.)

Administration Guides

Mac OS X Server Getting Started

System Imaging and Software Update Administration

User Management

Apple Knowledge Base Documents

You can check for new and updated Knowledge Base documents at http://www.apple.com/support.

Review Quiz

1. What is the difference between a local user account and a network user account?

2. How is a mobile user different from a network user?

3. Can a user be a member of more than one workgroup?

4. Can a computer be a member of more than one computer group?

5. What is the difference between a group and a workgroup?

6. In Workgroup Manager, how can you configure preferences for user, group, computer, and computer group accounts to avoid overrides?

7. Name two ways to review raw preference data in Workgroup Manager.

8. What folders are synchronized with mobile accounts?

Answers

1. In the case of a local user account, the home folder and account information are stored locally. But in the case of a network user account, the home folder is stored on a remote home folder server, and the account information resides in a shared domain.

2. A mobile user is a network user whose Mobility preference is managed. When you manage this preference, the next time the user logs in, Mac OS X Server creates two things: a copy of the user's account in the local domain of the user's computer, and a local home folder, which becomes the user's default home folder.

    Important: Any documents that were stored in the network home folder are not copied to the local home folder.

3. Yes.

4. Yes, in v10.5. No, in v10.4.

5. A group is a file-system designation. It is used to handle access to the file system (as in owner, group, others). It is specific to the file system, server, or computer. A workgroup is a directory-service record separate from any specific file system or server. It is used as a method of associating similar preferences for sets of user records.

6. You can avoid overrides by setting each preference for only one type of account. For example, you could set printer preferences only for computers, set application preferences only for workgroups, and set Dock preferences only for users. In such a case, no override occurs for these preferences because the user inherits them without competition.

7. Inspector and the Details pane of the preference management screen.

8. Only those in the Home folder hierarchy are synchronized in a mobile account.

Index

The Apple Pro Training Series

The official curriculum of the Apple Pro Training and Certification Program, the Apple Pro Training books are comprehensive, self-paced courses written by acknowledged experts in the field. Focused lessons take you step by-step through the process of creating real-world digital video or audio projects, while lesson files on the companion DVD and ample illustrations help you master techniques fast. In addition, lesson goals and time estimates help you plan your time, while chapter review questions summarize what you've learned.

Final Cut Pro 6
0-321-50265-5

Cut a scene from the USA Network television series *Monk*, create a promo for Seaworld's *Belief* documentary, master filters and effects as you edit a segment of BBC's *Living Color*. In this best-selling guide, Diana Weynand starts with basic video editing techniques and takes you all the way through Final Cut Pro's powerful advanced features. You'll learn to mark and edit clips, mix sound, add titles, create transitions, apply filters, and more.

Final Cut Pro 6: Beyond the Basics
0-321-50912-9

Director and editor Michael Wohl shows how to master advanced trimming techniques, make polished transitions, work with nested sequences, edit multi-camera projects, create fantastic effects, color-correct your video, and composite like a pro. Also covers Soundtrack Pro, and managing clips and media.

The Craft of Editing with Final Cut Pro
0-321-52036-X

Superbly fitted to a semester-length course, this is the ideal curriculum for a hands-on exploration of advanced editing. Director and editor Michael Wohl shares must-know techniques for cutting dialogue scenes, action scenes, fight and chase scenes, documentaries, comedy, music videos, multi-camera projects, and more. Two DVD-9s of professional footage and project files give students the chance to work with every genre as they learn.

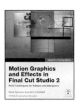

Motion Graphics and Effects in Final Cut Studio 2
0-321-50940-4

This practical approach focuses on just the parts of Final Cut Studio that editors and designers need to create motion graphics in their daily work.

Motion 3
0-321-50910-2

Top commercial artists show you how to harness Motion's behavior-based animations, particles, filters, effects, tracking, and 3D capabilities.

Soundtrack Pro 2
0-321-50266-3

Audio producer Martin Sitter is your guide to the only professional audio post application designed specifically for the Final Cut editor.

DVD Studio Pro 4, Second Edition
0-321-50189-6

Learn to author professional DVDs with this best-selling guide. Build three complete DVDs, including the DVD for the Oscar-nominated *Born into Brothels* documentary.

Color
0-321-50911-0

This guide to Apple's masterful new color grading software starts with the basics of color correction and moves on to the fine points of secondary grading, tracking, and advanced effects.

Apple Pro Training Series: Logic Pro 8 and Logic Express 8
0-321-50292-2

Create, mix, and polish your musical creations using Apple's pro audio software.

Apple Pro Training Series: Logic Pro 8 Beyond the Basics
0-321-50288-4

Comprehensive guide takes you through Logic's powerful advanced features.

Apple Pro Training Series: Shake 4
0-321-25609-3

Apple-certified guide uses stunning real world sequences to reveal the wizardry of Shake 4.

Encyclopedia of Visual Effects
0-321-30334-2

Ultimate recipe book for visual effects artists working in Shake, Motion and Adobe After Effects.

Encyclopedia of Color Correction
0-321-43231-2

Comprehensive training in the real-world color correction and management skills editing pros use every day in the field.

Aperture 1.5
0-321-49662-0

The best way to learn Aperture's powerful photo-editing, image-retouching, proofing, publishing, and archiving features.

Final Cut Express 4
0-321-53467-0

The only Apple-authorized guide to Final Cut Express 4 has you making movie magic in no time.

Optimizing Your Final Cut Pro System
0-321-26871-7

The ultimate guide for installing, configuring, optimizing, and trouble-shooting Final Cut Pro in real-world post-production environments.

Final Cut Pro for Avid Editors, Third Edition
0-321-51539-0

This comprehensive "translation course" is designed for professional video and film editors who already know their way around Avid nonlinear systems.

Final Cut Pro 6 for News and Sports Quick-Reference Guide
0-321-51423-8

This easy look-up guide provides essential techniques for broadcast studios using Final Cut Pro to edit news and sports.

Shake 4 Quick Reference Guide
0-321-38246-3

This compact reference guide to Apple's leading compositing software offers a concise explanation of the Shake interface, workspace, and tools..

Compressor 3 Quick-Reference Guide
0-321-51422-X

Learn essential techniques for audio and video compression, batch-encoding, test-clip workflows, exporting podcasts, and more.

QuickTime Pro Quick-Reference Guide
0-321-44248-2

An invaluable guide to capturing, encoding, editing, streaming, and exporting media.

Final Cut Server Quick-Reference Guide
0-321-51024-0

Final Cut Server delivers intuitive media asset management, review and approval tools, and workflow automation.

Xsan Quick-Reference Guide, Second Edition
0-321-43232-0

Apple's exciting new enterprise-class file system offers high-speed access to centralized shared data.

The Apple Training Series

Apple Training Series: Mac OS X Support Essentials, Second Edition
0-321-48981-0

Apple Training Series: Mac OS X Server Essentials, Second Edition
0-321-49660-4

Apple Training Series: Desktop and Portable Systems, Third Edition
0-321-33546-5

Apple Training Series: Mac OS X System Administration Guide, Volume 1
0-321-36984-X

Apple Training Series: Mac OS X System Administration Guide, Volume 2
0-321-42315-1

Apple Training Series: iLife '08
0-321-50190-X

Apple Training Series: iWork '08
0-321-50185-3